LGBT Youth in America's Schools

LGBT Youth in America's Schools

Jason Cianciotto and Sean Cahill

THE UNIVERSITY OF MICHIGAN PRESS | ANN ARBOR

Published in the United States of America by
The University of Michigan Press
Manufactured in the United States of America
⊗ Printed on acid-free paper

2015   2014   2013   2012   4   3   2   1

A CIP catalog record for this book is available from the British Library.

Library of Congress Cataloging-in-Publication Data

Cianciotto, Jason.
    LGBT youth in America's schools / Jason Cianciotto and Sean
Cahill.
        p.   cm.
    Includes bibliographical references and index.
    ISBN 978-0-472-11822-9 (cloth : alk. paper) —
    ISBN 978-0-472-03140-5 (pbk. : alk. paper) —
    ISBN 978-0-472-02832-0 (e-book)
    1. Lesbian students—United States.   2. Gay students—United States.
    3. Bisexual students—United States.   4. Transgender youth—
Education—United States.   5. Sexual minorities—Education.
    6. Homosexuality and education—United States.   I. Cahill, Sean (Sean
Robert)   II. Title.
    LC2575.C54   2012
    371.826'60973—dc23
                                                         2011045478

JASON CIANCIOTTO *would like to dedicate
this book to Jack Emery and Kathy Hartman,
devoted teachers and mentors at his high school,
and to his husband Courter Simmons.*

SEAN CAHILL *would like to dedicate this book to his
mother, Jeanne Parker Cahill, for her lifelong dedication to
education and her passionate advocacy for equality and respect
for all people, including gay men and lesbians, in the
Catholic Church as well as in American society.*

Acknowledgments

The authors would like to thank the following people (listed in alphabetical order) for their assistance with this book:

Michelle Agostini, Craig Bowman, Steve Brandwein, Samuel Buggeln, Eliza Byard, Larry Bye, Rea Carey, Chris Chen, Roddrick Colvin, Connie Cordovilla, Susan Cronin, Blair Darnell, Mitra Ellen, Chai Feldblum, Susan Fineran, Matt Foreman, Naomi Goldberg, Carole Goodenow, Brenda Greene, Pat Griffin, Adrian Guzman, Cathie Hartnett, Melody Herr, Sarah Holmes, Kenneth Jones, Courtney Joslin, Jason Jurjevich, Steve Kaufman, Sarah Kennedy, Joe Kosciw, Alana Krivo-Kaufmann, Kevin Kumashiro, Carolyn Laub, Arthur Lipkin, Elizabeth Lovinger, Sheri Lunn, Emily Marker, Martha Matthews, Lance McCready, Beth McFarland, Andrew Miller, Lisa Mottet, Brian Moulton, Bic Ngo, Donald Ofstedal, Luna Ortiz, Pauline Park, Charlotte Patterson, Clarence Patton, Eric Pliner, Dusty Porter, Beth Reis, Gary Remafedi, Paula Ressler, Eric Rofes, Francisco Roque, Charlie Rounds, Kathleen Russell, Caitlin Ryan, Emily Saltzman, Ritch Savin-Williams, Nathan Schaefer, Ron Schlittler, Bernard Schlotfeldt, James T. Sears, Roberta Sklar, Samuel Slater, Dean Spade, Kara Suffridini, Laura Szalacha, Dinh Tu Tran, Lyndel Urbano, Urvashi Vaid, Robert Valadez, Joan Varney, Dawn Walsh, Kim Westheimer, Olivia Yi, Beth Zemsky.

Special thanks to the Kevin J. Mossier Foundation, the National Gay and Lesbian Task Force, Gay Men's Health Crisis, and the Gay, Lesbian, and Straight Education Network.

Contents

SECTION 1 | A Comprehensive Review of
Social Science Research on
LGBT Youth and Their Experiences
in School

Introduction

From controversy over bringing a same-sex date to the prom to incidents of harassment and violence, every school year brings new headlines about the experiences of lesbian, gay, bisexual, and transgender (LGBT) youth in America's classrooms. In September 2010, unprecedented national attention to anti-LGBT bullying in schools occurred after several students, some as young as thirteen years old, completed suicide. All of them were frequently bullied and harassed at school because of their real or perceived sexual orientation or gender identity, and at least three were openly gay.[1] As pundits and activists on all sides of the LGBT rights debate argued over what needs to be done to protect students, these tragedies highlighted the fact that LGBT youth are simply "coming out" at younger ages, forcing teachers, school administrators, and policymakers to address a variety of school safety, curricular, and other education policy issues at the intersection of sexual orientation, gender identity, and public education.

In the 1970s and 1980s, surveys found that the average age at which youth self-identified as gay or lesbian was nineteen to twenty-one for men and twenty-one to twenty-three for women. As a result, the coming-out process for most young adults occurred either during college or after having established an independent life. More recent studies have found that lesbian, gay, and bisexual (LGB) youth first become aware of their sexual orientation between ages eleven and thirteen and come out to others around the age of fifteen.[2] There is a dearth of research on self-identification for transgender youth, but many also become aware during childhood that their gender identity does not match their biological sex.[3] Self-identification at an earlier age can expose LGBT youth to rejection, harassment, and violence at home and at school, creating a greater need for appropriate advice, comprehensive and age-appropriate sex education, and referrals to available resources from supportive adults.[4]

Access to support systems at home and at school is critical because violence and harassment against LGBT students is widespread. The 2007

National School Climate Survey of 6,209 LGBT students, conducted by the Gay, Lesbian, and Straight Education Network, found that 86 percent were verbally harassed at their school because of their sexual orientation and that 67 percent were verbally harassed because of the way they expressed their gender. Nearly half had been physically harassed because of their sexual orientation, and 61 percent felt unsafe at their school.[5] Data from a variety of state and federal government surveys also confirm that LGBT youth are more likely than their heterosexual peers to experience harassment and violence in school, including from teachers and school administrators.[6]

"Outed" by His Guidance Counselor and Forced to Read Aloud from the Bible at School

A Profile of Thomas McLaughlin

When Thomas McLaughlin was a thirteen-year-old student at Jacksonville Junior High School in Jacksonville, Arkansas, the assistant principal called him out of his seventh-period class and asked if his parents knew that he was gay. When Thomas replied no, the assistant principal said that Thomas had until 3:40 p.m. that day to tell them, or the school would. Too upset to sit through eighth period, Thomas went to his guidance counselor for help. Despite Thomas's protest, she called his mother and told her that Thomas was gay.[7]

This chain of events began when Thomas's science teacher overheard him refuse to deny that he was gay when another student was teasing him. Along with calling in the assistant principal, the science teacher also gave Thomas a four-page, handwritten letter. Referencing the Bible, it told Thomas he would be condemned to hell if he "chose" to be gay.[8]

Thomas's parents were accepting and understanding of his sexual orientation. However, back at school, the trouble had only just begun. While other students generally did not have a problem with Thomas's sexual orientation, several teachers and administrators did. One teacher told Thomas to stop talking about being gay because she found it "sickening." Another publicly scolded Thomas for talking with a female friend about which boys in class they thought were cute. (The female student was not disciplined.) Several teachers also attempted to silence Thomas by warning him that he was going to be beat up in school because he was gay, that the school would not protect him, and that if he did not keep quiet, he would end up like Matthew Shepard, the gay college student from Laramie, Wyoming, who, in 1998, was tied to a fence, beaten, and left to die.[9]

Over the course of the school year, the situation grew worse. After arguing with a teacher who had called him "abnormal" and "unnatural" for being gay, Thomas was sent to the assistant principal's office again. As part of his disciplinary action, the assistant principal forced Thomas to read aloud passages from the Bible that condemn homosexuality. When Thomas, who is also a Christian, told his friends about having to read the Bible aloud at school, he was suspended for two days. The principal also warned him that if he told anyone why he was suspended, he would immediately be expelled from school. When Thomas told his mother about the suspension and forced Bible readings, she called the American Civil Liberties Union (ACLU). "We're Christians," she said, "but this isn't the school's business. It's something for us, his parents, to talk about."[10]

On April 8, 2003, after repeated attempts to resolve this problem with various school administrators, the ACLU filed suit against Pulaski County Special School District on behalf of Thomas and his parents. The lawsuit charged that school officials violated Thomas's religious liberty and his rights to free speech, equal protection, and privacy. Thomas said he simply wanted to go to school without being harassed by his teachers: "All I want out of this is for me and other gay students to be able to go to school without being preached to and without being expected to lie about who we are."[11]

On July 17, 2003, in a court-ordered settlement, Thomas got his wish. Under the terms of settlement, school officials agreed not to disclose any student's sexual orientation to others, not to punish students for talking about their sexual orientation during noninstructional time, not to discriminate against students on the basis of their sexual orientation in disciplinary matters, and not to preach to students by any means, including forced Bible readings.[12]

In addition, the school district issued a formal apology to Thomas and his parents, expunged Thomas's disciplinary record, and agreed to pay twenty-five thousand dollars in damages and attorneys' fees. After the settlement, Thomas said, "I'm really glad

> that this is all over and that the ACLU is making the school treat gay students the way they should have been treated in the first place. No more students should have to go through what I did."[13]

LGBT youth who do not have access to support systems at home or at school can become dangerously isolated. A number of studies have found that many parents react negatively when their child comes out to them, with emotions ranging from shock, grief, disbelief, and self-guilt to anger and rejection. A small but no less significant percentage of LGBT youth may even be kicked out of their homes.[14] Many are also cut off by their friends and by members of their religious communities, harassed and attacked by their peers in school, and demeaned by society at large. For some LGBT youth, these situations lead to poor academic achievement and dangerous physical and mental health outcomes, including a higher incidence of substance abuse, homelessness, and suicide.

More than fifteen studies have consistently shown that gay and lesbian youth attempt suicide at higher rates than their heterosexual peers.[15] In a study of transgender youth in New York City, nearly half (45 percent) seriously thought about taking their own lives.[16] Of homeless youth in major metropolitan cities, 20 to 40 percent identify as gay or lesbian and may engage in sex work (prostitution) to feed and support themselves.[17] Transgender homeless youth face similar choices when rejected by their families. Homelessness and reliance on sex work to survive may be even more prevalent among LGBT youth of color, who already face social prejudice and stigmatization because of their race or ethnicity.[18] By coming out, they also risk rejection by members of their own racial or ethnic community and, therefore, intensified isolation.[19]

Despite the harassment and violence they experience on a daily basis, most LGBT youth display amazing strength and resiliency. In many instances, they have organized to demand policy changes that make schools safer and more inclusive, often without the support of the school officials responsible for protecting all students. After they graduate from high school, many continue working to increase awareness and understanding of the harassment and violence they experienced and the impact it had on their academic achievement, as well as on their mental and physical health. In cooperation with a broad coalition of advocates, these youth have led successful interventions in a growing number of schools and communities, including nondiscrimination and antiharassment policies, safe schools programs, and community- and school-based support groups that provide peer and adult mentors, role models, and age-appropriate information.

The ultimate reach of these initiatives goes beyond making schools safer for LGBT youth. A program that acknowledges and values the LGBT members of a school community changes the atmosphere for everyone, making it safer for other students perceived to be different. The children of LGBT parents, regardless of their own sexual orientation or gender identity, benefit greatly from an environment that allows them to be honest about their families.[20] In addition, many young people use anti-LGBT epithets against peers they perceive as different for a variety of gender-related reasons. They might target boys who do not like sports; who are introverted, studious, and sensitive; or who have many female friends. They might target girls who are athletic, tomboys, or aggressive; who do not wear makeup; or who have rejected boys' advances. While some of these youth may be lesbian, gay, bisexual, or transgender, it is likely that a substantial proportion, perhaps even most, are not.

This book was written to support the common goal that schools should be safe and affirming institutions of learning for all students, regardless of real or perceived sexual orientation or gender identity. It addresses this critical issue by combining a comprehensive and accessible review of social science research with analyses of school-based best practices; local, state, and federal laws; and the gaps in available academic research that affect LGBT students across the country. To contrast the quantitative information in the text, we included over a dozen real-world case studies of LGBT youth and their experiences in schools. These stories "put a face" to the data and are strategically incorporated to illustrate issues discussed in specific sections. To provide context and help the reader navigate to the information most relevant to his or her needs, this book is divided into three sections.

Section 1, a comprehensive review of decades of social science research on LGBT youth and their experiences at school, bridges the gap between academia and real-world practice by incorporating information from nearly two hundred studies, journal articles, books, and other sources of information about LGBT youth. In this section, chapter 1 defines and explores the universe of youth impacted by LGBT issues at school and answers basic questions, including how many LGBT youth there are and how the experiences of LGBT youth of color differ from those of their white peers. Chapter 2 summarizes research on the incidence of anti-LGBT harassment and violence in schools and its effects on the health and educational outcomes of students.

Section 2 provides a comprehensive review of school-based practices, laws, and policies that affect LGBT students. Chapter 3 summarizes federal, state, and local laws, including constitutional protections for LGBT students and state antibullying laws. Chapter 4 summarizes school-based programs and practices, from gay-straight alliances to the inclusion of LGBT issues in school curricula and textbooks. Chapter 5 is a detailed analysis of specific provisions of the federal No Child Left Behind Act that affect the experiences of LGBT students. Chapter 6 reviews the history and impact of abstinence-only programs in sex education, including how such programs portray homosexuality and affect the spread of HIV and other sexually transmitted diseases in youth, particularly among youth of color.

Section 3 completes the book with a detailed research agenda designed to inspire the scholars, researchers, and graduate students whose work will inform future public policy. In this section, chapter 7 addresses political and methodological issues affecting research on LGBT youth and students, summarizing a variety of research on ways to standardize and accelerate the availability of reliable information about this population. Chapter 8 enumerates specific research questions and projects that would help fill existing knowledge gaps about LGBT students and issues in schools, and chapter 9 includes a brief conclusion and a set of policy recommendations.

1 | Lesbian, Gay, Bisexual, and Transgender Youth: A Critical Population

Methodological Barriers to Research on LGBT Youth

Conducting research on the experiences of LGBT youth, the harassment and violence they endure, and the effects of this abuse on their mental health, physical health, and educational performance is fraught with technical challenges. A number of problems, including a lack of funding and political barriers that complicate researchers' attempts to collect information from youth, make it difficult to capture a random, representative sample of LGBT youth. For example, a provision in the No Child Left Behind Act, which is discussed further in chapter 5, requires all school districts to develop written policies and procedures, in consultation with parents, regarding any third-party survey of students that includes questions about political affiliations or beliefs, mental problems, sexual attitudes or behavior, illegal or antisocial behavior, critical appraisals of family members, religious beliefs of the student or parent, or income.[1] (This would include, for example, the Youth Risk Behavior Survey conducted by the Centers for Disease Control and Prevention [CDC], which includes optional questions about sexual orientation and behavior as well as many other health issues.) At a minimum, these policies must specify how parents will be notified about such surveys and how they will be given the opportunity to prevent their children from participating in them.

As written, this provision does not dramatically influence researchers' ability to collect information. Prior to the passage of the legislation, many schools chose to notify parents about all surveys administered to students, allowing parents to request that their child not participate. In practice, however, few parents exercise this opt-out option, and it has had no substantial impact on survey results.

By comparison, policies that require parents to opt *in* by sending in prior written permission, or "active permission" for participation, make collecting reliable data extremely difficult. Once in place, active parental

9

consent regulations make it virtually impossible to collect data on large representative samples of students in schools. At least three states—Alaska, New Jersey, and Utah—require the prior written informed consent of a parent before a survey can be administered to a student.[2] Alaska's opt-in law prevented the state from obtaining a high enough response rate for it to participate in the 2001 Youth Risk Behavior Survey.[3]

Although volunteer-based research methodologies, which use self-selecting participants, are commonly employed in many academic disciplines, they can be problematic for research on small, minority populations. For participants in studies about sexual orientation or gender identity, self-identification often comes with risk, both real and perceived. Consequently, LGBT research participants may choose to withhold information about their sexual orientation or gender identity. Even though most studies are anonymous, fear of the consequences of coming out still prevents many people from participating. The issues of self-selection and coming out tend to skew research on LGBT youth toward those who are most comfortable with their identities at younger ages and are more likely to experience negative outcomes, making more broadly-based research especially difficult.[4]

Some argue that researchers who rely on self-selected volunteers are likely to overlook important developmental characteristics of those who experience same-sex attraction but do not necessarily consider themselves lesbian, gay, or bisexual.[5] Because of the perception that being gay entails being harassed at school, some adolescents choose not to categorize themselves according to existing labels, instead describing their same-sex relationships in terms of desires or attractions. Consequently, studies that ask youth to self-identify as "lesbian" or "gay" yield lower numbers compared to studies that ask questions about same-sex attraction, sexual behavior, or both.[6]

To address these problems, researchers use population-based data, which can include a large number of students in one region or even nationwide. Since the late 1980s, state and federal agencies have used this method to conduct surveys on a broad range of issues critical to teen health and safety. The CDC, for example, coordinates the nationwide Youth Risk Behavior Survey every two years. Although none of these population-based studies focuses exclusively on LGBT youth, answers to the questions they include about same-sex sexual behavior offer important and sometimes striking information about health and safety risks that disproportionately affect LGB students. Unfortunately, none of them includes questions specific to gender identity.

From Isolation to Activism

A Profile of Louie Garay

After coming out to several friends at his Catholic middle school when he was fourteen years old, Louie Garay began experiencing isolation and harassment—experiences that only grew stronger after he started attending an all-boys preparatory seminary high school.[7] Because of inadequate support from teachers and school staff and a lack of dedication to his studies, Louie was expelled after his freshman year. Although this was quite stressful and upsetting at the time, leaving that school allowed Louie to transfer to Global Studies High School, closer to his home in Brooklyn, New York.

Fueled by his frustration at the inadequate support from his former school, Louie decided to become politically active and change his new school environment to make it more supportive. He learned of the annual Equality and Justice Lobby Day at the New York State Capitol in Albany, sponsored by the Empire State Pride Agenda (ESPA), and arranged for his new school to approve the trip. Despite meeting all requirements, school officials rejected the trip at the last minute. (It is unclear whether this was because of homophobic school officials or clerical errors.) Regardless, Louie, his mother, and a fellow classmate decided to join ESPA's trip anyway. According to Louie, this event was the beginning of his activist journey.

After returning from Albany, Louie became more involved with ESPA and began participating in programs for youth at New York City's LGBT community center. Louie and several of his classmates founded his high school's first gay-straight alliance (GSA), which caused quite a stir in south Brooklyn. Shortly afterward, several school officials from neighboring districts who also wanted to start GSAs at their schools contacted Louie for assistance. The GSA had about twenty consistent members and worked with teachers and staff on school initiatives to provide a safe and supportive environment for LGBT students. For example, the GSA, along with other student groups, organized the school's first No Name-Calling Week, which brought students, teachers, and staff to a new level of understanding of how bullying and verbal harassment causes a great deal of harm.[8] Although much of Louie's student activism and school involvement created opportunities for him to connect with school officials and develop leadership skills, he still dealt with occasional harassment from students.

By the time Louie was a senior, he became a trailblazer at his school and a leader in the larger LGBT community in New York City. He collaborated with a variety of national LGBT rights organizations, including the Gay and Lesbian Alliance Against Defamation (GLAAD); the Gay, Lesbian, and Straight Education Network (GLSEN); and PRIDE, a Puerto Rican LGBT group. He also participated in an initiative sponsored by Gay Men's Health Crisis that supports young gay men of color who participate in the House and Ball community.[9] Working with these and other groups, Louie conducted outreach and education to support LGBT youth and to prevent the transmission of HIV and other sexually transmitted diseases. During his final year at Global Studies High School, Louie even became the first openly gay president of the school's student government.

While Louie developed into an out and proud leader at his high school, his mother became more politically active as a member of a Families of Color and Allies (FCA) chapter of the national support, education, and advocacy organization Parents, Families, and Friends of Lesbians and Gays (PFLAG). As a result of her participation and Louie's involvement with the group, he was asked to join the board of PFLAG-FCA as its youth advisor. Throughout Louie's struggles in school, his parents grew from supportive confidants to active allies. His mother participated in numerous events to raise awareness of LGBT issues, and both parents opened their homes to several of Louie's friends who became homeless after coming out to their families.

Louie's unfaltering activism also garnered national recognition. On June 29, 2009, he and his mother were chosen to represent PFLAG–FCA at the White House's LGBT Pride reception. Wearing a brand new suit, which he purchased only hours before arriving, Louie met President Barack Obama and First Lady Michelle Obama as an out, young, gay man with his supportive, activist mother—an accomplishment he never thought possible. Participating in this historic event was a formative experience that, according to Louie, solidified his journey as an activist. Louie plans to continue inspiring other LGBT youth to realize their boldest dreams.

How Many LGBT Youth Are There?

The problems endemic to the scientific study of LGBT students make it difficult to determine exactly how many LGBT youth there are in the United States. Data from population-based studies allow for estimates of the prevalence of homosexuality and bisexuality among adolescents. (As of 2010, we could find no population-based studies that asked questions about gender identity.) How homosexuality and bisexuality is defined affects what percentage of the population is viewed as lesbian, gay, or bisexual. Measuring attraction finds the highest rates, while measuring sexual behavior or self-identification reports lower rates. Various studies conducted over the past decade and a half indicate that the percentage of the population that is homosexual and bisexual is between 4 and 6 percent.[10]

The 1996 National Longitudinal Study of Adolescent Health, a comprehensive study of more than twelve thousand youth in grades 7 through 12, found that 6 percent of participants between the ages of thirteen and eighteen reported same-sex attraction: 1 percent reported that they were only attracted to members of their own sex, and 5 percent reported attraction to both sexes.[11] Similarly, a 1999 review of eight population-based studies by the Safe Schools Coalition of Washington State found that 4 to 5 percent of teens in secondary schools identified themselves as lesbian, gay, or bisexual; had engaged in same-sex sexual activity; or had experienced same-sex attraction.[12] Additional surveys had similar findings:

- The 2001 Massachusetts Youth Risk Behavior Survey reported that 5 percent of respondents either self-identified as gay or bisexual or reported same-sex sexual experiences.[13]
- The 2001 Vermont Youth Risk Behavior Survey found that 3 percent of students reported same-sex sexual experiences.[14]

The 2002 National Survey of Family Growth found that 6.5 percent of men and 11 percent of women from fifteen to forty-four years of age reported a same-sex sexual experience. When asked if they thought of themselves as heterosexual, homosexual, bisexual, or something else, 2.3 percent of men answered homosexual, 1.8 percent answered bisexual, and 5.7 percent said something else or did not give an answer (3.9 percent and 1.8 percent, respectively). Among women, 1.3 percent answered homosexual, 2.8 percent answered bisexual, and 5.6 percent said something else or did not give an answer (3.8 percent and 1.8 percent, respectively). Roughly 4.1 percent of respondents identified as homosexual or bisexual.[15]

When questioned about their sexual attractions, 92 percent of men from eighteen to forty-four years of age said they were attracted only to women, 3.9 percent said mostly to women, and 3.2 percent said mostly to men or equally to men and women. For women, 86 percent said they were attracted only to men, 10 percent said mostly to men, and 3.4 percent said mostly to women or equally to men and women.[16]

How one asks about sexual orientation affects response rates. A 2006 study reported that self-administered surveys that do not require a human interviewer find much higher rates of reported homosexuality and bisexuality. The study compared results from interviews involving a human interviewer and results using a technique called telephone audio computer-assisted self-interviewing (T-ACASI). Those taking the self-administered survey were 50 to 60 percent more likely to report same-sex attraction than those who took a traditional telephone survey with a human interviewer.[17]

Very few studies estimate the transgendered population, because of the complexity associated with defining "transgender" and what one considers gender variant (a category that includes transsexuals, cross-dressers, androgynous people, and those who are gender nonconforming). In 1998, *Time* magazine reported that an estimated twenty-five thousand Americans had had sex reassignment surgery and that another sixty thousand were candidates for it.[18] The American Psychiatric Association estimates that one in thirty thousand adult men and one in one hundred thousand women undergo sex reassignment surgery.[19] It is likely that the percentage and number of people who are transgender is much smaller than the share of the population that is gay, lesbian, or bisexual.

To estimate the number of LGBT youth in public schools in the United States, researchers should focus on students in public school grades 7 through 12 (ages thirteen through eighteen), because they are more likely to be aware of their sexual attractions, sexual orientation, or gender identity and out to their families and friends. For the 2007–8 school year, the U.S. Department of Education estimated that there were 22.4 million students in this grade range.[20] Given the studies indicating that 4 to 6 percent of the U.S. population is homosexual or bisexual, we estimate that between 896,000 and 1.34 million students in grades 7 through 12 may identify as LGB. This estimate is conservative: it is likely that many youth either are afraid to report same-sex attraction on a survey or are simply not yet aware of their sexual orientation or gender identity. However, it does provide a rough estimation of the number of students directly affected by school policies related to LGBT issues and anti-LGBT harassment or violence.

Transgender Youth

Transgender is an umbrella term used to describe a wide range of identities and experiences, including, but not limited to, transsexual people (who may or may not pursue medical treatments to change their bodies); cross-dressers (including drag queens and drag kings); and men and women, regardless of sexual orientation, whose appearance or characteristics are perceived to be gender atypical. In its broadest sense, the term encompasses anyone whose identity or behavior falls outside of stereotypical gender norms. That includes people who do not self-identify as transgender but who are perceived as such by others and are thus vulnerable to the same social oppressions and physical violence as those who actually identify with any of these categories.[21]

Gender identity refers to how people understand themselves: as boys or girls, men or women, or something else altogether. Gender expression refers to all the ways that people express their gender identity to the outside world, including through dress, appearance, and behavior. Transgender youth include those who identify with a gender different from their birth sex. Some transgender youth are transsexual and may seek to modify their bodies through hormones and/or gender reassignment surgery in order to bring their physical appearance in line with their gender identity.[22]

Transgender and gender-nonconforming youth face significant challenges "integrating a complex gender identity with their cultural and ethnic backgrounds, personal characteristics, and family circumstances. They are faced not only with the task of developing a sexual identity, but also with reconciling their gender identity with the traditional gender expectations associated with their biological sex."[23] This can lead to increased risk of negative mental and physical health outcomes, as well as pervasive harassment and violence at school.[24] According to GLSEN, transgender students are at great risk: over 53 percent report being physically harassed because of their gender expression, as compared with 44 percent of LGB students reporting physical harassment because of their sexual orientation. In other words, transgender students were 20 percent more likely to suffer physical harassment than LGB students.[25] One activist argues,

> Given the bullying and discrimination faced by "sissy" boys, "tomboy" girls, gay teens, and [transgender] students, school administrators have a special obligation today to set an example of tolerance for diversity. They must make sure every student knows that gender stereotyping—and the violence that often accompanies it—no longer has a place in our nation's schools.[26]

In general, transgender people may face constant danger of emotional or physical harm. For example, they encounter workplace discrimination, may be asked to show identification that does not match their identity, or may be obliged to use unsafe public restrooms several times each day. Given that transgender youth often do not have the same access to resources as adults do and that they may depend on adults who do not approve of their gender identity or expression, the harassment and discrimination they face can be even more pervasive given the younger ages at which transgender people are coming out.[27]

There are no longitudinal, population-based data on the prevalence or experiences of transgender youth in public schools. Of the 6,209 LGBT youth surveyed by GLSEN in 2007, 5 percent (297) identified as transgender, 4 percent (248) as "[an]other gender identity" (e.g., genderqueer, androgynous).[28] These transgender students reported even higher levels of verbal harassment and physical assault than their non-transgender peers, were more likely to miss school due to safety concerns, and were more likely to report that they were not going to college.[29]

A study conducted in the United Kingdom in 2002 analyzed 124 transgender youth who were receiving mental health treatment at St. George's Hospital in London.[30] The average age of the youth in the program was eleven; 32 percent were biologically female, 66 percent were biologically male, and 2 percent were intersex, meaning they were born with ambiguous genitalia. Although 75 percent of the youth in the study stated that they wished they were of the opposite sex, only 21 percent stated a belief that they belonged to the opposite sex. Many of these youth exhibited problems at school and in social relationships:

- 16 percent of all the youth in the study and 28 percent of the females refused or were afraid to go to school.

- 11 percent did not attend school at all.
- 22 percent experienced discipline problems.
- 52 percent cited difficulty relating to their peers.
- 33 percent of all the youth and 43 percent of the males experienced harassment or persecution by their peers.

The study concluded that these youth require long-term support and understanding, particularly at school, given the higher incidence of harassment and violence they experience. The fact that boys were harassed more often may indicate that gender nonconformity is more socially acceptable for girls.[31]

Basing an estimate of the proportion of transgender youth in a school-age population primarily on a clinical subpopulation raises serious conceptual and methodological issues, and it may also overestimate the extent of mental health issues not gender-related in that subpopulation. Apart from the groundbreaking research conducted by GLSEN, the experiences of transgender youth have not been well documented. More inquiry is needed to better understand their experiences and what kinds of interventions might best mitigate the harassment and other obstacles they face. Breaking the silence around transgender issues, including positive representations of transgender individuals in the classroom, are important steps toward creating a more hospitable environment for all gender-nonconforming youth.[32]

Judge Rules That School Must Allow Transgender Youth to Express Her Gender Identity While Attending School

A Profile of "Pat Doe"

Doe v. Yunits, a case decided by a Massachusetts Superior Court in 2000, was the first reported case on behalf of a transgender student.[33] The fifteen-year-old plaintiff, know only as "Pat Doe," began wearing women's makeup and clothing to school when she was in the seventh grade. Her outfits included tight skirts, high-heeled shoes, and a dress once worn to a semiformal dance. Although this attire was not so different from what many girls in Pat's school wore, school officials singled her out and treated her differently because she was transgender.[34]

When Pat began eighth grade in the fall of 1999, the principal required that she report each morning so that he could determine whether her clothing was appropriate. If Pat came to school in clothing deemed too feminine, she was sent home to change. She was frequently too upset to return. Eventually, Pat stopped going to school altogether. The next year, the administration told her she could not enroll if she continued to wear women's clothing. Pat's grandmother, "Jane Doe," who had raised Pat since she was one month old, filed suit against the school district with the help of the Boston-based Gay and Lesbian Advocates and Defenders.[35]

On October 12, 2000, superior court judge Linda E. Giles ruled that the school had discriminated against Pat on the basis of her sex by treating her differently from other girls simply because she was biologically male. She also ruled that Pat must be allowed to express her self-identified gender while attending school. The court explained that Pat's decision to wear women's clothing "is not merely a personal preference but a necessary symbol of her very identity." Furthermore, to force her to wear male clothing would be to stifle her selfhood "merely because it causes some members of the community discomfort." The school district's attorney, Edward Lenox, argued that Pat's wearing feminine clothing constituted a "pattern of behavior that has been disruptive." Judge Giles responded that Pat could not be reprimanded for wearing clothing and accessories that would be considered acceptable on other female students. Furthermore, Judge Giles suggested that rather than view Pat as a disruption to the educational process, the situation could be seen as an educational opportunity. She wrote that "exposing children to diversity at an early age serves the important social goals of increasing their ability to tolerate differences and teaching them respect for everyone's unique personal experience."[36]

When Pat returned to school, twenty of her fellow classmates, in a show of protective solidarity, shielded their friend from the media and urged the public to be more sensitive. As they walked home with Pat on her second day back, a friend remarked, "[She's] mad cool. I don't know why people have to hate . . . [her]; all they have to do is get to know [her]."[37] Six months after the ruling, Pat's attorney, Jennifer Levi, remarked on the significance of the case. "Now schools know," she said, "that they can easily and happily incorporate a transgender student."[38]

Intersex Youth

Like LGBT youth, youth with intersex conditions suffer the negative consequences of not fitting into prevailing ideas about sex and gender. The term *intersex* refers to a variety of conditions in which a person has or had reproductive or sexual anatomy that does not fit the typical definition of "male" or "female."[39] Intersex youth are distinct from transgender youth and can have any sexual orientation or gender identity. Overall, there are at least fifteen different medical causes of intersexuality, and only a small percentage of these cases result in ambiguous genitalia at birth. Other intersex conditions manifest at puberty, while still others manifest later in life. Frequencies of intersex conditions range widely, from "late-onset adrenal hyperplasia," found in 1 in 66 births, to "complete gonadal dysgenesis," found in 1 in 150,000 births.[40]

Doctors perform surgery on one or two babies per thousand births in an effort to "correct" ambiguous genitalia. The Intersex Society of North America, along with other groups, reports that these surgeries are harmful to many intersex people and that performing cosmetic genital surgery on infants is often not in the best interest of the child. Instead, they recommend that a child be assigned and raised either male or female and be given choices when older about whether or not to pursue surgery.[41]

At school, where anti-LGBT attitudes reinforce prevailing notions about what it means to be a girl or a boy, intersex youth are likely to feel great discomfort and shame about their intersex status. Intersex youth may live in fear of others learning of their condition. Education about the existence of intersex individuals is a necessary first step to eradicating this fear. Greater understanding and acceptance of the fluidity of sex and gender would benefit not only intersex youth but all young people who exhibit gender-nonconforming characteristics.

Gender Nonconformity: Making the Connection

Research on anti-LGBT violence in public schools has focused heavily on sexual orientation. As students identify as gay or lesbian at younger ages, they are harassed in school at younger ages. This simple correlation, however, does not account for the majority of violence and harassment that occurs in elementary and middle schools—sometimes long before these youth are even aware of sexual orientation and gender identity issues. Even in high school, a girl who is certain of her heterosexual identity may be called "dyke" simply because she has short hair and plays softball. This is because a lot of anti-LGBT harassment is actually a response to gender nonconformity, or behavior and mannerisms that do not match socially acceptable standards of behavior for males and females.

Gender-conforming children are those who prefer sex-typical activities and same-sex playmates; gender-nonconforming children are those who prefer sex-atypical activities and opposite-sex playmates.[42] Not all children who exhibit primarily gender-nonconforming behavior grow up to identify as LGBT. Many—perhaps most—grow up to be heterosexual, and all youth, regardless of their sexual orientation, exhibit some behaviors that could be perceived as gender nonconforming. Regardless of their sexual orientation or gender identity, many youth experience violence and harassment because they do not conform to gender-stereotypical behavior in their attire, interests, or mannerisms. Violations of these stereotypes and gender roles (which can be as innocuous as a boy who is more artistic than athletic) may cause harassment and victimization that begins long before a child is aware of his or her sexual orientation or gender identity.

Youth who are gender noncomforming and identify as LGBT may be even more likely to experience harassment.[43] A 1998 study of school counselors' experiences with lesbian and gay students found that the majority of reported incidents of harassment targeted male students who acted "too feminine."[44] The 2002 Preventing School Harassment Survey, which surveyed over twenty-four hundred students in California, found that nearly a quarter (23 percent) of all students were harassed because they were not "as masculine as other guys" or "as feminine as other girls." LGB students were nearly twice as likely (42 percent) and transgender students were nearly three times as likely (62 percent) to report harassment based on gender noncomformity.[45]

A 2006 study supported by the National Institute of Mental Health confirms the link between gender atypical behavior and verbal, physical, and sexual harassment or violence, referred to by the researchers as sexual orientation violence (SOV). A two-year longitudinal study of 528 LGB youth ages fifteen to nineteen found that those who were considered gender atypical in childhood experienced more victimization and suffered more long-term mental health consequences.

Three fourths of the youth felt different from their peers as they were growing up. This perception of difference occurred, on average, at about age 8, or in late childhood. This is a period in which gender expectations become increasingly salient to children, and their sex role–related behavior comes under increasing scrutiny and evaluation by parents, peers, and school personnel. . . .

Youth who felt different, were called sissies or tomboys by others including parents, and who were discouraged by parents from acting in gender atypical ways experienced significantly more lifetime verbal and physical SOV than those who did not have these experiences. Gender atypical youth were verbally attacked for the first time at earlier ages, if they felt different, were considered different, or were called sissy or tomboy by parents. As to physical SOV, youth reporting gender atypicality received more physical attacks during their lifetime. First physical attacks occurred at earlier ages for youth who were called sissies or tomboys and who reported that their parents discouraged their gender atypicality.[46]

When they were growing up, over half of the males in this study were called sissies, and two-thirds of the females were called tomboys. Gender atypical behavior also elicited negative responses from parents, which, for a small percentage, ranged from punishing or restricting the behavior of their children to sending their children to therapy. Youth who were called sissies or tomboys when they were growing up were two to three times more likely to meet the diagnosis criteria for post-traumatic stress disorder than those who were never called sissies or tomboys.[47]

LGBT Youth of Color: The "Tricultural" Experience

In GLSEN's 2007 National School Climate Survey, 6 percent of LGBT youth identified as African American/black; 13 percent as Hispanic or Latino/a; 4 percent as Asian Pacific Islander; 6 percent as Native American, American Indian, or Alaska Native; and 5 percent as multiracial.[48] Although youth from minority communities face challenges that reflect the unique multidimensionality of their lives, there is a paucity of research about the intersection of race, ethnicity, and sexual orientation among youth.[49] In GLSEN's survey, a little more than half of the LGBT youth of color experienced verbal harassment based on their race or ethnicity.[50] LGBT youth of color may confront a "tricultural" experience: they face homophobia from their respective racial or ethnic group, racism from within a predominantly white LGBT community, and a combination of the two from society at large.[51] They are also at increased risk for being stigmatized and bullied in school because of their sexual orientation and gender identity, as well as their race or ethnicity.[52] Feeling that they must choose between various aspects of their identity can be particularly burdensome.

Research into the influence of ethnicity on the development of a sexual orientation indicates that some milestones in identity development, such as labeling same-sex attractions and same-sex romantic or sexual involvement, are consistent among all ethnicities, while others, such as disclosing to family members and having opposite-sex romantic and sexual relationships, vary according to ethnic group.[53] A small study of fifteen minority gay male youth found no difference between racial or ethnic groups when analyzing the disclosure of sexual orientation. Instead, attitudes toward marriage and religion and the use of a second language played a much larger role in coming out. Racial or ethnic minority youth who had families with more "traditional" values were less likely to come out at all.[54] A larger study published in 2006 found significant differences between racial and ethnic groups in being out to one's parents.[55] Unfortunately, there is no research comparing how transgender youth of color and white youth develop and disclose their gender identities.

LGBT youth of color are likely to face different challenges and stressors in consolidating their racial, ethnic, and sexual identities than white, non-Hispanic LGBT youth.[56] The significance of sexuality can vary greatly among different cultural and ethnic groups. Identity is influenced, in part, by such cultural factors as values and beliefs regarding sexuality, stereotypes about gender roles and expectations about childbearing, religious values and beliefs, and the degree of acculturation or assimilation into mainstream society. The tight-knit family structures important to many immigrant communities and communities of color can make the coming-out process more difficult for some LGBT youth.[57] As Trinity Ordona, a cofounder of Asian/Pacific Islander PFLAG in San Francisco notes, "The families are the core of the culture. When a gay Asian comes out and gets kicked out of the family, it's like being severed from the heart. But if you get the family on your side they will stand and protect you."[58]

For children, racial and ethnic identity is an important point of commonality with their families, which provide a vital support system for living in a society in which racism persists.[59] Even when children experience hostility in the outside world because of their race or ethnicity, they come home to a supportive environment anchored by a shared culture. In contrast, LGBT youth cannot expect to find similar support around sexuality or gender issues at home.[60] In addition, conservative religious beliefs dominate some ethnic minority and immigrant communities. Two-thirds of the 2,700 Black Pride Survey respondents in the year 2000 said homophobia was a problem in the black community. Forty-three percent reported mostly negative experiences in black churches and mosques, while another 31 percent reported equally positive and negative experiences.[61]

The age at which youth become aware of same-sex attraction and the degree to which they are comfortable coming out to school friends may vary along racial and ethnic lines. Though not generalizable to all LGBT youth, a study of 139 gay men found that Latinos became aware of their same-sex attraction at a younger age compared to white and African American youth. White youth, however, were more likely to come out to their families. The same study found that Asian American youth were more likely to have sex at an earlier age—three years earlier, on average—than other racial or ethnic groups. The majority of African American youth in the study engaged in sex before labeling their sexual identity, while Asian American youth overwhelmingly engaged in sex only after labeling themselves as gay or bisexual.[62] A 1996 study reported that African American youth had more optimistic attitudes than whites about coming out to their friends, believing that their heterosexual peers would accept them. Most had already come out to their best friends with positive results.[63]

Some researchers have proposed that there are differences in the coming-out process based on race and culture. In one study, Asian American, African American, and Latino youth were less likely than white youth to disclose their sexual orientation to family members. Low levels of disclosure of sexual orientation to others were associated with higher levels of internalized homophobia among Latino and Asian American youth. This dynamic was not the case for African American and white youth.[64] White youth may be more likely to hide their sexual orientation in school, citing fears of harassment and violence.[65] Some researchers suggest that white adolescent students feel less comfortable coming out because they are not accustomed to minority status and have not developed the same coping skills as minority youth.[66]

LGBT youth of color often experience racism in white-dominated LGBT communities, organizations, and support networks, which may disproportionately be of service to white, suburban, middle-class LGBT youth.[67] Such LGBT communities may offer fewer resources for urban youth, who are more likely to be black or Latino, and the institutions that do exist may be perceived as "white," inaccessible, or irrelevant to their experiences. For example, some students in a California high school reported that the local Project 10 program, a chapter of the first major school-based program developed to provide education and counseling on the subject of sexual orientation, did not serve the purpose for which it was intended.[68] During the 1997–98 academic year, Lance McCready investigated the reasons why black gay males were reluctant to be involved with Project 10. About one of the students interviewed, the researcher wrote,

> At [the high school], where social groups are often defined by race, identifying himself as gay (a social identity he and other Black students perceived as White) in every situation would put him at odds with his Black peers. Consequently, he chose to de-emphasize his sexuality and involve himself in extracurricular clubs and activities (such as student government) that are legitimated by Black students. Downplaying his sexuality also meant that Project 10 was off limits—to align himself with Project 10 meant risking harassment and public ridicule.[69]

Although sizable and well-organized LGBT communities of color exist, particularly in large urban areas, LGBT youth of color may choose not to connect with them because they fear they will be harassed by their peers. Though these youth are stigmatized on the basis of both race and sexual orientation or gender identity, many find inadequate support as they navigate among three, often compartmentalized communities.[70]

The few researchers and educators who have examined the relationship between sexuality, race, and the harassment faced by LGBT youth of color often treat LGBT students' race as an add-on to their sexuality or gender identity.[71] Initiatives to make schools safer for LGBT students and to integrate LGBT issues into the curriculum sometimes lack an understanding of how the experiences of youth of color differ from those of white LGBT students. The information that is available seems to assume that because of the stigma of being both a racial and sexual minority, LGBT youth of color have a more difficult school experience. However, that may not always be the case. One researcher found that African American youth who experience same-sex attraction actually had significantly higher self-esteem then their white, Asian, or Hispanic peers.[72] While these findings do not discount other studies that have documented the negative experiences of LGBT youth of color, they do highlight the need for more research on the different ways that white youth and youth of color cope with coming out at school.

Children of LGBT Parents

Historically, estimates of the number of children in the United States being raised by gay or lesbian parents ranged widely from one to fourteen million.[73] More recent analysis of data from the U.S. Census Bureau estimated that over 270,000 children were living in households headed by same-sex couples in 2005.[74] (There are no available estimates on the number of children who have a parent who identifies as bisexual or transgender.)

Estimates of the number of lesbian or gay parents in the United States range from two to eight million.[75] U.S. Census data also provide estimates of the number of unmarried same-sex couples with children. Of the nearly six hundred thousand same-sex couples counted in the 2000 census, 34 percent of female unmarried-partner households (i.e., lesbian or bisexual female couples) and 22 percent of male unmarried-partner households (i.e., gay or bisexual male couples) had at least one child under the age of eighteen living with them. The percentage of unmarried female same-sex couples is not that much lower than the percentage of married opposite-sex households with children (46 percent) or the percentage of unmarried opposite-sex households with children (43 percent).[76]

These children are enrolled in schools throughout the United States, not just in urban areas. For example, the following rates of parenting by female or male same-sex unmarried partners were reported by the U.S. Census in predominantly rural states:

Alaska: 37 percent of unmarried same-sex male couples and 39 percent of unmarried same-sex female couples
Mississippi: 31 percent of unmarried same-sex male couples and 44 percent of unmarried same-sex female couples
South Dakota: 34 percent of unmarried same-sex male couples and 42 percent of unmarried same-sex female couples[77]

Analysis of census data also revealed some interesting statistics regarding the intersection of LGB parenting with race and ethnicity: black[78] and Latino[79] same-sex couples were nearly twice as likely as white same-sex couples to be raising children.[80] In a 2000 survey of LGBT African Americans, 21 percent of respondents reported being biological parents, and 2 percent reported being adoptive or foster parents.[81] Another study found that one in four black lesbians lived with a child for whom she had child-rearing responsibilities, while only 2 percent of black gay men reported households with children.[82] Clearly, many LGB people are parents, and parenting appears to be even more prevalent among LGB people of color.

LGBT individuals pursue different paths to parenthood. Some have children from previous or current heterosexual relationships; others have children after coming out, through donor insemination, surrogacy, or adoption. Some parents are couples; others are single parents.[83] The vast majority of professional organizations, including the American Academy of Pediatrics,[84] the National Association of Social Workers,[85] and the American Psychological Association (APA),[86] recognize that gay and lesbian parents are just as good at parenting as heterosexual parents and that children thrive in gay- and lesbian-headed families. As one APA publication reports, "not a single study has found children of gay or lesbian parents to be disadvantaged in any significant respect relative to children of heterosexual parents."[87] These conclusions are likely true of bisexual parents as well. Although there is a lack of research focusing specifically on bisexual parents, it is highly probable that there are bisexuals in the same-sex couples included in the samples of many of these studies.[88]

Debate over same-sex marriage and other laws and policies that affect the ability of LGBT people to foster or adopt children has focused on whether the development of sexual orientation or gender identity and the psychological and personal development of children raised in families headed by same-sex couples differs significantly from the development of children raised by heterosexual parents. However, research has found little difference in the psychological adjustment and well-being of children raised by gay or lesbian parents.

More than 25 years of research on the offspring of non-heterosexual parents has yielded results of remarkable clarity. Regardless of whether researchers have studied the offspring of divorced lesbian and gay parents or those born to lesbian or gay parents, their findings have been similar. Regardless of whether researchers have studied children or adolescents, they have reported similar results. Regardless of whether investigators have examined sexual iden- tity, self-esteem, adjustment, or qualities of social relationships, the results have been remarkably consistent. In study after study, the offspring of lesbian and gay parents have been found to be at least as well adjusted overall as those of other parents.[89]

In fact, research on gay or lesbian families with children suggests that the quality of parenting is far more influential in the development of children than is the gender[90] or sexual orientation[91] of parents.[92] For ex- ample, a study of data from the National Longitudinal Study of Adoles- cent Health found no statistically significant difference in delinquency, victimization, and substance use between children being raised in fami- lies headed by female same-sex parents and those headed by different- sex parents. Rather, good family relationships were associated with lower tobacco, drug, and alcohol use.[93] Another study of the same data found that "regardless of family type, adolescents whose parents described closer relationships with them reported higher quality peer relations and more friends in school."[94]

While the overall health and well-being of children in gay- or lesbian- parent families is very similar to those in heterosexual-parent families, research has found differences, likely related to family structure and en- vironment, that many would consider positive.

> Without a doubt, many differences between children growing up in lesbian-, gay-, and heterosexual-parented homes do exist. For instance, the young adult offspring of lesbian mothers report feel- ing fewer antigay sentiments than do the offspring of heterosexual mothers. With regard to parental divisions of labor within cou- ples, lesbian mothers report sharing child-care duties more evenly than do heterosexual parents. Although not relevant to policy de- bates, these and other differences have been reported in the re- search literature.[95]

Researchers have also begun to identify the effect that societal homo- phobia may be having on the children of LGBT parents. A study that compared children raised by lesbian parents in the United States with children raised by lesbian parents in the Netherlands found that the chil- dren in the United States were less likely to be open about having lesbian mothers and experienced more homophobia.[96] According to Abigail

Garner, the founder of Families Like Mine, an organization dedicated to decreasing the isolation of people who have LGBT parents and giving voice to their experiences, "It wasn't having a gay father that made growing up a challenge, it was navigating a society that did not accept him and, by extension, me."[97]

Homophobia also leads to harassment and violence against the children of LGBT parents at school. A 1998 study of school counselors and their perceptions of the gay and lesbian students in their schools found that many of the students targeted for harassment had gay or lesbian parents.[98] Nearly one-third of the twenty-four hundred students in the seventh through twelfth grades who participated in the Preventing School Harassment Survey in California disagreed or strongly disagreed that their school is safe for students with LGBT parents.[99]

> In one school, a sixth-grader was labeled a "fag" by classmates who discovered that he had lesbian parents. Other children would point pencils at his behind and make sexual innuendos, while teachers who witnessed this harassment failed to intervene. The harassment spiraled out of control, culminating in physical violence. He was thrown against his locker and kicked in the head by a boy wearing cleats. Moments later, he yelled at one of his attackers, and he was later punished for using inappropriate language. His mothers, with the help of a lawyer, quickly had their son transferred to another school.[100]

Analysis of data from the National Lesbian Family Study found that at ten years old, 43 percent of children in the study reported experiencing homophobia:

> At first when I was in second grade some kids said some things to me on the bus. Now they don't. . . . I ignored them. I felt bad.

> The only time I remember is once last year a girl told me my moms were going to hell. I probably turned away and told a teacher. It's hard to remember [how I felt]—probably sad, definitely annoyed, not at the point of tears.

> Teachers don't allow kids to make negative comments about skin color or gender, but they don't stop them from saying negative things about gays.[101]

Children in this study also reported that schools were less likely to reprimand students for making homophobic comments than for sexist, religious, or ethnic insults.[102]

In 2008, GLSEN released the results of a survey of 588 LGBT parents of a child in grades K–12 (in public or private school) and 154 students in middle or high school with an LGBT parent. Nearly 60 percent of parents reported that they were "sometimes," "often," or "frequently" worried that their children will have problems in school because of having an LGBT parent. Nearly one-quarter of the youth in the study reported that they felt unsafe at school because of having an LGBT parent. Sixty-four percent of students heard derogatory, homophobic remarks in school "frequently" or "often," and 18 percent "frequently" or "often" heard negative remarks specifically because of having an LGBT parent. Even more students (28 percent) heard negative remarks about LGBT families from school faculty or staff.[103]

There is very little research specifically on the children of transgender parents. A small study published in the *International Journal of Transgenderism* in 1998 noted that opposition to transsexuals' continuing in a parenting role during and after their transition to the opposite sex is still very high among psychiatrists, psychologists, and society at large. This opposition is largely due to unsubstantiated concerns that the children of transgender parents will be confused about their own gender identity during critical years of child development and will be subjected to bullying and ostracism at school. However, the small body of research that is available does not support these concerns. A small study of eighteen children, each with one transsexual parent, found that none became transsexual, despite continued contact with their transsexual parent, and that only three of them experienced some teasing when their peers found out about their parents. In each case, it was quickly resolved with the help of supportive teachers and school administrators.[104] The fourteen-year-old daughter of a female-to-male transsexual parent summarized her experience in this way:

> My mother is not happy in the body she is in. My mom is a lot happier since starting to live as who she wants to be. When I was thirteen, my mother said, "I want to be a man; do you care?" I said, "No. As long as you are the same person inside and still love me. I don't care what you are on the outside." It's like a chocolate bar; it's got a new wrapper, but it's the same chocolate inside.[105]

While further research is needed on the experiences of children with transgender parents, the author of this 1998 study concluded that these children are more likely to be hurt by a traumatic separation from their parent than because of that parent's gender identity.

Children of LGBT parents hear messages—from society, from their school-age peers, and even from school personnel—that their families are, at best, nontraditional or, at worst, a threat to them and to Western civilization. Heterocentric assumptions are pervasive in society and tolerated, if not magnified, in public schools.[106] Most early childhood education programs and teachers are ill-equipped to address the needs of these youth.[107] So the inclusion of LGBT parents in school partnership can only aid students.

> It is well established that the development of school, family, and community partnerships can help children succeed in school and later in life. By extension, it can be assumed that efforts to improve communication among school professionals, sexual minority parents, and the entire school community will be a tremendous help to the success of children with sexual minority parents.[108]

Educators and administrators who work to create safer and more inclusive schools assist not only LGBT-identified students but also children in LGBT families and children who come from other nontraditional families.[109]

LGBT Youth in Foster Care

An estimated 5 to 10 percent of youth in the foster care system are gay or lesbian.[110] The lack of institutional acknowledgment of LGBT youth in foster care leads to a hostile atmosphere that forces them to hide their sexual orientation or gender identity and subjects them to physical, verbal, and emotional harassment and abuse.[111] One of the problems faced by transgender youth in foster care is not being allowed to dress according to their gender identity. One study found that 78 percent of LGBT youth ran away from foster homes because of the hostile treatment they received due to their sexual orientation or gender identity. Sadly, 100 percent of LGBT youth surveyed in group homes run by New York City's Administration on Children's Services reported being verbally harassed, and 70 percent suffered physical abuse because of their sexual orientation.[112]

Youth in the foster care system are also more likely to encounter difficulty finding a long-term living situation and to suffer multiple interruptions in their education. This discontinuity, combined with their experience of harassment and alienation in schools, places these students at an elevated risk for dropping out. The New York City Child Welfare Administration, the Council of Family and Child Care Agencies, and the Child Welfare League of America have all endorsed reforming the foster care system to better aid LGBT youth.[113]

Homeless LGBT Youth

Though the number of homeless youth who identify as LGBT is difficult to determine, the National Network of Runaway and Youth Services estimates that anywhere from 20 to 40 percent of homeless adolescents identify as gay or lesbian.[114] It has been estimated that more than 40 percent of homeless youth in large cities like New York and Los Angeles are LGBT.[115] Additional research shows that over one-third (35 percent) of homeless youth identify as gay, lesbian, or bisexual.[116] According to a 2002 report by the Urban Justice Center, 4 to 10 percent of youth in the juvenile justice system in New York identify as LGBT.[117] The 1991 National American Indian Adolescent Health Survey found that gay Native American youth were significantly more likely than their heterosexual peers (28 percent vs. 17 percent, respectively) to have run away from home within the previous twelve months.[118]

A 2002 study was the first to compare the risks faced by homeless LGBT youth to those faced by their heterosexual counterparts. From 1995 to 1998, data were collected from homeless youth thirteen to twenty-one years of age. The majority of participants identified as white (53 percent) and heterosexual (78 percent). Of the 22 percent of the participants who identified as other than heterosexual, 85 percent identified as bisexual, with only 14 percent identifying as exclusively gay or lesbian. Only one participant (1 percent) identified as transgender.[119]

The study indicated that LGBT youth and heterosexual youth left their homes for similar reasons, including an inability to get along with their parents and domestic violence. But LGBT youth left their homes, returned, and ran away again almost twice as frequently. LGBT youth were also more likely to leave home as a result of physical abuse and parental alcoholism. Only twelve LGBT youth (14 percent) said that they ran away because of conflicts with their families over their sexual orientation. The LGBT homeless youth experienced higher levels of victimization than their heterosexual counterparts, and since the time that they first became homeless, gay male homeless youth had been sexually victimized more frequently than their heterosexual counterparts. These youth were also more likely to abuse drugs and alcohol and experienced a higher incidence of the symptoms of depression. The LGBT homeless youth had sex with more partners and were also younger, at an average age of thirteen, when they had their first sexual experience. The majority also reported that they did not use a condom during sex "most of the time."[120]

While the process of coming out to family and friends at school is difficult for the majority of LGBT youth, many are fortunate enough to have a support network to rely on for guidance and acceptance. This is almost completely absent for homeless LGBT youth, who were almost entirely ignored by researchers and policymakers until recently. The homeless shelters that exist are often segregated by sex and do not properly integrate transgender youths according to their gender identity. Left on their own to support themselves, many LGBT youth are arrested for "survival" crimes, such as robbery or sex work.

LGBT Youth and Their Families

LGBT youth often feel estranged from their families because they feel the need to hide their emerging sexual orientation or gender identity. One study found that coming out or being discovered as gay by family or friends, along with antigay harassment, induced the most common stressors among youth.[121] This stress is magnified when youth are prematurely discovered to be gay by their parents, which happened to 33 percent of the predominantly black and Hispanic gay and bisexual male adolescents interviewed in a 1996 study. A slightly higher percentage (38 percent) chose to disclose their sexual orientation to their parents.[122] Youth who voluntarily tell their parents about their sexual orientation are more likely to come out to their mothers than to their fathers. In 1998, a study found that 60 to 80 percent of gay and lesbian youth came out to their mothers, while 30 to 65 percent chose to come out to their fathers.[123] A study of 528 LGB youth that was published in 2006 had similar findings: approximately 60 percent came out to their mothers, but only 27 percent told their fathers.[124]

When parents find out that their child is lesbian, gay, bisexual, or transgender, responses range from warm acceptance to open hostility. A study published in 1987 found that 26 percent of adolescent males were forced to leave their homes because of their families' conflict over their sexual orientation.[125] Available research indicates that the experiences of gay and lesbian youth who come out to their parents have not gotten much better over time. A 1993 study of 120 lesbian and gay men ages fourteen to twenty-one found that 42 percent of the women and 30 percent of the men reported negative responses from their families after coming out to them.[126] A study published in 1996 found that only 11 percent of gay and lesbian youth experienced supportive responses after coming out to their parents, while 20 percent of mothers and 28 percent of fathers were rejecting or completely intolerant.[127]

There is little academic research available on how parents react to the gender expression of their transgender children. However, in one small study of twenty-four transgender youth ages fifteen to twenty-one, between 35 and 73 percent reported being "sometimes" or "often" verbally abused by their parents because of their gender expression, and between 13 and 36 percent reported "sometimes" or "often" being physically abused. These youth were more likely to report attempting suicide than those who experienced less abuse at the hands of their parents.[128]

A groundbreaking study published in 2009 in the journal of the American Academy of Pediatrics was the first to examine the relationship between family rejection of LGB youth and the development of health and mental health problems in adulthood. This survey of 224 LGB young adults (ages 21 to 25) found that higher rates of family rejection were significantly correlated with negative health outcomes. Participants who reported higher levels of family rejection during adolescence were 8.4 times more likely to report having attempted suicide, 5.9 times more likely to report high levels of depression, 3.4 times more likely to use illegal drugs, and 3.4 times more likely to report having engaged in unprotected sexual intercourse, compared with LGB youth who reported no or low levels of family rejection.[129]

The Strength and Resiliency of LGBT Youth

Because many researchers and advocacy groups passionately advocate for the safety of LGB youth, a lot of information is collected regarding the difficulties these youth face. (Unfortunately, there has been less attention paid specifically to the experiences of transgender youth, good and bad.) While the existing research is significant in establishing the need for nondiscrimination policies, gay-straight alliances (in-school support groups for LGBT, questioning, and straight students), and other policy interventions, many LGBT youth are happy, healthy, and display remarkable strength and resiliency.[130] Even after they experienced harassment or violence at school, some youth reported feeling well supported and cared about because of the interventions of friends, family, or school administrators. "I don't feel as scared as I did. I'm a whole lot angrier now," asserted one youth. "[I am] much stronger. Very sure of who I am," said another. Many youth are also able to use these negative experiences to develop self-empowering, proactive behaviors. According to one youth, "I joined a club at school to combat racism, sexism and homophobia. Hopefully that will help." Another reported, "[Harassment] has made me a lot more active, made me try to push harder to fix what's wrong at my school."[131]

Many LGBT youth are also thriving in their school environments and are proud of who they are and what they are accomplishing.[132] They have remarkable strengths, talents, and skills at their disposal; are able to develop positive and productive coping strategies; and can tap into existing support networks or even create their own.[133] They do not just advocate for themselves; they also educate their peers and teachers in the process.[134] For example, in Massachusetts in 1993, hundreds of LGBT youth successfully lobbied the legislature to pass a law banning sexual orientation discrimination in the state's public schools. It was the first time most legislators had met an openly gay youth. Many LGBT students are also one another's role models and sources of support, learning from each other's experiences.[135] Through these experiences, they gain a sense that they can make a difference and contribute positively to their communities.[136]

While the statistics regarding LGBT youth and suicide demand immediate intervention, a large study of 11,940 adolescents revealed that the majority of the sexual minority youth who were surveyed (85 percent of males and 72 percent of females) reported no suicidal ideation at all.[137] Another study of 221 LGB youth found that participants who had not considered or attempted suicide "possessed internal and external qualities that enabled them to cope well in the face of discrimination, loneliness, and isolation."[138]

What are those "internal and external qualities"? New research has found that when youth are in environments that support the development of their sexual orientation or gender identity safely, they can thrive emotionally and psychology. For example, a study of 350 youth ages fifteen to nineteen who attended LGBT youth support programs in the New York City area found that participation in a same-sex relationship increased self-esteem in males and decreased internalized homophobia in girls.[139] This suggests, for example, that schools that treat students in same-sex and opposite-sex dating relationships equally, such as by allowing LGBT youth to take a same-sex date to the prom, are helping to support healthy developmental milestones.

Still, little attention has been given to explaining why the majority of sexual minority youth grow up to be healthy despite widespread homophobia. The small but growing body of research on protective factors that support resilience in LGBT youth in schools has found a number of unique protective factors, including

- school policies that explicitly prohibit harassment based on sexual orientation;
- teacher training to create supportive school climates;
- social supports geared toward sexual minority students, whether in the form of peer support in school clubs or institutional support through clearly identified policies, resources, and support for sexual minority students.[140]

In fact, research in California has found that when students attend schools that have

(1) specific anti-harassment policies, (2) teachers who intervene when they hear slurs, (3) a GSA or similar student club, and (4) information and support related to sexual orientation and gender identity, they score higher on multiple scales of resilience, including feeling that adults care, feeling that teachers are fair, and feeling that students have a voice and can make contributions at their school.[141]

Section 2 of this book includes a more detailed review and analysis of these school-based policies that can significantly influence the experiences of LGBT youth. The need for more research on LGBT youth and resiliency is discussed in more detail in chapter 7.

Of course, it would be far better for youth to develop increased self-esteem and personal acceptance without having to deal with harassment and violence in the first place. In many of the cases discussed in the next chapter, parents and school administrators do little or nothing to protect them. School districts that believe they do not need to address the needs of LGBT students or, worse, that they "have no gay or lesbian students"[142] are woefully mistaken.

2 | A Grave Picture of Harassment and Violence in Schools

The following conversation took place between a six-year-old elementary school student and his father:

> Daddy, do you know what a "faggot" is?
> Why do you ask?
> [My friend] called me one at recess.[1]

This is but one striking example of the epidemic of anti-LGBT harassment and violence in American schools. Numerous studies have documented pervasive harassment and violence perpetrated by students, and even some school faculty and staff, against students from elementary school through senior high. This little boy's question illustrates that the violence and harassment is about more than sexual orientation.

Students routinely use terms such as *fag, sissy, fairy, queer,* or *gay* to tease and berate peers who do not conform to gender-role stereotypes, as well as to express disgust and disdain for something they simply do not like.[2] The exclamation "That's so gay!" is used by children around the United States to connote negativity. A study in Iowa found that high school students on average heard twenty-five antigay remarks per day, with teachers who hear such slurs failing to respond 97 percent of the time.[3] In a study of 528 LGB youth in New York City, 72 percent reported that the first time they were verbally harassed because of their sexual orientation occurred in school.[4] GLSEN's 2007 National School Climate Survey reported that over 73 percent of LGBT youth across the nation heard antigay slurs from other students "frequently" or "often" and that 63 percent heard those slurs from faculty or school staff.[5]

Verbal harassment is not harmless behavior. "It's not just name calling," stressed one student interviewed for a study conducted by Human Rights Watch in 2001, "I don't know how schools can isolate it like that. When are they going to see it as a problem? When we're bloody on the ground in front of them?"[6] Sadly, it may not stop even then. A 1993

Massachusetts study of high school students found that gay teens are twice as likely as their straight peers to be threatened or injured with a weapon at school.[7] GLSEN's 2007 survey found that over 40 percent of LGBT youth were shoved, pushed, or otherwise physically harassed because of their real or perceived sexual orientation and that over 30 percent were physically harassed because of their gender expression.[8] Another study found that school was the most frequently reported location where LGB youth were physically assaulted.[9]

A five-year study conducted by the Safe Schools Coalition of Washington State documented 111 incidents of anti-LGBT violence in seventy-three different schools, including thirty-eight cases of ongoing verbal harassment, seventeen incidents of physical harassment, and eight gang rapes in which a total of eleven students were molested, including two sixth-graders. Most of these incidents occurred in a classroom or in school hallways, and more than one-third of the cases involved female offenders. As a result of this violence, ten students dropped out of school, ten students attempted suicide, and two students successfully completed suicide.[10]

Anti-LGBT Harassment and Violence in Elementary and Middle Schools

Jamal was in third grade when he wrote the first of the following letters to his mother and in seventh grade when he wrote the second letter to teachers at his school:

> Dear Mom,
> Bobby hit me on the bus. I did not do anything. What he did was put his earphones on my ear, and then I moved it away and he said, "Don't hit me, you little fagite [sic]." Then he hit me real hard. I wanted to cry. Then he said, "I'll hit you so hard you will want to cry forever." Why does everyone pick on me? Why? I think I am ugly like people say. I don't think I look nice at all.
> Bye bye,
> Jamal

> I have been called gay, faggot and a girl most of my life. I have recently had a new name added . . . "gay prick." I have reached out for help so many times it's unbelievable. Nothing much has hap-

pened except a phone call home. I am still being teased and embarrassed in front of people and also my friends. . . . I have been putting up with this since elementary school. And let me tell you this—the longer you let this continue, the worse it will get. And it will be twice as hard to deal with it.[11]

When people think of violence and harassment against LGBT students, they think of incidents occurring in high school and maybe middle school. The experiences of elementary students like Jamal are often anecdotal and tolerated as immature childhood behavior. Because people mistakenly believe that it does not happen, there is little documentation of anti-LGBT harassment in elementary schools. But because violence is targeted at youth who do not conform to stereotypical gender roles, regardless of their sexual orientation or gender identity, this victimization can begin at very young ages. Through observing adults or their older brothers and sisters, elementary students know that it is bad to call someone a "fag," even if they do not understand what it means. Consequently, interventions at the high school level come too late for many children who are teased, bullied, and tormented from the very first day they set foot in elementary school.

A five-year study by the Safe Schools Coalition of Washington State documented numerous anti-LGBT incidents in elementary schools. For example:

- After hearing taunts like "Get away, gay boy!" from his peers over a four-month period, a second grader, upset that no one would play with him and afraid to go to school, finally reported the incidents to his mother. The school intervened by teaching the class that name-calling would not be tolerated. According to the boy's mom, "[It's made me] more aware that [the teasing] starts younger than I would have thought. These are second-grade kids. I don't know *how aware* they are of sexual orientation at that age."
- An eleven-year-old boy was attacked by a large group of classmates after his diary, in which he described feeling like a girl inside and wondered if he were a lesbian, was stolen. The classmates sold his diary for ten dollars per page and, when they attacked him, took some of his clothes off and tried to force him to wear girl's clothes. This youth, who eventually identified as transgender, waited until age sixteen before talking to school administrators about these experiences.

- A twelve-year-old sixth grader was attacked and repeatedly gang-raped by four other sixth graders and two high school students at a camp sponsored by an elementary school. One of the attackers vomited on him and threatened to kill him if he told anyone about the incident.

Incidents of violence and harassment were more pervasive in middle and junior high schools:

- Since the beginning of the school year, a seventh grader was repeatedly teased and harassed by students in the hallways. The students called him "flute boy" because he played flute in the school symphony. One demanded, "How come you look so gay? Are you gay?" The boy's family reported that he cried nearly every day and no longer wanted to go to school. But when the boy's mother reported these incidents to a school counselor she trusted, the counselor was hesitant to intervene because she did not want the harassment to get worse.
- After her seventh-grade son was harassed daily at school by being called a "faggot" and a "pervert" and told, "Queers burn in hell," the boy's mother complained to the school principal, who assured her that the staff would get sensitivity training, even though it was the students who were doing the harassing. Later in the year, after a game of "smear the queer," the boy started a fight with two other students after a classmate told him that standing up for himself would end the teasing. When the fight was over, the boy was sent to the nurse's office with cuts, bruises, a lump on his neck from being hit by a soda bottle, a sprained ankle, and a broken arm. He was reprimanded by school administrators for starting the fight and was suspended for the rest of the day.[12]

None of the largest population-based studies cited in this book collected information from students below the sixth-grade level. These horrific accounts of violence and harassment, though specific to just one state, clearly underscore the need for more research and intervention on behalf of elementary and middle school students nationwide.

Unchecked harassment against young children in elementary school predictably escalates into violence as they grow older, especially in smaller school systems in which the student population remains fairly consistent. A nineteen-year-old high school senior who had been harassed since first grade explains,

> It was horrible. At first they made fun of me because I was different. Then it was because I was gay. They'd call me things like "fag" and "cocksucker." It went on through middle school and got really bad in high school. After I came out it was like I had a death wish or something. I was pushed around, thrown into lockers. I can see it all in my head. It was just constant. Everybody was always harassing me.[13]

The 626 LGBT students in middle school who participated in GLSEN's 2007 School Climate Survey were more likely than those in high school to experience verbal and physical harassment and physical assault. For example, over 80 percent of LGBT middle school students heard homophobic remarks from other students at school, compared to just over 70 percent of LGBT high school students. Nearly 60 percent of LGBT middle school students experienced physical harassment, compared to just over 40 percent of LGBT high school students. LGBT students in middle school were also twice as likely to be physically assaulted at school (e.g., punched, kicked, or injured with a weapon) than their peers in high school (39 percent vs. 20 percent, respectively).[14]

GLSEN also found that LGBT middle school students who were victimized at school were unlikely to receive help and support from teachers and school administrators.

> Many middle school students who were harassed or assaulted in school never reported the incident to adult authorities—57% never told school staff and 50% never told a parent or other family member. Among middle school students who did tell school authorities about an incident, less than a third (29%) said that reporting resulted in effective intervention by school staff.[15]

LGBT students in middle school were also less likely than those in high school to have access to support programs like gay-straight alliances and LGBT-inclusive curricular resources.

The Middle School Safety Study, a survey of over fifteen hundred middle school students in California, found that LGB students (54 percent) were significantly more likely than straight students (33 percent) to experience social bullying (having mean rumors or sexual jokes told about them or bias-based bullying, including being bullied or harassed based on sex, perceived sexual orientation, disability, body size, or looks). LGB students (39 percent) were also more likely than straight students (25 percent) to experience physical bullying (being pushed, shoved, hit, or threatened or injured with a weapon; being in a physical fight; or having property damaged or stolen). As a result, the LGB students reported that they did not feel as safe as straight students in school, particularly in unsupervised places.[16]

"You're So Gay"

A Profile of Carl Joseph Walker-Hoover

Eleven-year-old Carl Joseph Walker-Hoover completed suicide after frequent teasing and bullying by other kids at school, who called him "girlie, "gay," and "fag." A student at New Leadership Charter School in Springfield, Massachusetts, Carl did not identify as gay. He would have celebrated his twelfth birthday on April 17, 2009. Carl was a Boy Scout, and he played on the 5A football team, the Martin Luther King Jr. Community Center basketball team, and the soccer team of his parish, Holy Name Church. He loved to learn and was active in his church, playing a wise man in the Christmas play.[17]

According to Carl's mother, Sirdeaner, he just happened to be someone his peers targeted. After complaining to his mother about being bullied so much, she decided to take action. She spoke to his principal, teachers, and guidance counselor, and she became more active in the school's parent-teacher organization. However, the teasing and threats continued, and Carl started acting out in school, becoming increasingly fearful and feeling even more alienated. On April 6, 2009, Sirdeaner found her son with an extension cord wrapped around his neck, hanging from the third floor rafter of their home. In the letter left behind for his mother, Carl explained that he simply could not take it anymore. He apologized, expressing his love for his family and that he wanted his little brother to have his Pokémon card collection.[18]

Anti-LGBT Harassment and Violence in High Schools

There is far more information about the experiences of LGBT high school students—in part because many become aware of their attractions or begin to self-identify during their high school years—allowing for a much clearer picture of experiences of secondary school students. A study from the United Kingdom published in 2001 found that although 93 percent of openly gay and bisexual students in British high schools experienced verbal harassment and bullying, only 6 percent of schools had a nondiscrimination policy that included sexual orientation.[19] The lack of attention and intervention on behalf of these students led one researcher to claim that this institutional neglect is "nothing less than state-sanctioned child abuse."[20] The high school environment in the United States is no better.

Analysis of data from the 1996 National Longitudinal Study of Adolescent Health, which included more than 12,000 students in U.S. high schools, revealed that LGB youth were more likely then heterosexual youth to have been in a fight that resulted in the need for medical attention and more likely to have witnessed violence. Bisexual youth were also more likely to be jumped and violently attacked. This study also found that gay youth were more likely to *perpetrate* violence against their peers. This was accounted for by the fear and need to defend themselves they feel because of the violence and harassment they regularly endure.[21]

Gay Student Sues School and Wins $900K Settlement

A Profile of Jamie Nabozny

> The story of Jamie Nabozny, a student from Wisconsin, is a tragic example of how verbal harassment can escalate into life-threatening violence in high school. In elementary school, although shy and quiet, Jamie was a good student and enjoyed going to school. In seventh grade, however, Jamie realized that he was gay. When other students at Ashland Middle School in Wisconsin learned of his sexuality, the torment began. What started as name-calling and spitting quickly turned to more violent attacks. In a science lab, for example, Jamie was the victim of a "mock rape" by two boys who told him he should enjoy it, while twenty other students looked on and laughed. In response to the attack, the middle school principal told Jamie and his parents that "boys will be boys" and that if

Jamie "was going to be so openly gay, he had to expect this kind of stuff to happen."[22] This "kind of stuff" continued throughout middle school and escalated in high school, when he was attacked several times in the bathroom and urinated on. On the school bus, he was routinely pelted with objects, including steel nuts and bolts. But the most serious assault occurred in eleventh grade, when Jamie was surrounded by eight students and kicked in the stomach repeatedly while other students stood by. A few weeks later, Jamie collapsed due to internal bleeding caused by the attack and was rushed to the hospital.[23]

Despite frequent meetings with school officials, the identification of his attackers, and the intervention of his parents, the school took no meaningful disciplinary action against Jamie's abusers.[24] Throughout his time at Ashland High School, Jamie tried to kill himself several times. He dropped out of school twice and eventually decided to leave for good: "In December of my eleventh-grade year, we had a meeting with my parents and guidance counselor at school, and we decided the best thing for me to do was to leave. [The guidance counselor] said, 'I've tried to help you through this whole thing and nobody's willing to do anything.'" Jamie left Ashland, moved to Minneapolis, and earned a GED. He also began to get involved in the local LGBT community, working for a while with District 200, a community center for LGBT youth.[25]

While in Minneapolis, Jamie was diagnosed with post-traumatic stress disorder related to his experiences in middle and high school. Jamie initially just wanted to put the Ashland experiences behind him and move on. However, a trip to the Gay and Lesbian Community Action Center in Minneapolis changed his mind. Having moved out of his parents' home at seventeen, Jamie had gone to the center in search of foster parents. It was there that a crime victims' advocate told Jamie that what had happened to him was illegal and that the school should be held responsible. Jamie remembers his thoughts at the time: "I didn't realize what was being done to me was illegal or wrong. I just thought it's a small town; they're very prejudiced, homophobic. I almost felt it was OK what they did to me—that they could get away with it. I knew it wasn't right, but I didn't know that it was illegal." The crime victims' advocate secured a lawyer for Jamie, and a suit was filed within a few days. Unfortunately, the lawyer turned out to be "quite homophobic and did not want to be labeled as a gay rights advocate. She didn't want this to be a gay case."[26] The federal district judge presiding over Jamie's lawsuit ruled that Jamie's school could not be held liable for the actions of its students, and the case was dismissed.[27]

However, Lambda Legal Defense and Education Fund offered to represent Jamie on appeal, arguing, "Jamie's rights to equal protection and due process were violated when the school refused to protect him from antigay abuse." In July 1996, in a precedent-setting decision, the federal appellate court ruled that public schools have a constitutional obligation to prevent the abuse of lesbian and gay students. Then, in November 1996, a jury unanimously found Jamie's middle and high school principals liable for failing to protect him during four years of brutal antigay abuse, and he was awarded more than nine hundred thousand dollars in damages.[28] The case succeeded in bringing national attention to violence and harassment against LGBT students in public schools. As for Jamie's personal message, he said, "It really had become much more about everyone else and less about me. . . . I'm going to go on, and I'm going to be OK . . . But there's a lot of people who aren't, some people don't make it out of high school because they kill themselves. . . . It's very important to me that [LGBT students] know they don't have to take the abuse. They don't have to go through this stuff."[29] Jamie Nabozny's victory was the first in a series of court rulings that have held school districts responsible for failing to protect LGBT students from discrimination, violence, and harassment.

According to a summary of fifteen lawsuits written by GLSEN and the National Center for Lesbian Rights, school districts paid between forty thousand and almost one million dollars in damages between 1996 and 2002 due to discrimination, violence, and harassment against LGBT students. The lawsuits have occurred throughout the United States, from California to Kentucky, even in states that do not have legislation or department of education regulations specifically protecting students on the basis of sexual orientation or gender identity. Unfortunately, the threat of an expensive lawsuit has not translated into a safer environment for many LGBT students. GLSEN's 2007 National School Climate

Survey of 6,209 students in fifty states and the District of Columbia found that violence and harassment is still pervasive:

- more than 73 percent of LGBT students heard insults like "faggot" or "dyke" frequently or often from other students at school;
- 23 percent heard homophobic remarks from faculty at least some of the time;
- nine out of ten students heard "gay" used in a negative way often or frequently at school;
- nearly half had been verbally harassed at school often or frequently because of their sexual orientation;
- 17 percent had been physically harassed often or frequently because of their sexual orientation;
- over 10 percent of the students were often or frequently physically harassed because of their gender expression;
- more than two-thirds of LGBT students said that they felt unsafe in school because of a personal characteristic, such as their sexual orientation or gender expression.[30]

A study of 350 LGB youth, supported in part by the National Institute of Mental Health, had similar findings:

> More than half (59%) experienced verbal abuse in high school, 24% were threatened with violence, 11% had objects thrown at them, 11% had been physically attacked, 2% were threatened with weapons, 5% were sexually assaulted, and 20% had been threatened with the disclosure of their sexual orientation. Over half (54%) experienced three or more instances of verbal abuse in high school. Males reported significantly more verbal attacks, threats of violence, and objects being thrown at them. Males were also physically attacked more often: 15% of males and 7% of females had been assaulted. Few youths were threatened with weapons (2%) or sexually assaulted (5%); however, 20% were threatened with the disclosure of their sexual orientation.[31]

Cyberbullying and LGBT Youth

New research on cyberbullying, "an aggressive, intentional act carried out by a group or individual, using electronic form of contact, repeatedly and over time,"[32] indicates that it may disproportionately impact LGBT youth. A 2008 CDC study found that up to 35 percent of youth report being victims of cyberbullying.[33] In comparison, a 2010 study by researchers at the University of Iowa found that 54 percent of youth who identify as or are perceived to be LGBT report being bullied online within the last thirty days.[34]

The advent of cyberbullying is linked to the increased use of online social media by youth. A 2010 study found that 84 percent of homes in the United States have a computer with Internet access and that 53 percent of teens ages fifteen to nineteen have an account on a social networking site like Facebook or MySpace that they use for at least one hour per day.[35] One-third of teens have a computer in their room, and 85 percent have their own cell phone, allowing significant autonomy when accessing the Internet and receiving or sending text and video messages.[36]

When researchers at GLSEN specifically analyzed responses from the 295 students in the 2007 School Climate Survey who identified as transgender, they found even more frequent incidence of harassment and assault:

- 90 percent of transgender students heard derogatory remarks, such as "dyke" or "faggot," sometimes, often, or frequently in school.
- 90 percent of transgender students heard negative remarks about someone's gender expression sometimes, often, or frequently in school.
- A third of transgender students heard school staff make homophobic remarks, sexist remarks, and negative comments about someone's gender expression sometimes, often, or frequently in the past year.
- Almost all transgender students had been verbally harassed (e.g., called names or threatened) in the past year at school because of their sexual orientation (89 percent) and their gender expression (87 percent).
- Over half of all transgender students had been physically harassed (e.g., pushed or shoved) in school in the past year because of their sexual orientation (55 percent) and their gender expression (53 percent).
- Over a quarter (26 percent) of transgender students had been phys-

ically assaulted (e.g., punched, kicked, or injured with a weapon) in school in the past year because of their gender expression.

As was the case with LGB students in GLSEN's survey, the majority of transgender youth (54 percent) who were victimized did not report it to school officials, and of those who did, only 33 percent believed that those officials handled the situation effectively.[37]

Sexual Harassment in Public Schools

Much of the verbal harassment directed at LGBT or gender-nonconforming youth can actually be classified as sexual harassment. Seventy-two percent of the students surveyed by GLSEN reported being sexually harassed at school at least once within the past year.[38] Another nationwide study found that 63 percent of students experienced sexual harassment by a peer of the same sex, including:

- Sexual comments, jokes, gestures, or looks;
- Sexual messages or graffiti on bathroom walls and in locker rooms;
- Sexual rumors;
- Being shown sexual pictures, photographs, illustrations, messages, or notes;
- Being identified as gay or lesbian through the use of derogatory terms like "fag" or "dyke";
- Being touched, pinched, or grabbed in a sexual way;
- Being blocked or cornered in a sexual way;
- Being forced to kiss or forced to endure other unwelcome sexual behavior.[39]

While sexual harassment by a member of the opposite sex is more commonly reported in the workplace, members of the same sex often perpetrate peer-to-peer harassment in schools.[40] This creates a hostile environment regardless of the sexual orientation or gender identity of the students being victimized. In a study conducted by the American Association of University Women Educational Foundation in 1993, 86 percent of all students who were sexually harassed claimed that being labeled gay or lesbian, regardless of their true sexual orientation, was more distressing than physical abuse, especially for boys.[41] A study of Midwestern high school students found that male and female adolescents were distressed more about being harassed by same-sex peers than about harassment by peers of the opposite sex.[42]

Students who openly identify as LGBT experience more sexual harassment (much of which is based on gender nonconformity) than their heterosexual peers.[43] Young gay and bisexual girls are more likely to be sexually harassed, called sexually offensive names, and touched or grabbed in a sexual way.[44] "People would grab my breast area," recalled one lesbian high school student. "They'd come up and grab my waist, put their arm around me." Gay and bisexual male students are also victims of sexually suggestive remarks or gestures. "Guys will grab themselves, or they'll make kissing noises," reported another high school student. "They mimic homoerotic acts. They'll mimic anal sex, oral sex."[45]

Attention to and the prevalence of sexual harassment in schools has been increasing. In 1991, the U.S. Department of Education reported only eleven same-sex sexual harassment claims by elementary and secondary school students. In 1999 and 2000, the combined number increased to 274 for elementary and secondary education schools, and there were 111 claims concerning postsecondary educational institutions.[46] Despite the increased reporting, efforts to protect students who are sexually harassed have been largely unsuccessful. For example, in Utah, a same-sex harassment lawsuit filed by a high school football player against his teammates was dismissed by a court "on the grounds that the boy failed to prove that he had been a victim of any discriminatory effort."[47] His teammates taped his genitals (he was naked) to a towel rack and then exposed him to a girl brought into the locker room against her will. School administrators called the incident "hazing" and did not feel that the behavior of his teammates was abnormal.[48]

Efforts to curtail sexual harassment in public schools have been hampered by the belief that sexual harassment in school is a normal adolescent behavior. This view ignores both the cruelty inherent to many instances of harassment and the mental health effects of that cruelty on its victims. These effects can include loss of appetite, loss of interest in school, nightmares or disturbed sleep, feelings of isolation from family and friends, and feeling sad, nervous, threatened, and angry.[49]

As a result of these symptoms, the school performance of students who are sexually harassed often declines. They are more likely to cut class or be absent or truant, to have lower grades, and to lose friends. Students who are forced to endure long-term harassment may also be more likely to retaliate out of anger and self-defense. This can lead to physically threatening situations and even make the victim appear to be a perpetrator.[50]

The Impact of Anti-LGBT Harassment and Violence

The threat of violence and harassment makes school an unsettling and unsafe place for LGBT students. Some find it difficult to concentrate in class and focus on schoolwork. Many, fearing discovery of their sexual orientation or gender identity, hesitate to participate in school activities. As a result, they distance themselves from the school environment both emotionally and physically, becoming truants or dropping out altogether.[51] This has a lasting, negative impact on LGBT youth, inhibiting their development and their successful transitions to adulthood.[52]

A number of studies highlight the problem of chronic truancy among LGBT students. According to GLSEN, 33 percent of LGBT youth reported missing at least one entire day of school in the previous month because they felt unsafe, compared to just 5 percent of students surveyed in a national sample of secondary school students.[53] Transgender youth were even more likely to skip school than their LGB peers.[54] Students reporting same-sex behavior in the 1993 Massachusetts Youth Risk Behavior Survey were more than three times as likely as their heterosexual peers to skip school because they felt unsafe.[55] In 1995, the same survey indicated that self-identified LGB students were almost five times as likely as heterosexual students to have missed school because of fears about safety.[56] In 1999, 20 percent of Massachusetts students who described themselves as LGB reported that they had skipped school in the previous month because of feeling unsafe at or en route to school, compared with only 6 percent of other students.[57] The 2001–2 California Healthy Kids Survey (CHKS) of nearly 240,000 seventh, ninth, and eleventh graders found that those who were harassed because of their actual or perceived sexual orientation were over three times more likely to report missing school because they felt unsafe than students who were not harassed (27 percent vs. 7 percent).[58]

In addition to the impact that missing school has on LGBT students' academic achievement, it costs school districts millions of dollars per year in unrealized income. Analysis of CHKS data found that over one hundred thousand school absences per year in middle and high schools in California can be attributed to harassment based on actual or perceived sexual orientation.

Based on the state's school expenditures over a nine-month school calendar year, the cumulative cost to school districts in the State of California is an estimated minimum of $39.9 million each year due to school absences when students feel unsafe to attend school due to fear of being bullied based on their actual or perceived sexual orientation.[59]

Given that LGBT students have higher truancy rates, it is not surprising that some also score lower on other indicators of school performance and satisfaction. A study published in 2001, using data from the 1996 National Adolescent Health Survey, was among the first to analyze the differences in several school outcome measures between students who identified as being attracted to members of the same sex or both sexes and students who were only attracted to the opposite sex.[60] Female students who identified as being attracted to both sexes (i.e., with a bisexual sexual orientation) were significantly more likely to report that they had trouble getting along with other students, difficulty paying attention in class, and difficulty getting their homework done than their heterosexual peers. They also had lower grade point averages (GPAs).

Bisexual females had more negative school attitudes, did not feel like a part of their school community, and had significantly more negative feelings about their teachers than heterosexual female students. Females with only same-sex attractions also had more negative school attitudes and lower GPAs than heterosexual female students. Surprisingly, the same study found that adolescent boys who reported same-sex attraction exclusively did not significantly differ from their heterosexual peers in school outcomes, including GPA. The results of this study call for more research focusing on why male and female students who were attracted to both sexes reported more problems at school than those who were only attracted to the same sex or the opposite sex and why female students tended to have more negative experiences and outcomes overall.[61]

A 2002 report from the New York State Department of Education identified the torment experienced by many LGBT youth as one of the leading causes for their dropping out of school.[62] It proposed that administrators be flexible in accommodating individual student situations, including the sexual orientation or gender identity of students who are LGBT, in order to reduce the student dropout rate. It also recommended training teachers and staff about cultural differences. The most effective programs in the New York study attempted to generate and sustain a welcoming community within the school and sought to involve the parents of the children the school served. Collaborating with neighborhood communities may be particularly crucial in addressing the needs of LGBT students of color, who may also be coping with issues of alienation beyond the schoolyard that impact their ability to participate and learn at school.

The key findings of research conducted by GLSEN on the academic achievement and educational aspirations of LGBT students include the following:

- LGBT students were twice as likely not to plan to pursue any type of postsecondary education than a national sample of students, yet LGBT students were also more likely than a national sample of students to plan to pursue an advanced degree (Master's, PhD, JD).
- Students who experienced higher frequencies of physical harassment because of their sexual orientation or gender expression were less likely to say they would go on to college.
- Students who were frequently physically harassed because of their sexual orientation or gender expression reported lower grades than other students.[63]

Victims of severe physical harassment (occurring often or frequently) because of their sexual orientation or gender expression reported GPAs almost half a grade lower than those who were targeted less often (2.8 vs. 2.4). The frequency of physical assault also correlated with higher percentages of students reporting that they missed at least one day of school in the past month because they did not feel safe.[64]

According to the 1995 Massachusetts Youth Risk Behavior Study, LGB youth were more than four times as likely to have been threatened with a weapon on school property than their heterosexual peers (33 percent and 7 percent, respectively).[65] In the most extreme cases, the combination of violence and powerlessness experienced by LGBT youth may also lead them to bring weapons onto school property. Based on the results of the 1995 Vermont Youth Risk Behavior Study, some researchers have argued that male youth with multiple same-sex sexual partners were more likely to be victims of violence at school and therefore more likely to carry weapons both in and out of school.[66] Analysis of the 1996 National Adolescent Health Study found that youth who indicated same-sex romantic attraction were more likely than their peers to perpetrate extreme forms of violence against others, such as pulling a gun or knife or shooting or stabbing someone. While previous findings have indicated that LGB youth are more likely to carry weapons, this study is the first to suggest that these same students are willing to use them. The authors of the analysis suggest that the use of weapons results primarily from fear of being a victim of violence and from the need for self-defense.[67]

The harassment and violence that LGBT students experience has a negative impact on their mental and physical health in indirect ways as well. Recent research supported by the National Institute of Mental Health found statistically significant relationships between verbal, physical, and sexual harassment and assault (referred to by the researchers as sexual orientation violence, or SOV) of gender atypical LGB youth and negative mental health outcomes, including post-traumatic stress disorder (PTSD).

> More cases of PTSD were found among those who were gender atypical in childhood than among those who were not. PTSD was associated with increased physical SOV, in particular, and with the upset experienced at the first verbal SOV. Thus, youth who are gender atypical in childhood and who are victimized may have elevated mental health and trauma symptoms, and some may have PTSD.[68]

A 2002 study indicated that LGB youth who experienced three or more incidents of harassment within the preceding year engaged in behaviors putting their health at risk at a higher rate than their heterosexual peers who were similarly harassed.[69] Substance abuse by LGBT youth is linked to being marginalized by society, seeking relief from depression and isolation, and attempting to alleviate the stress associated with stigma.[70] Students reporting same-sex behavior on the 1993 Massachusetts Youth Risk Behavior Study were nine times more likely to report using alcohol on each of the thirty days preceding the survey, and 10 to 15 percent of LGB youth appeared to abuse alcohol and/or use marijuana regularly, compared to 1 to 4 percent of students reporting only heterosexual attraction and behavior.[71] In a 2002 study of data for Massachusetts and Vermont from the 1995 Youth Risk Behavior Survey, gay, bisexual, and questioning male students reported significantly higher marijuana and cocaine use than did lesbian, bisexual, and questioning females.[72] Another study, analyzing 1996 National Adolescent Health Study data, indicated that youth attracted to both males and females were at a somewhat higher risk for substance use and abuse than were heterosexual youth.[73] More recent analysis of data from a longitudinal study of over thirteen thousand youth confirms that LGB youth are more likely to begin drinking at earlier ages than their heterosexual peers and are at higher risk of binge drinking.[74]

LGBT youth, faced with the stress caused by victimization and isolation and often lacking positive sources of peer support and socialization, may engage in unprotected sex or other risky sexual behaviors, which increases their risk of contracting sexually transmitted diseases, including HIV.[75] A Minnesota study of gay and bisexual males between the ages of thirteen and twenty-one conducted from 1989 to 1991 found that nearly one-quarter had had a sexually transmitted disease.[76] A San Francisco study found that almost one-third of gay and bisexual young men reported contracting at least one sexually transmitted disease.[77] A study of 334 homeless and runaway adolescents and young adults in San Francisco found that 33 percent of the gay and bisexual males and 3 percent of the lesbian and bisexual females were HIV-positive, as opposed to 1 percent of the heterosexual males and none of the heterosexual females in the study.[78]

Given the health and other long-term impacts of anti-LGBT harassment and violence in schools, it is not surprising that LGB youth are at higher risk for suicide. This increased risk is not due to being gay but, rather, because of psychosocial stressors associated with being gay, including gender nonconformity, victimization at home and in school, lack of social support, homelessness, and substance abuse.[79] A controversial 1989 U.S. government study, which found that gay and lesbian youth were almost three times more likely to attempt suicide than their heterosexual peers, was among the first to bring national attention to this issue.[80] These findings have been supported by numerous additional studies. Analysis of data from the 1995 Massachusetts Youth Risk Behavior Survey confirmed that students who self-identify as LGB or who are unsure of their sexual orientation were over three times more likely to report attempted suicide in the previous year.[81] Data from the same survey four years later showed that nearly half of LGB students had considered suicide during the previous year.[82]

More recent studies that include larger, representative samples of youth continue to confirm higher suicide risk. In 2007, the *American Journal of Public Health* published the results of a study of over fourteen thousand youth ages eighteen to twenty-six who participated in the federal National Longitudinal Study of Adolescent Health. Nearly 5 percent of youth who identified as LGB in the study reported attempting suicide, compared to 1.6 percent of non-LGB youth.[83] LGB youth who attempt suicide are at higher risk for long-term psychological distress, including depression and anxiety, reenforcing the need for support systems at home and in school.[84]

A few researchers have questioned whether the magnitude of difference between LGB and non-LGB youth suicide risk is inflated due to problems in research design. Dr. Ritch C. Savin-Williams at Cornell University hypothesized that LGB youth who participate in studies through their connection to programs at LGBT community centers or who are willing to identify as LGB on a government survey may be at higher risk for suicide than the population of LGB youth as a whole. Additionally, many of the surveys used to assess suicide risk do not ask questions that differentiate between reported and more serious suicide attempts, such as those that are life-threatening and require medical attention. In 2001, Savin-Williams published the results of a study of 226 youth ages 17 to 25 recruited from introductory college courses in human development and sexuality. While he did find that the LGB men and women in his study were more likely to report suicide attempts, the magnitude of difference decreased significantly when only "true" and "life-threatening" attempts were considered. For example, lesbian or bisexual and heterosexual women reported the same incidence of life-threatening attempts (3 percent). However, gay or bisexual men were still significantly more likely to report a life-threatening attempt (6 percent) than heterosexual men (0 percent).[85]

In 2005, a study of 528 LGB youth in the New York City metropolitan area incorporated the critiques of Savin-Williams and other researchers concerned about the impact of research design. While nearly 33 percent of the LGB youth in that study reported a past suicide attempt, 15 percent were "serious" attempts, about half of which required medical attention. The researchers compared their findings to comparable epidemiological data from New York City, which showed that approximately 11 percent of high school students reported planning suicide. They concluded that, when making a reasonable assumption that many of the attempts reported in the epidemiological data were not serious, their findings again confirmed that LGB youth attempt suicide at higher rates than heterosexual youth.[86]

The impact and prevalence of anti-LGBT violence in public schools is a national tragedy. It affects all youth, regardless of sexual orientation or gender identity, because they experience or are forced to witness harassment and violence against their peers on a daily basis. Whether they identify as LGBT or simply do not specifically conform to what American society deems appropriate for male and female behavior, LGBT youth are publicly demeaned and demoralized while many teachers and administrators turn a blind eye. Though there is a continued need for more nationwide, population-based research, the preponderance of evidence shows that anti-LGBT violence is harmful to childhood and adolescent development and well-being and is also life-threatening. Efforts to curtail this harassment and mediate its effects on students are critical.

SECTION 2 | A Comprehensive Review of School-Based Practices and Federal, State, and Local Laws and Policies That Affect LGBT Students

3 | Federal, State, and Local Policy Interventions

In response to the need to protect youth in schools, some students, parents, teachers, and administrators are creating ways to protect and support LGBT students. Interventions include gay-straight alliances, nondiscrimination policies, safe schools programs, and curricula designed to provide positive and inclusive examples of the contributions that LGBT people have made to American and world culture. Unfortunately, such programs are often met with harsh resistance from antigay organizations and activists, who falsely claim that "homosexuals recruit public school children"[1] and that "there is evidence that harassment of gay teens may neither be as frequent, as severe, nor as disproportionate, as some pro-homosexual rhetoric would suggest."[2] By summarizing initiatives that have succeeded despite such opposition, we hope to inspire and equip parents, teachers, and school administrators to protect and nurture LGBT youth.

A variety of policies and support systems can help communities combat and eventually eliminate anti-LGBT harassment and violence in their public schools:

- The equal protection clause of the U.S. Constitution and existing federal laws, including Title IX of the Education Amendments Act of 1972 and the Equal Access Act of 1984, offer LGBT students some protection from harassment and violence, as well as the freedom to create and attend gay-supportive clubs on school campuses.[3]
- States can pass, implement, and enforce comprehensive nondiscrimination and antibullying legislation that explicitly includes protections based on sexual orientation and gender identity of students.
- School districts can implement and enforce nondiscrimination and antiharassment policies that protect LGBT students and teachers.

- Teachers can include LGBT culture and history in curricula and create a safe environment by not tolerating anti-LGBT harassment; those who are either LGBT or LGBT-friendly can also serve as role models for both their gay and straight students and coworkers.[4]
- Gay-straight alliances or other support groups can give LGBT students and their straight allies a place to meet on school property in a safe and supportive environment; their very existence is symbolic of a school's commitment to a safe and inclusive environment for all students.

Combined, these resources can comprehensively meet the needs of LGBT students. A pilot study of the Massachusetts Safe Schools Program found that clear nondiscrimination policies that are backed by financial resources and support from key administrators, educators, and community and student leaders are at least as important as GSAs in creating more tolerant and safer environments for LGBT students.[5] The decentralized nature of the U.S. public education system demands that each individual school district act to implement such measures, especially because efforts to mandate these protections and curriculum changes at the federal level have been unsuccessful.

The Equal Protection Clause of the U.S. Constitution

The equal protection clause of the Fourteenth Amendment to the U.S. Constitution requires that all government agencies treat similarly situated persons in the same way. Federal courts have held that public schools have an obligation under the equal protection clause to protect students from harassment and discrimination based on their sexual orientation or gender identity.[6]

An equal protection claim requires the student to show that school officials did not abide by antiharassment policies when dealing with sexual orientation harassment or that the student was treated differently from other similarly situated students. In other words, if school administrators or teachers enforce rules against harassment for heterosexual students, but fail to enforce the same rules for LGBT students, then an equal protection violation may have occurred. The same claim can be made when school districts take disciplinary action against LGBT students but not heterosexual students for similar behaviors.[7]

Additionally, if school officials fail to stop anti-LGBT harassment or violence either because they believe that a student who is out of the closet should expect to be harassed or simply because they are uncomfortable addressing the situation, the school can be held liable for failing to provide equal protection for that student.[8]

Schools also must treat transgender students the same way they would treat students of the same gender identity. For example, if a female-identified transgender student is prevented from wearing the same type of clothing that other female students are allowed to wear in school, that school may be violating the equal protection clause. A transgender student's right to dress according to his or her gender identity is also protected under the First Amendment and due process clause of the Constitution.[9]

School Held Liable for Failing to Protect Students from Harassment

A Profile of Alana Flores

Alana Flores met her first girlfriend the summer before her sophomore year of high school, but she did not come out of the closet until the end of her senior year. Nonetheless, she endured harassment and death threats at Live Oak High School in Morgan Hill, California, because other students believed she was gay. For three years, threatening notes and pornographic images were repeatedly taped to her locker. One note threatened, "Die, Die . . . Dyke Bitch, Fuck off. We'll kill you."[10] When Alana went to a teacher for help, the teacher only asked, "Why does that word bother you? Are you a lesbian?"[11] The harassment continued, and Alana went to her principal for help, but he did nothing to stop the harassment. When Alana asked for a new locker, the principal replied, "Yes, sure, sure, later. You need to go back to class. Don't bring me this trash anymore. This is disgusting."[12] The threats and the failure of school officials to stop them, combined with Alana's own reluctance to accept her sexual orientation, kept Alana in the closet and reinforced her fear of coming out. By her senior year, the stress became too much, and she attempted suicide.[13]

While in the hospital after her suicide attempt, Alana told her parents that she was a lesbian and about the constant harassment and death threats. Her family expressed unconditional love and support and stood by her when, nine months after graduation, she decided to file a lawsuit against the school for failing to protect her from pervasive and ongoing harassment. The ACLU and the National Center for Lesbian Rights (NCLR) represented Alana and five other plaintiffs who joined the case, including one student who was hospitalized after a group of male students shouted "faggot" and other homophobic slurs while hitting and kicking him at a bus stop in full view of the bus driver.[14] All of the plaintiffs had endured significant emotional distress related to harassment and violence that occurred on school property. Some suffered from flashbacks and felt generally unsafe in the world.[15]

The plaintiff's lawyers were able to document a long history of anti-LGBT harassment at Live Oak High School, including a 1993 incident reported in the school's newspaper, the *Oak Leaf*. The paper described graffiti reading, "Kill all gays. Keep it in the closet," which had been written in an area where a few gay students tried to organize a support group. NCLR lawyer Leslie Levy argued that the history of harassment "was so open and obvious that teachers and administrators had to know about it"; that "it was clear that the school district, in almost every instant [*sic*], failed to respond appropriately"; and that this failure violated the equal protection clause of the U.S. Constitution.[16] On April 8, 2003, the U.S. Court of Appeals for the Ninth Circuit issued a historic decision in *Flores v. Morgan Hill Unified School District*.[17] Holding that school officials had failed in their constitutionally mandated duty to treat LGB students equally by not protecting them from harassment, the court ordered them to eliminate any harassment of LGB students in the future.[18]

After winning the case, NCLR executive director Kate Kendell commented, "This decision is long overdue. Finally, it's clear that schools can no longer stand back and turn a blind eye to the kind of debilitating harassment that so many lesbian, gay and bisexual students face everyday." Matt Coles, director of the Lesbian and Gay Rights Project of the ACLU, added, "The court made it very clear that going through the motions is not enough. Schools have to really deal with the problem of antigay harassment."[19] Alana explained why she chose to sue the school in the first place: "I could have graduated from Live Oak, moved on with my life, and never looked back. But there was always something in me that said that's not the right thing to do, because it could happen to somebody else, over and over and over again."[20] Unfortunately, many youth will continue to experience harassment and violence at schools across the country due to their real or perceived sexual orientation. Thanks to Alana, the ACLU, and the NCLR, however, students can demand that schools be held responsible for failing to protect them.

Existing Federal Law: Title IX and The Equal Access Act

Although they do not explicitly protect students based on sexual orientation or gender identity, Title IX of the Education Amendments of 1972 and the Equal Access Act are federal laws that provide some protection for LGBT students. Usually associated with access to sports programs, Title IX[21] guarantees equal educational opportunities regardless of a student's sex, and it also prohibits schools from limiting or denying a student's participation in any school program on the basis of sex. Specifically, Title IX provides that "[n]o person in the United States shall, on the basis of sex, be excluded from participation in, be denied the benefits of, or be subject to discrimination under any educational program or activity receiving Federal financial assistance."[22] Claims under Title IX are tenable under the following conditions:

1. school personnel have actual knowledge of the harassment;
2. school officials demonstrate deliberate indifference or take actions that are clearly unreasonable;
3. the harassment is so severe, pervasive, and objectively offensive that it can be said to deprive the victim(s) of access to the educational opportunities or benefits provided by the school.[23]

Title IX does not explicitly protect LGBT students from harassment based on their sexual orientation or gender identity,[24] but if an LGBT student can show that he or she was harassed because of gender nonconformity or was the victim of same-sex sexual harassment because of his or her sexual orientation, that student may have a Title IX claim.[25]

In guidelines that clarify the applicability of Title IX to sexual harassment in public schools, the U.S. Department of Education explains how Title IX protects LGBT students:

Although Title IX does not prohibit discrimination on the basis of sexual orientation, sexual harassment directed at gay or lesbian students that is sufficiently serious to limit or deny a student's ability to participate in or benefit from the school's program constitutes sexual harassment prohibited by Title IX. . . . For example, if a male student or a group of male students target a gay student for physical sexual advances, serious enough to deny or limit the victim's ability to participate in or benefit from the school's program, the school would need to respond promptly and effectively . . . just as it would if the victim were heterosexual. On the other hand, if students heckle another student with comments based on the student's sexual orientation (e.g., "gay students are not welcome at this table in the cafeteria"), but their actions do not involve conduct of a sexual nature, their actions would not be sexual harassment covered by Title IX. . . . Gender-based harassment, which may include acts of verbal, nonverbal, or physical aggression, intimidation, or hostility based on sex or sex-stereotyping, but not involving conduct of a sexual nature, is also a form of sex discrimination to which a school must respond, if it rises to a level that denies or limits a student's ability to participate in or benefit from the educational program.[26]

Title IX does not hold a school responsible for the behavior of students who harass; it holds a school accountable for failing to correct harassment once school officials have been notified. A U.S. Supreme Court ruling in 1999 reinforced this policy, specifically stating that schools are liable for student-to-student sexual harassment if the school has been informed of the problem. In its decision, the Court wrote that schools are liable for monetary damages "only if they were 'deliberately indifferent' to information about 'severe, pervasive, and objectively' offensive harassment among students."[27] This has been critical to the outcome of a number of lawsuits filed by students who were harassed because of their real or perceived sexual orientation.

In 2004, the U.S. Court of Appeals for the Third Circuit affirmed a district court ruling that the Belafonte School District in Pennsylvania was not liable under Title IX for sexual harassment a student experienced over the course of three years because he was effeminate. Each time the student complained, the school district responded with appropriate disciplinary action against the offending students and even sponsored assemblies and enacted policies that addressed student harassment. The district also distributed memorandums to school faculty and staff soliciting assistance with reporting and preventing future incidents.[28] In contrast, one year later, a federal district court in Kansas ruled that Dylan Theno, a heterosexual student who was the victim of antigay harassment in the Tonganoxie School District, had an actionable claim under Title IX because the school failed to take appropriate action to protect him. In response, the school district agreed to pay Dylan $440,000 in damages. According to the court,

> the plaintiff was harassed because he failed to satisfy his peers' stereotyped expectations for his gender because the primary objective of plaintiff's harassers appears to have been to disparage his lack of masculinity.... [The harassment was] so severe, pervasive, and objectively offensive that it effectively denied [him] an education in the Tonganoxie school district.[29]

The Equal Access Act[30] (EAA) was passed by a bipartisan majority of Congress and signed into law by President Ronald Reagan in 1984. The purpose of the bill was to counteract perceived discrimination against religious speech in public high schools, while maintaining the constitutional separation of church and state. The legislation was developed after two federal appellate courts held that student-led religious groups could not meet on school property before or after school hours. The law was eventually challenged in the Supreme Court, which ruled that it was constitutional in 1990.[31] Under the EAA, a school cannot deny equal access to student activities because of the "religious, political, philosophical, or other content of the speech at such meetings."[32] This also had an unexpected, secondary effect: it provided legal standing for the formation of gay-straight alliances in all public schools that allow any other school-sponsored clubs. In 2000, a federal judge in California ruled that under the Equal Access Act, schools could not pick and choose among clubs based on what they think students should or should not discuss.

> The [school] Board members may be uncomfortable about students discussing sexual orientation and how all students need to accept each other, whether gay or straight.... [But they] cannot censor the students' speech to avoid discussion[s] on campus that cause them discomfort or represent an unpopular viewpoint. In order to comply with the Equal Access Act ... the members of the Gay-Straight Alliance must be permitted access to the school

campus in the same way that the District provides access to all clubs, including the Christian Club and the Red Cross/Key Club.[33]

In the same ruling, the judge recognized that violence and harassment against gay students was "widespread" and that his ruling was not just about promoting tolerance for diverse points of view: "As any concerned parent would understand, this case may involve the protection of life itself."[34]

Proposed Federal Legislation: The Safe Schools Improvement Act and the Student Nondiscrimination Act

In 2007, the National Safe Schools Partnership—a coalition of over thirty education, health, civil rights, law enforcement, youth development, and other organizations—released recommendations to the U.S. Congress for bridging gaps in federal law that would promote school improvement, safety, and student achievement. The partnership proposed that this objective be carried out through amendment of the Elementary and Secondary Education Act (ESEA) so that bullying and harassment is defined

- With specific reference to conduct that causes harm to students, defined as conduct that adversely affects one or more students, depriving them of access to educational opportunities or benefits provided by their schools.
- To clarify that it can be based on any grounds set forth by a district or state; and to enumerate specific bases related to the highest frequency of such incidents, including conduct that is based on a student's actual or perceived race, color, national origin, sex, disability, sexual orientation, gender identity, or religion.
- To exclude any action that would constitute protected free expression.[35]

Specifically, the coalition made three recommendations:

1. Federal law should ensure that schools and districts have comprehensive and effective student conduct policies that include clear prohibitions against bullying and harassment;
2. Federal law should ensure that schools and districts focus on ef-

fective prevention strategies and professional development designed to help school personnel meaningfully address issues associated with bullying and harassment; and

3. Federal law should ensure that states and districts maintain and report data regarding incidents of bullying and harassment in order to inform the development of effective federal, state, and local policies that address these issues.[36]

To achieve these objectives, the coalition recommended passage of two pieces of legislation: the Safe Schools Improvement Act (SSIA) and the Student Nondiscrimination Act.

The SSIA was first introduced in the House of Representatives on June 23, 2007, by Representative Linda Sánchez (D-CA), with seventy-eight cosponsors (seventy-five Democrats and three Republicans).[37] It amends the Safe and Drug-Free Schools and Communities Act (Title IV of ESEA as amended by the No Child Left Behind Act) to require schools and districts receiving federal funds to adopt codes of conduct that specifically prohibit bullying and harassment, including on the basis of sexual orientation and gender identity. It also requires states to collect and report data on bullying and harassment to the Department of Education.[38] The bill was referred to the House Committee on Education and Labor, where no further action was taken. It was reintroduced in the House again in 2009, with 117 cosponsors,[39] and for the first time in the Senate in 2010 by Senator Robert Casey (D-PA), with eleven cosponsors (all Democrats).[40]

On July 8, 2009, Sirdeaner Walker, the mother of Carl Joseph Walker-Hoover, testified in support of the SSIA before the House Subcommittee on Early Childhood, Elementary, and Secondary Education and the Subcommittee on Healthy Families and Communities. At age eleven and just a few months before his mother's testimony, Carl completed suicide as the result of pervasive bullying and harassment in school (see his profile in chapter 2). The following are excerpts from Mrs. Walker's testimony:

> . . . My name is Sirdeaner Walker, and four months ago, I would not have dreamed that one day I would be testifying on Capitol Hill. I was an ordinary working mom, looking after my family and doing the best I could as a parent.
>
> But my life changed forever on April 6, 2009.
>
> That was the night I was cooking dinner when my son, Carl Joseph Walker-Hoover, went to his room where I imagined he'd

be doing his homework or playing his video games. Instead, I found him hanging by an extension cord tied around his neck.

He was 11 years old.

Carl liked football and basketball and playing video games with his little brother. He loved the Lord and he loved his family. What could make a child his age despair so much that he would take his own life?

That question haunts me to this day, and I will probably never know the answer.

What we do know is that Carl was being bullied relentlessly at school. He had just started secondary school in September, and we had high hopes, but I knew something was wrong, almost from the start.

He didn't want to tell me what was bothering him, but I kept at him, and he finally told me that kids at school were pushing him around, calling him names, saying he acted "gay," and calling him "faggot."

Hearing that, my heart just broke for him. And I was furious. So I called the school right away and told them about the situation. I expected they would be just as upset as I was, but instead, they told me it was just ordinary social interaction that would work itself out.

I desperately wish they had been right. But it just got worse. By March, other kids were threatening to kill him.

I did everything that a parent is supposed to: I chose a "good" school; I joined the PTO; I went to every parent-teacher conference; I called the school regularly and brought the bullying problem to the staff's attention. And the school did not act. The teachers did not know how to respond.

After Carl died, I could have stayed at home and mourned him, but instead, I've chosen to get involved, to speak out about school bullying—and I have learned a lot in a short time.

And the most important thing I've learned is that bullying is not an inevitable part of growing up. It can be prevented. And there isn't a moment to lose.

Since my son died on April 6, I met the mother of another 11-year-old boy who was also being seriously bullied at school and killed himself. And I know there are others. This has got to stop.

School bullying is a national crisis, and we need a national solution to deal with it. That is why I am here today. Teachers, administrators and other school personnel need additional support and clear guidance about how to ensure that all kids feel safe in school. Congress can make sure they have that guidance and support by making anti-bullying policies mandatory in all of our nation's schools.

Policies that make it clear exactly what kind of behavior will not be tolerated. Policies that include training teachers and other school personnel to recognize bullying and harassment and enforce the rules with immediate, appropriate discipline. Policies that recognize that to prevent bullying, we have to teach young people to treat each other with respect. . . .

. . . The Safe Schools Improvement Act would help achieve the goals I have outlined today and I urge the subcommittees to move this legislation forward. . . . We cannot afford to wait for another child to drop out of school, struggle academically or even worse, take his own life before we take this problem seriously.[41]

In the spring of 2011, the SSIA was reintroduced in the Senate by Senator Robert Casey, this time with 30 cosponsors, and in the House by Representative Sanchez, with over 100 cosponsors. As of September 2011, neither version had passed out of committee.

Modeled after Title IX of the ESEA, the second piece of legislation supported by the National Safe Schools Partnership is the Student Nondiscrimination Act (SNDA). First introduced in the House on January 27, 2010, by Representative Jared Polis (D-CO), with 124 cosponsors (122 Democrats and two Republicans), the bill was referred to the House Committee on Education and Labor.[42] The Senate version of SNDA was introduced by Senator Al Franken (D-MN) on May 20, 2010, with twenty-four cosponsors (all Democrats), and was referred to the Senate Committee on Health, Education, Labor, and Pensions.[43] SNDA prohibits school programs or activities that receive federal funding from discriminating against any public school student based on actual or perceived sexual orientation or gender identity. SNDA also prohibits discrimination against any public school student because of the actual or perceived sexual orientation or gender identity of a person with whom a student associates or has associated. Discrimination, as defined by SNDA, also includes harassment of a student. SNDA also prohibits retaliation based on an individual's opposition to conduct made illegal by the bill, and it affirms the right of any individual who believes he or she has been harmed under its provisions to pursue legal recourse.[44]

In a press release in support of SNDA, the ACLU highlighted the story of Constance McMillen, a student it represented in a lawsuit against the Itawamba County School District in Fulton, Mississippi, as an example of the need for SNDA.[45] On April 2, 2010, officials cancelled a school prom in order to prevent Constance from attending with a same-sex date and from wearing a tuxedo. Blamed for the cancellation of the prom, Constance was harassed by other students at school, and when an alternative prom was organized by students' parents, Constance was directed to a "decoy" prom to prevent her from attending.[46]

The ACLU argued that the school violated Constance's First Amendment right to free expression, and the U.S. District Court for the Northern District of Mississippi agreed. In July 2010, the Itawamba County School District settled with Constance out of court, agreeing to pay her thirty-five thousand dollars to end the lawsuit. The school district also agreed to implement a nondiscrimination policy including sexual orientation and gender identity as protected categories, the first of its kind in the state. Constance, who eventually transferred to and graduated from a high school in a different district to escape harassment, was happy with the settlement "not for the money, but the policies. . . . That's going to change things for so many people at my school."[47]

While the federal court ruled in favor of Constance's First Amendment claim in this instance, a different court may have interpreted Constance's claim under the First Amendment differently and ruled against her. SNDA would make the discrimination she experienced explicitly illegal. Under SNDA, public school students, whether at a school prom or any other school-sponsored activity, would be protected from discrimination based on their actual or perceived sexual orientation or gender identity. In March 2011, SNDA was reintroduced in the Senate by Senator Al Franken, this time with 34 cosponsors, and in the House by Representative Polis, with 134 cosponsors. As of September 2011, neither version had passed out of committee.

State and Local Laws and Policies

In addition to federal laws that protect students, the majority of states have laws or regulations that prohibit discrimination, harassment, and/or bullying in schools. However, most of these laws do not explicitly include sexual orientation or gender identity as enumerated categories of protection. GLSEN warns that such enumeration is critical to ensuring the safety of LGBT students,[48] a position supported by a critical U.S. Supreme Court ruling in 1996. In *Romer v. Evans,* the Court ruled against an amendment to the Colorado Constitution that prevented the state from passing legislation or adopting policies that prohibited discrimination based on sexual orientation.[49] In his majority opinion, Justice Anthony Kennedy not only declared that LGB Americans have the same right to seek government protections from discrimination as any other group, but he also declared that specific enumeration of sexual orientation in such laws was critical: "Enumeration is the essential device used to make the duty not to discriminate concrete and to provide guidance for those who must comply."[50] This is among the reasons why groups like GLSEN argue that student antibullying and nondiscrimination laws should specifically include sexual orientation and gender identity as protected categories. State laws and policies without them may still leave LGBT students vulnerable.

As of September 2011, sixteen states and the District of Columbia had laws that addressed discrimination, harassment, and/or bullying of students based on sexual orientation and gender identity, among other enumerated categories (see fig. 1): Arkansas [51,] California,[52] Colorado,[53] Connecticut,[54] District of Columbia,[55] Illinois,[56] Iowa,[57] Maine,[58] Maryland,[59] Minnesota,[60] New Hampshire,[61] New Jersey,[62] New York,[63] North Carolina,[64] Oregon,[65] Vermont,[66] and Washington.[67] Additionally, Massachusetts,[68] and Wisconsin[69] banned discrimination, harassment, and/or bullying based on sexual orientation (gender identity was not included as a protected category). Twenty-seven states prohibited discrimination, harassment, and/or bullying in schools but did not enumerate categories of protection: Alabama,[70] Alaska,[71] Arizona,[72] Delaware,[73] Florida,[74] Georgia,[75] Idaho,[76] Indiana,[77] Kansas,[78] Kentucky,[79] Louisiana,[80] Mississippi,[81] Missouri,[82] Nebraska,[83] Nevada,[84] North Dakota,[85] Ohio,[86] Oklahoma,[87] Pennsylvania,[88] Rhode Island,[89] South Carolina,[90] Tennessee,[91] Texas,[92] Utah,[93] Virginia,[94] West Virginia,[95] and Wyoming.[96]

The state board of education in Hawaii had a policy prohibiting school employees from bullying, harassing, or discriminating against a student based on sexual orientation or gender identity and expression. The state also had a regulation that prohibited students from bullying, cyberbullying, or harassing a fellow student on the basis of sexual orientation or gender identity and expression.[97] New Mexico's Public Education Department also had a regulation that prohibits bullying and harassment of students based on sexual orientation, but gender identity is not included as a protected category.[98] In addition to their statewide laws

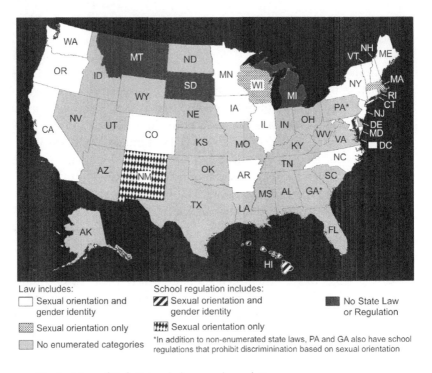

Law includes:
☐ Sexual orientation and gender identity
▒ Sexual orientation only
▒ No enumerated categories

School regulation includes:
▨ Sexual orientation and gender identity
▤ Sexual orientation only

■ No State Law or Regulation

*In addition to non-enumerated state laws, PA and GA also have school regulations that prohibit discriminination based on sexual orientation

Fig. 1. Map of Safe Schools laws and regulations

that do not include enumerated categories of protection, Pennsylvania and Georgia also have school regulations that prohibit discrimination based on sexual orientation.[99] Only three states—Michigan, Montana, and South Dakota—did not have a law prohibiting discrimination, harassment, and/or bullying of students.

Given the U.S. Supreme Court's ruling in favor of nondiscrimination laws with enumerated protections, we excluded states that do not include sexual orientation or gender identity as enumerated categories from our analysis of the proportion of the public school student population (K–12) protected by such laws (see fig. 2). To show any change in proportion of students protected over time, our calculations included the 2000, 2005, and 2010 academic school years.

As illustrated in figure 2, only 2 percent of the over forty-seven million K–12 public school students in the United States in 2000 were protected by a statewide law that addressed discrimination, harassment, and/or bullying based on sexual orientation and gender identity.[100]

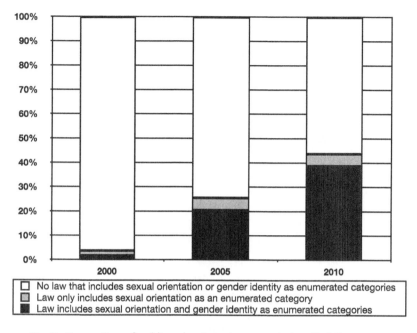

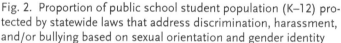

☐ No law that includes sexual orientation or gender identity as enumerated categories
▨ Law only includes sexual orientation as an enumerated category
■ Law includes sexual orientation and gender identity as enumerated categories

Fig. 2. Proportion of public school student population (K–12) protected by statewide laws that address discrimination, harassment, and/or bullying based on sexual orientation and gender identity

However, by 2005, 21 percent of the public school student population was covered by a fully inclusive law. By the beginning of the 2010 school year, the proportion of students covered nearly doubled: 39 percent were protected by a fully inclusive law. Despite the progress made over the past decade in passing inclusive state nondiscrimination and antibullying laws, nearly twenty-eight million students (56 percent) in 2010 attended public schools in a state that did not specifically protect them from discrimination and harassment based on their real or perceived sexual orientation or gender identity.

In the absence of statewide laws, some school districts have implemented nondiscrimination and antiharassment policies with enumerated protection for LGBT students. This strategy may be effective in states with political leadership that is indifferent or even hostile to passing more comprehensive statewide laws. In *Sexual Orientation and School Policy: A Practical Guide for Teachers, Administrators, and Community Activists,* Ian Macgillivray describes "High Plains School District's"[101] struggle to establish, implement, and enforce a districtwide nondiscrimination policy to protect LGBT students. This true story is an example of successful community-based activism that accomplished its goals without relying on state and federal statutes or constitutional protections.

Traditionally, the relatively affluent city of High Plains had been supportive of the LGBT community and local gay rights policies. In 1992, the High Plains School District's school board easily adopted a policy outlining procedures for resolving conflicts, including those related to sexual orientation. The policy was rarely discussed, however, and had drifted into relative obscurity within a few years.

Prompted by a 1992 state ballot initiative limiting legal recourse for LGB persons, "Trisha," an openly gay teacher, founded a group called the Coalition in 1993 to offer support to LGBT youth. The Coalition later became known as the High Plains Safe Schools Coalition (HPSSC). Having previously organized classes for teachers, administrators, and other staff on how to work with LGBT youth, Trisha felt that a more structured approach would be more effective in advocating for the school district to adopt specific goals to support LGBT students. HPSSC discussed the possibility of integrating LGBT issues into the curricula but, sensing the conservative slant of the current school board, opted instead to focus on continuing the classes and on getting sexual orientation included in the diversity goal of the district's strategic plan, the set of districtwide policies that serve to guide each school's goals.

Through networking with school district administrators and several community meetings, HPSSC got the attention of the school board. It framed its advocacy as a request for the formation of a committee to provide recommendations to the board on ways to promote tolerance and respect for all people. The first two meetings went well, and the HPSSC provided to the board testimony by local experts and LGBT youth on issues related to discrimination.

By the third meeting, however, conservative parents and community members had heard about HPSSC's work and had organized campaigns opposing the change in district policy. Supporters (including members of the local chapter of Parents, Families, and Friends of Lesbians and Gays) and protesters (including members of Boy Scouts of America) were in full force, making for a contentious, emotionally charged meeting. After a heated session of community input, the school board failed to pass the inclusion of sexual orientation issues in the curriculum (citing these issues as "values instruction") or to form a committee to further explore HPSSC's proposal.

The school board president proposed a compromise by way of a districtwide nondiscrimination policy that would state, "[The High Plains School District] will not tolerate discrimination, harassment, or violence against anyone, including students or teachers, regardless of race, ethnicity, gender, sexual orientation, or religion, and will encourage respect for all people." Another board member, who proposed that the policy needed language stating how the district would handle discrimination should it occur, moved to amend the president's original statement to continue, "study and recommend to the board ways to encourage tolerance and respect for all people, clarify the board's policy intent to prohibit harassment and discrimination, resolve conflicts that arise, and develop accountability procedures for those instances where conflicts are not resolved." Citing the "extremely broad language of that statement," the motion failed. The board president reintroduced her previous statement, and it passed. High Plains School District nondiscrimination policy now read,

> The Board affirms that there shall be no discrimination against anyone in the school system on the basis of race, age, marital status, creed, color, sex, disability, or national origin.
> The High Plains School District will not tolerate discrimination, harassment, or violence against anyone, including students and staff members, regardless of race, ethnicity, gender, sexual orientation, age, disability, or religion.

HPSSC saw this as a victory, since its primary goal of integrating sexual orientation into both the curricula and the district's diversity goal had resulted in a districtwide nondiscrimination policy addressing sexual orientation. Trisha summarized, ". . . we were sitting there going, 'Oh my God. They're writing a policy! We're getting a policy out of it, not a committee!' [laughing] And, 'Okay, who cares about the curriculum stuff. That's gonna come later anyway. . . . once it's in the policy, that's so much more than what we were asking for. We can really build on that. We can really take it and run.'" Meanwhile, protestors, pleased that the board had stopped short of integrating LGBT issues into the curricula, were fine with the policy as a compromise.

The nondiscrimination policy was implemented, then published in a 1995 edition of *Students' and Parents' Rights and Responsibilities,* a handbook distributed to all students each school year. HPSSC continued to offer classes for staff on LGBT issues. But by 1998, HPSSC found that discrimination against LGBT students persisted in High Plains School District. Many teachers and administrators were unaware of the policy, and few, if any, resources were available to gay youth seeking protection from bullying and discrimination. By this time, a new, less socially conservative school board had been elected, and HPSSC saw this as an opportunity to advocate for better enforcement of the nondiscrimination policy and to reintroduce efforts to integrate sexual orientation into the diversity goal.

In 1998, the board began reconsideration of the district's diversity goal and invited input from the community. Both HPSSC and Concerned Citizens, a group opposing the integration of sexual orientation in the diversity goal, participated in the debate. HPSSC's efforts secured support from local churches and a synagogue, community organizations, government officials, and a state senator. It presented testimony by LGBT youth on the harassment and discrimination they experienced in the district's schools, as well as information on the legal implications of this issue, including Title IX protections.

The debate continued for months and ultimately came down to semantics. The proposed inclusion of sexual orientation in the diversity goal accompanied a directive to "value diversity and promote understanding." Opponents preferred the word *respect* over *value*, claiming that it would avoid the impression that students would be forced to "value homosexuality." Further, they did not support spelling out the protected classes, stating that this was limiting. The board met with both groups, together and separately, in an effort to come to a compromise regarding the language and content of the diversity goal.

Finally, by a vote of five to two, the board decided to include the phrase "value diversity," a victory for HPSSC. The statement and beliefs of the High Plains School District's diversity goal now read as follows:

STATEMENT
Value Diversity and Promote Understanding

BELIEFS
1. All human beings have inherent worth.
2. All students, regardless of race, ethnicity, gender, sexual orientation, age, disability or religion, deserve a quality education.
3. HPSD will not tolerate discrimination, intimidation, harassment or violent based on race, ethnicity, gender, sexual orientation, age, disability or religion.

4. Healthy school communities respect differences, welcome diversity and promote cultural plurality.
5. Racial, ethnic and cultural diversity should be evident across all employee groups and central administration.

Macgillivray presents strategies that HPSSC successfully utilized to build community and district support, including

- Establish relationships with other diversity groups (e.g., groups advocating for equity for students of color)
- Cultivate understanding between opposing groups by organizing face-to-face meetings
- Build alliances with community organizations and individuals
- Present testimony of LGBT youth
- Meet with individual schools' governance teams, including students, staff, and parents, and ask them to rate their schools on various LGBT discrimination scales, including prevalence of anti-gay remarks, number of LGBT-related books in the library, whether or not nondiscrimination policies are clearly posted, whether harassment reports are readily available, etc.
- Approach individuals on a personal level
- Keep the school's Gay-Straight Alliance (GSA) strong and organized
- Encourage professional development for staff
- Ensure that nondiscrimination regulations are clearly drafted
- Ensure that enforcement involves both discipline and education
- Be aware of existing nondiscrimination policies and laws
- Anticipate common barriers (e.g., lack of top-down support, staff misunderstanding and/or unawareness of policies, lack of implementing resources, fear, stigma, etc.)

Whether or not there is a statewide law protecting students from anti-LGBT discrimination and bullying, school districts that fail to protect students risk lawsuits based on violations of the equal protection clause, the due process clause, and the First Amendment of the U.S. Constitution, as well as Title IX of the Education Amendments Act of 1972. The majority of cases brought against school districts to date have either been won by the students or settled in their favor, and such settlements are costly. In fifteen lawsuits involving anti-LGBT harassment or discrimination, compiled and summarized by the NCLR and GLSEN, school districts have paid between $40,000 and $962,000 in settlements to the parents of harassed students. These figures do not include district attorney's fees, which, in many cases, were far greater than the settlement itself. A number of lawsuits were also settled for undisclosed amounts, making it difficult to quantify the true cost of failing to protect students. For example, in California's *Ray v. Antioch,* which was settled for an undisclosed amount, the plaintiff had urine-soaked towels thrown on him and was beaten by another student because he was perceived to be gay and because one of his parents is transgender.[102]

As summarized in table 1, five of the fifteen cases that resulted in settlements were in states that had nondiscrimination and antiharassment laws at he time of filing, including California and Minnesota. Some of these lawsuits have even been filed in states that do not have statutes explicitly prohibiting bullying based on sexual orientation or gender identity, including Kentucky, Missouri, and Nevada. However, even in states with laws specifically protecting them, LGBT students continue to experience harassment and violence. While the passage and enforcement of such laws is necessary, education and intervention at the local level must also continue to be a priority.

In addition to the fifteen lawsuits summarized by the NCLR and GLSEN, additional lawsuits that have happened since 2002, highlighted by the ACLU, have resulted in nearly two million dollars awarded to students who have been victims of anti-LGBT harassment in schools.[103]

Although many settlements have required teachers and staff to receive sensitivity training, state legislation does not usually mandate the inclusion of LGBT-positive curricula or safe schools training for students. However, school districts throughout the country should follow the lead of these court rulings, by taking proactive steps to support and protect LGBT students from harassment and discrimination, rather than waiting for a lawsuit. Concurrently, they should provide education and training to their students and employees.

Parental Notification and "No Promo Homo" Laws

Parental notification laws in four states—Arizona,[104] California,[105] Nevada,[106] and Utah[107]—require students to obtain the written consent of their parents before they participate in classes in which such topics as sex, sexuality, and HIV are discussed. (These laws do not, however, require prior written consent if teachers want to discuss discrimination or harassment related to a student's sexual orientation or gender identity.) State parental notification laws with opt-out provisions are also common. They allow parents to remove their children from classes or assemblies that include education on sexuality, HIV, sexually transmitted diseases, or even death. Such laws exist in several dozen states and the District of Columbia, varying in their provisions and scope.[108]

In 2003, the legislature in Massachusetts considered a bill that would have converted its parental opt-out policy into a more restrictive, opt-in law. The new policy would have also expanded the scope of parental control beyond "curriculum which primarily involves human sexual education or human sexuality issues"[109] to also encompass "school sanctioned program or activity, which primarily involves human sexual education, human sexuality issues, or sexual orientation issues."[110] The bill did not become law.

TABLE 1. Summary of 15 Lawsuits Against Public School Districts That Failed to Protect Students from Anti-LGBT Discrimination and/or Harassment

Name of Case	State	Date of Settlement	Monetary Award
Nabozny v. Podlesny	Wisconsin	1996	$962,000
*Wagner v. Fayetteville Public Schools**	North Carolina	1998	None
*Iverson v. Kent**	Washington	1998	$40,000
Vance v. Spencer County Public School District	Kentucky	2000	$220,000
*Lovins v. Pleasant Hill Public School District**	Missouri	2000	$72,000
O. H. v. Oakland Unified School District	California	2000	Undisclosed
Ray v. Antioch Unified School District	California	2000	Undisclosed
Montgomery v. Independent School District	Minnesota	2000	Undisclosed
*Putman v. Board of Education of Somerset Independent Schools**	Kentucky	2000	$135,000
Snelling v. Fall Mountain Regional School District	New Hampshire	2001	None
*Dahle v. Titusville Area School District**	Pennsylvania	2002	$312,000
Gay/Straight Alliance Network v. Visalia Unified School District	California	2002	$130,000
Henkle v. Gregory	Nevada	2002	$451,000

*Settled out of court

A number of states have also passed laws preventing even mention of the word *homosexual* by teachers in the classroom or mandating that homosexuality be presented in an exclusively negative way. South Carolina bans discussion of "alternative sexual lifestyles from heterosexual relationships including, but not limited to, homosexual relationships, except in the context of instruction concerning sexually transmitted disease."[111] Arizona law prohibits instruction that "promotes a homosexual lifestyle, portrays homosexuality as a positive alternative lifestyle, or suggests that it is possible to have 'safe' homosexual sex."[112] Alabama requires any mention of homosexuality to be made within the context "that homosexuality is not a lifestyle acceptable to the general public."[113] Texas requires any mention of gay-related issues to be followed by the admonition that homosexual conduct is a criminal offense in the state, yet its sodomy laws were struck down in 2003.[114] Utah prohibits the "advocacy" of homosexuality.[115]

Some expected that state laws requiring schools to teach that homosexual conduct is illegal would be changed or struck down in light of the 2003 U.S. Supreme Court ruling in *Lawrence v. Texas,* which held that sodomy laws—which made homosexual sex a criminal offense in those states—violate the U.S. Constitution.[116] However, these laws remain in effect as of August 2011.

In the meantime, these laws are having an adverse impact on students. Kay Coburn, an administrator with the Temple (Texas) Independent School District, told Human Rights Watch in 2002 that there is "no discussion of homosexuality" or "any message in the curriculum about how homosexuals might protect themselves from HIV. Abstinence is the only message. The traditional family is where you have sex. The curriculum doesn't address sex outside this structure."[117] Cheryl Cox, a health teacher and member of her Robinson (Texas) High School Health Education Advisory Council, noted that coverage of homosexuality and other "lifestyle options" was "not needed or necessary. . . . I can't see it ever being acceptable to discuss homosexuality, as it's a very conservative community. It's a topic that I'm not supposed to be talking about because of the standards set forth by the community and by the health advisory board."[118] Terry Cruz, an abstinence educator in Laredo, Texas, told Human Rights Watch that "probably the only time I touch on the subject [of homosexuality] is with HIV, referring to how HIV originally started."[119]

Fear of "promoting homosexuality" due to these provisions sometimes prevents school districts from protecting LGBT students. In response to violence and harassment against gay students, the West Virginia Attorney General's Office searched for a program that would promote tolerance through school curricula. The state received eighty thousand dollars in federal grants from the U.S. Department of Justice to implement a model program from Maine that included training manuals for teachers. However, when the West Virginia Family Foundation, a conservative Christian group, found references in those manuals to making LGBT students feel safer, they brought two hundred people to a state board of education meeting wearing antigay T-shirts and accused the attorney general of "promoting homosexuality." The program was immediately suspended.[120] Anti-LGBT activists around the country have forced LGBT youth to defend themselves not only against their peers but also against the parents, administrators, and religious leaders who have targeted schools as the primary sphere for their moralistic crusades.

> Schools are battlegrounds for the right. So much of their "cultural war" is waged over curricula, teachers' roles, parental rights, censorship, and privatization. Queer youth are on the front lines of these battles, often in isolation and without organizational support. In the name of family and community moral standards, the right fights against any mention of homosexuality in schools, whether in books, sex education classes, counseling sessions, or through the presence of openly queer youth and teachers. This enforced silence leaves our schools riddled with homophobia and provides no opportunities for young people to learn truths about queer lives and to have open discussions of their own sexuality.[121]

Although some state "no promo homo" laws are written to specifically cover sexuality and health education, others use such sweeping language that their scope is unclear, and they have a chilling effect not only on discussions of sexual orientation and gender but on scholarship in general. As a result of such a law in New Hampshire, teachers decided not to discuss Shakespeare's *Twelfth Night* because a female character disguises herself as a man. They also declined to show a video about Walt Whitman that mentioned he was gay.[122]

In contrast, California law explicitly states that "instruction or materials that discuss gender, sexual orientation, or family law and do not discuss human reproductive organs or their functions" are not subject to parental opt-out provisions.[123] In effect, for any school programs that do not reference sexual health or the prevention of HIV or other sexually transmitted diseases—such as programs that promote tolerance or the prevention of bullying and harassment—parents need not be notified in advance, and parents do not have an opt-out option with respect to their children's participation.

Legislation Censoring Books and Textbooks

State lawmakers have considered laws banning books that portray LGBT people in a neutral or positive light. For example, in 2004 and 2005, legislation was introduced in Alabama and Arkansas to censor books that, according to representatives, "promote the gay agenda" and the teaching of homosexuality as a "normal" lifestyle. In Alabama, state representative Gerald Allen (R-Cottondale), who sponsored legislation banning same-sex marriage in 2004, introduced a bill that would prohibit the use of public funds for "the purchase of textbooks or library materials that recognize or promote homosexuality as an acceptable lifestyle."[124] If the proposed bill did not fail in the state legislature, it would have barred any representation of homosexuality in schools, libraries, and state-funded universities.[125] Similarly, Arkansas state representative Roy Ragland (R-Marshall) proposed a bill in 2005 that would have forced the state's school districts to only purchase textbooks that define marriage as between one man and one woman. Ragland said that the legislation was aimed at bringing schoolbooks in line with the state constitution, which was amended by voters in 2004 to ban same-sex marriage.[126] However, this bill failed in the state senate.[127]

---

4 | School-Based Programs and Practices

Teachers, Administrators, and Staff

In a 1991 study of 289 school counselors, one in five reported that counseling adolescent lesbian or gay students was or would be gratifying. An almost equal number reported just the opposite. Seventy-one percent reported having counseled at least one lesbian or gay student, although only 25 percent believed they were competent to do so.[1] In a 1993 study of 120 gay and lesbian adolescents, the same researchers also found that only one-quarter of students felt able to talk with their school counselors about their sexual orientation; none of the respondents identified school personnel as being a major source of support.[2] Given the low level of interest and competence reported by counselors in the earlier study, such an outcome was predictable.

Many teachers and other school staff members hesitate to discuss sexual orientation or LGBT issues in general. For heterosexual teachers, the reason may be moral or religious objections or a lack of knowledge or understanding. For LGBT teachers, such reticence may stem from fears of eliciting parental complaints or jeopardizing their jobs.[3] One teacher from rural Georgia, recalling what happened after she came out to her principal, said he told her that "if the parents found out, he didn't need that kind of shit in his life, and he'd hang me out to dry."[4] Human Rights Watch reported that these kinds of fears were expressed most often in states and school districts that do not have nondiscrimination policies.

A study of fifteen lesbian and gay educators found that their apprehensions about disclosing their sexual orientation centered on harassment and discrimination, job loss, and accusations of child molestation or "recruiting" students into the "gay lifestyle."[5] Many gay and lesbian teachers have grown wary of charges of pedophilia. Anti-LGBT activists and right-wing politicians regularly conflate homosexuality with pedophilia and claim that gay men are more likely to molest children than heterosexual men, a claim regularly repudiated by social science research. A 2000 report titled *Homosexuals Recruit Children,* published by the Traditional Value Coalition, even claims that "homosexual militants" have an ongoing "campaign to legalize sex with children" and are "pushing for aggressive recruitment programs in public schools." The report concludes, "Since homosexual couples can't reproduce, they will simply go after *your* children for seduction and conversion to homosexuality."[6] Such hate-filled lies are all too typical of organizations on the far right.

Social Science Research Finds No Link between Sexual Orientation and Child Sexual Abuse

Any notion of a link between pedophilia and homosexuality has been definitively refuted by peer-reviewed social science research. A study in the *Journal of the American Medical Association* noted that 90 percent of pedophiles are men and that 98 percent of these individuals are heterosexual.[7] One researcher explained this statistic by noting, "Gay men desire consensual sexual relations with other adult men. Pedophiles are usually adult men who are sexually attracted to pre-pubescent children. They are rarely sexually attracted to other adults."[8] In fact, gay men and lesbians may be *less* likely than heterosexuals to sexually abuse children. Two peer-reviewed studies that examined the sexual orientation of convicted child molesters found that less than 1 percent in one study and 0 percent in the other were lesbian or gay.[9]

About four in five cases of child sexual abuse reported to child protection authorities involve a girl who is abused. But because the sexual abuse of boys is less likely to be reported, it is estimated that one-quarter to one-third of all sexually abused children are boys, while two-thirds to three-quarters are girls.[10] Because 90 percent of child molesters are men, some have argued that "homosexual child abuse" is widespread and that homosexuals abuse children at a rate higher than their proportion of the population.[11] Such claims are based on the false belief that men who sexually abuse boys are homosexual. In fact, the overwhelming majority of men who sexually abuse children live their lives as heterosexual men. A review of existing social science literature on the relationship between sexuality and child sexual abuse that was published in 2000 found that "a gay man is no more likely than a straight man to perpetrate sexual activity with children."[12] Further, "cases of perpetration of sexual behavior with a pre-pubescent child by an adult lesbian are virtually nonexistent."[13]

A review of 352 medical records of children evaluated for sexual abuse during a twelve-month period at a Denver children's hospital found that less than 1 percent had been abused by a gay man or a lesbian. Of 269 adult perpetrators of child abuse identified among the 352 cases of abuse, only two were gay or lesbian. The vast majority of the children in the study (82 percent) "were suspected of being abused by a man or a woman who was, or had been, in a heterosexual relationship with a relative of the child." The review concluded that in this sample, "a child's risk of being molested by his or her relative's heterosexual partner is over 100 times greater than [the risk of being molested] by someone who might be identifiable as being homosexual, lesbian, or bisexual."[14] In an earlier study of convicted male child molesters in Massachusetts, none of the 175 men were found to have an exclusively homosexual adult sexual orientation or to be primary attracted to other adult men.[15]

Despite the evidence to the contrary, LGBT people are often characterized as a threat to youth, and some argue that gay people should not be allowed to teach, parent, or serve as Boy Scout troop leaders. Some conservatives have even suggested that nondiscrimination laws protecting LGBT people and the recognition of their rights will lead to an increase in child molestation. One author noted that due to fear of accusations of pedophilia, LGBT adults are the "only oppressed group that is severed from its relationships with youth. Youth then experience the absence of adult mentoring, support, counseling, or befriending of both queer and non-queer adults."[16] Because LGBT youth usually grow up in heterosexual households, they often lack role models with an understanding of their unique situations and remain without access to accurate information about their sexuality, their community, and themselves.[17] Researchers found that the majority (77 percent) of the supportive adults in the lives of the seventeen LGB youth they interviewed were not family members.[18]

Literature on the emotional development of ethnic minority children has revealed a definitive need for affirmative adult role models from their own racial or ethnic backgrounds. Similarly, research has shown that having an openly gay role model improves health outcomes for gay youth.[19] An exploratory study with twelve self-identified LGBT youth found that they perceived peers and unrelated adults to be more supportive than family members. Peers and adults who were also LGBT provided especially valuable information and support. Unfortunately, the participants reported that their teachers, counselors, coaches, and administrators "strove to uphold the heterosexual model as normative," in direct conflict with the students' emerging sexual identity.[20] In a study of 101 school counselors, only six indicated that there was at least one faculty member at their school who was openly gay or lesbian.[21]

Fortunately, some students are able to rely on teachers, counselors, or coaches who are LGBT or who are, in some way, perceived to be accepting.[22] According to Human Rights Watch, when LGBT students reported positive school experiences, they attributed them to the presence of supportive teachers.[23] In GLSEN's 2007 National School Climate Survey, eight out of ten respondents reported that they knew of at least one school staff member supportive of LGBT students at their school. Students who had support from faculty or staff were less likely to miss school because of feeling unsafe, and they were more likely to have higher GPAs and to go to college. These positive numbers increased as the number of supportive teachers and faculty members increased. Only 15 percent of students with many (six or more) supportive teachers/staff members said they did not plan to go to college, compared with 27 percent of LGBT students with no support from teachers/staff members.[24] Students' awareness of which teachers and school staff are supportive can come from a multitude of sources, including rumors, a passing expression of tolerance, a poster or a book in a classroom, and the enforcement of an antiharassment policy.[25]

While the school environment is often hostile toward LGBT students, supportive teachers can help them avoid a broad range of problems often associated with being young and LGBT.[26] In their analysis of National Adolescent Health Study data, one group of researchers found that "feelings about teachers play the largest role in predicting the troubles of both boys and girls with bisexual attractions in school—paying attention, getting homework completed, and getting along with other students."[27] Data from the 1998–99 *Nuestras Voces* study of Latino gay and bisexual men show that the presence of an adult gay role model while growing up increased self-esteem, lowered psychological distress, and lessened the likelihood of engaging in high-risk sexual behavior later in life.[28]

The presence of out gay men and lesbians among teachers, administrators, and staff has a positive impact on all members of a school community.[29] The insight that students gain from experiences with openly LGBT teachers in the school environment can be significant. A survey of eleven former students in their late twenties and early thirties did not elicit any intense concerns about having had a gay teacher while in middle school. The experience even seems to have left them with a more open-minded perspective on issues related to sexual orientation. Though further research is needed with a larger population, the results of this study suggest that openly LGBT teachers can be important role models for both LGBT and heterosexual students.[30]

Reporting on the decision of a Massachusetts teacher to come out to members of his school community, one author writes,

> His motivations for taking this action were twofold: first, he did it for the students. "It was an attempt to alleviate some of the fear, shame, loneliness, and despair of kids in high school today that I also felt as a closeted teen," he told me. And second, he did it for himself and other staff members. "It takes much more energy to be closeted than it does to be out," he continued. "All of the energy I used in worrying that I would say the wrong thing is now freed up for other things. I think I'm a much more effective teacher now on many levels."[31]

The response to this teacher's acknowledgment of his sexual orientation was mixed. While some students and parents expressed concern, there were also messages of support and encouragement from the community. One father wrote, "I . . . support your courageous statements. You will undoubtedly pay a price for your honesty, yet others would pay a price for your silence, and that price could be fatal."[32]

Staff Development and Training

The failure of many teachers and counselors to serve LGBT youth originates from a lack of training. Advocacy groups and educators who support the inclusion of training on sexual orientation and gender identity and expression in tolerance programs assert that prejudice and harassment can only be overcome by talking directly and frankly about the issue and through providing resources for in-school mentoring and support.[33] The use of staff training as an essential tool for creating a school atmosphere free of anti-LGBT harassment and discrimination is also supported by a small but growing body of research. School staff should be equipped with the tools and knowledge necessary to assist students who are struggling with their own or another's sexual orientation or gender identity and to identify and intervene on behalf of students who are harassed, discriminated against, or facing detrimental health consequences as a result of prejudice.[34] In addition to providing the tools to deal with such situations, training gives teachers, administrators, and other staffers the opportunity to work out their feelings related to sexual orientation and gender diversity and to learn how to handle the discomfort of colleagues, students, and parents around such issues.[35]

Published in 1998, a study of 101 junior and senior high school counselors found that only 8 percent felt they had a high level of competence in counseling LGBT youth; almost the same percentage indicated they had little or no competence. Eighty-nine percent of the counselors said they would be interested in such training.[36] Most of the teachers interviewed for a 2001 Human Rights Watch report also said their teacher training programs had not addressed harassment or discrimination based on sexual orientation or gender identity.[37] Analysis of data from the 2004 California Safe Schools Policy Survey, conducted by the California Safe Schools Coalition, found that the majority of school districts in the state who participated in the survey do not require middle and high school teachers to attend trainings on how to deal with discrimination and harassment based on sexual orientation. Of the trainings that do occur, the majority do not include training on how to deal with harassment or discrimination that occurs because of gender identity, appearance, and behavior. Lack of resources, expertise, and time were the most frequently cited reasons for lack of training. This is despite the fact that California law explicitly protects students from discrimination and harassment based on sexual orientation and gender identity.[38]

A survey of over fifteen hundred primary and secondary school principals, conducted in 2007 by GLSEN in collaboration with the National Association of Secondary School Principals, found that while half of principals say that harassment of students is a serious problem in their school, only 20 percent have engaged their schools in efforts to create a safe environment specifically for LGBT students. Nearly 70 percent of principals believe that professional development for school personnel would be most helpful in reducing that harassment of LGBT students.[39] This is supported by a study by the Massachusetts Safe Schools Project, which found that students in schools where the staff had been through training sponsored by that organization were twice as likely to report feeling supported by teachers and counselors than were students in schools without trained staff.[40] Clearly, there is a growing need for effective training curricula and programs for teachers and school staff.

The ACLU, the NCLR, and GLSEN offer training workshops for school districts seeking to address and prevent anti-LGBT harassment and violence.[41] These workshops show teachers and administrators how to create a safe environment for LGBT students and are designed to alert school districts to their responsibility to change any environment hostile to LGBT youth and to provide the skills and resources needed to promote an environment intolerant of harassment. The ACLU emphasizes that its workshop is not about sex or teaching morality.

> [I]t is about safety, equal access and equal protection. It is about making sure every student feels that they can achieve their best in school in an environment free of hostility. And it is about taking proactive steps to prevent the antigay attitudes that may exist in a school from turning into harassment and escalating into violence.[42]

Staff development and training workshops can have a significant effect on the experiences of LGBT students. One student described her experience at a new school with more supportive teachers, compared to the previous school she attended, as follows:

> It's wonderful here. My science and English teachers are so nice. If someone says "fag" or "dyke," they stop them. My teachers are really good about stopping homophobic words from being spread. There was one girl who used to give me complete hell. She'd tell me I'm fruity, stuff like that. The teacher took her into the hall and talked to her. My teachers are really cool.[43]

Unfortunately, most students never receive this kind of support. The most common response to anti-LGBT harassment and violence is no response at all. One student interviewed by Human Rights Watch described the lengths to which he went to document the harassment he experienced, only to be completely ignored by his school principal.

> I took a folder, wrote down dates and times every time I was harassed. I took it down to the principal. He said, "Son, you have too much time on your hands to worry about these folks. I have more

important things to do than worry about what happened two weeks ago." I told him, "I wanted to give you an idea of what goes on, the day-to-day harassment." He took the folder away from me and threw it in the trash. That was my freshman year, first semester. After that I realized [the school] wasn't going to do anything.[44]

Staff development and training programs about anti-LGBT harassment, in conjunction with nondiscrimination policies that include sexual orientation and gender identity, can effectively address the ignorance, fear, and apathy that prevent effective intervention on behalf of such students. Teachers interviewed by Human Rights Watch emphasized that students would benefit from staff training programs like the one described in the ACLU publication *Making Schools Safe*.[45] According to one teacher in Georgia, "If a model was in place, something designed to stop violence and take advantage of what teachers always refer to as 'teachable moments,' there's a lot of kids that would embrace it."[46]

The New York City Department of Education began implementing a training program for teachers and school administrators in 2007 as part of its Respect for All initiative (for more on this initiative, see the section on safe schools programs later in this chapter).[47] The formal training program prepares teachers, guidance counselors, and other staff members to address bullying, harassment, and intimidation of students.[48] In the first year, sixty-nine trainings were delivered to over one thousand educators from nearly 250 New York City schools serving students grades six and above. Representatives from the remainder of New York City's school districts were scheduled to attend additional trainings over the following two school years. Curricula for these two-day trainings included group discussions, mini-lectures, videos, and role-playing exercises designed to increase participants' awareness of anti-LGBT bias and behaviors in school and to stress the importance of intervening when anti-LGBT harassment occurs. Attendees were also provided with materials they could use with students, including a poster that identified district antibullying policies and the names of staff to contact to report incidents of harassment and bullying.[49]

The Respect for All curriculum was created based on a foundational program theory designed to increase participants'

• Awareness of prevalence of anti-LGBTQ ["Q" stands for "questioning"] behaviors in school;
• Self-awareness regarding own behaviors and professional practices;

- Knowledge of LGBTQ-related terminology;
- Empathy for LGBT students;
- Understanding of the importance of intervening in anti-LGBTQ remarks;
- Knowledge of and access to LGBT-related resources; and
- Self-efficacy related to the desired behaviors.

The expected outcomes and results of the training included

- An increase in participants' intervention in anti-LGBTQ behaviors;
- An increase in participants' engagement in efforts to create safer schools;
- An increase in participants' communication with students and other staff about LGBTQ issues; and
- A decrease in participants' use of hurtful language.[50]

GLSEN conducted an evaluation of the first year of the training program through pre- and post-training surveys completed by 813 of the participants and through a series of focus group interviews. According to GLSEN,

> Findings from the Year One evaluation demonstrate that this training program is an effective means for developing the competency of educators to address bias-based bullying and harassment, and to create safer school environments for LGBTQ students. The findings suggest that providing such training to all school staff, including administrators, would result in an even stronger effect on the school environment.[51]

Curricula and Textbooks

Even schools that recognize the need for the protection of LGBT students and teachers can make positive changes to curricula.[52] In many schools, the only time LGBT issues are discussed is in health classes, where homosexuality is only discussed within the context of sexually transmitted diseases and AIDS. Teachers should include discussions about LGBT people in other classes as well. Such curricular expansion might involve a discussion of the Mattachine Society, the Daughters of Bilitis, and the Stonewall Riots in the context of social change movements in recent U.S. history or the inclusion of a novel by a gay author like James Baldwin in a class on American literature.[53] Information on the family lives of same-sex couples should be included in life planning curricula, and school libraries should include books on the history of the LGBT rights movement.[54] The National Education Association, among other groups, supports the inclusion of LGBT issues in curricula and textbooks,[55] and recent research indicates that such inclusion can have a significant impact on school climate and safety.

The California Safe Schools Coalition analyzed data from the Preventing School Harassment and Safe Schools Policy surveys to determine what effect LGBT-inclusive curricula may have on school safety. Over three hundred school districts participated in the 2006 study, and an overwhelming majority (83 percent) reported that they include LGBT issues in their tolerance curriculum for all or some of their high school students. Smaller majorities reported including LGBT issues for some or all of their middle school students (64 percent) and elementary school students (54 percent). All students, LGBT and straight, reported feeling safer in schools that include LGBT issues in their curricula. Nearly three-quarters of LGBT students in schools with LGBT-inclusive curricula (73 percent) reported feeling safer, compared to 58 percent of those in schools with no inclusion. The difference was not as large but still significant for straight students (83 percent vs. 77 percent). Students attending schools with inclusive curricula also reported that they were less likely to have rumors or mean lies spread about them or to be made fun of because of the way they look or the way they talk and that there was less anti-LGBT bullying in their schools.[56]

While schools in more progressive states, such as California, are beginning to see the positive effects of LGB-inclusive tolerance curricula, the majority of textbooks used across the United States in other subjects either exclude or devote very little attention to LGBT issues and history. A review of five content analyses of textbooks for the high school and college levels published from 1992 through 2005 found very brief mentions of LGBT issues, often within a negative context.[57] For example, an analysis published in 2005 of twenty high school textbooks in five subject areas (personal and social education, moral education, family economics, human biology, and Catholic moral and religious education) found that 95 percent of the 610 textbook pages reviewed did not reference same-sex sexuality at all; 133 pages only defined sexuality as heterosexual, and only 33 pages mentioned same-sex sexuality at all. Almost 80 percent of the time, same-sex sexuality was mentioned in negative contexts, including sexually transmitted diseases, sexual abuse, and prostitu-tion.[58] A content analysis of eight textbooks for courses on the founda-tions of education, used in teacher preparation programs, also found lit-tle inclusion and coverage of LGBT issues. Of the nearly 214,700 estimated lines of text analyzed, only 3 percent were dedicated to LGBT content.[59]

GLSEN's 2007 National School Climate Survey confirms that LGBT-related curricula and resources are not available to most students. Less than half of the students surveyed were able to access information about LGBT history, people, or events in their school library, and even less (30 percent) were able to access this information on the Internet at school. Only 15 percent of students reported that LGBT issues were included in their textbooks or assigned readings, and the majority (87 percent) were not taught about LGBT history, people, or events in any of their classes. Of the small portion who were taught about LGBT-related topics in their classes, only one out of ten were exposed to positive representations.[60]

There were also significant differences in availability and access to these resources between youth in rural communities and those in subur-ban or urban communities:

- Only 9 percent of rural students reported that LGBT issues were taught in class, compared with 14 percent of suburban students and 15 percent of urban students.
- 20 percent of rural students reported that LGBT issues were repre-sented in their textbooks, compared with more than 43 percent of suburban students and 37 percent of urban students.
- 24 percent of rural students reported that LGBT resources were available in their school libraries, compared with 45 percent of suburban students and 32 percent of urban students.
- 22 percent of rural students had access to LGBT resources via In-ternet connections at school, compared to 42 percent of suburban students and 32 percent of urban students.[61]

GLSEN also found that LGBT students in the South are disproportion-ately unsupported when compared to LGBT students in any other re-gion. Students from the South were least likely to have a gay-straight al-liance at their school, least likely to have LGBT resources in their school library and access to LGBT community resources from the school Inter-net, and least likely to report having a comprehensive protective school policy about bullying and harassment in their schools.[62]

Multicultural education with curricular integration of LGBT issues reduces the alienation felt by LGBT students who do not see themselves reflected in school materials. It also makes all students more aware of a greater diversity of human experience. The development of LGBT students is enhanced through their exposure to their diverse and rich cultural history; even heterosexual students exposed to LGBT-inclusive education may come to better understand themselves and their own sexuality.[63] Unfortunately, there is an overall lack of support for the inclusion of LGBT-related materials in school curricula. In 1993, Massachusetts governor William Weld and his education department rejected two key recommendations of the Governor's Commission on Gay and Lesbian Youth: that schools purchase library books positively portraying gay men and lesbians and that curricula incorporate gay issues wherever appropriate. This rejection came a year before Weld's reelection and at the height of the Children of the Rainbow curriculum controversy in New York, during which the proposed adoption of a multicultural curriculum that included two minor references to gay people and gay families was defeated amid charges that it "promoted" homosexuality. Seven years later, however, Massachusetts amended the state's Equal Educational Opportunity regulations regarding curricula and sexual orientation:

1. All public school systems shall, through their curricula, encourage respect for the human and civil rights of all individuals regardless of race, color, sex, religion, national origin or sexual orientation.
2. Teachers shall review all instructional and educational materials for simplistic and demeaning generalizations, lacking intellectual merit, on the basis of race, color, sex, religion, national origin or sexual orientation. Appropriate activities, discussions and/or supplementary materials shall be used to provide balance and context for any such stereotypes depicted in such materials.[64]

Safe Schools Programs

Massachusetts launched the country's first safe schools initiative nearly two decades ago, after the Governor's Commission on Gay and Lesbian Youth documented the hostile school climate pervasive in most of the state's schools and its negative impact on gay and lesbian students, the children of gay parents, and other students who were perceived as somehow different. The Safe Schools Program sought to fulfill four recommendations made by the Massachusetts Board of Education in 1993:

- develop policies that protect gay and lesbian students from harassment, violence, and discrimination;
- offer school personnel training in violence prevention and suicide prevention;
- offer school-based support groups for gay, lesbian, and heterosexual students;
- provide school-based counseling for family members of gay and lesbian students.[65]

The Massachusetts legislature appropriated funds to support the Safe Schools Program through the Department of Education and the Department of Public Health. Within a few years, more than 140 schools across the commonwealth had gay-straight alliances, and many teachers and counselors were trained in how to deal with antigay harassment and violence. The program showed results very quickly. One study found that in schools with gay-straight alliances, 35 percent of students said LGB students could safely choose to be open about their sexuality. In schools without GSAs, only 12 percent said students could openly identify as LGB safely. It also discovered that in schools where the faculty had undergone training on gay issues, 54 percent of students said that gay students felt supported by teachers and counselors. In schools that had not undergone faculty training, only 26 percent of students said that gay students felt supported.[66]

The Massachusetts Safe Schools Program was a national model until 2002, when Governor Jane Swift vetoed funding for the program—the only such program fully funded by state money at the time. In other states and municipalities with safe schools programs, private funding is the primary source of support. These initiatives cannot succeed without the dogged determination of community-based supporters. Even in Massachusetts, many urban and rural communities did not have GSAs and had not conducted promised teacher trainings until recently. Most safe schools activity occurred in white, suburban, middle- and upper-class communities. However, the number of GSAs in Boston schools has significantly increased, and more safe schools work has been done in other cities with large communities of color. In California, over eight hundred GSAs exist across the state, in urban, rural, and suburban school districts.[67] Minneapolis, St. Paul, and Chicago also have many GSAs in their public schools, which are predominantly comprised of students of color. However, GSAs were still less likely to exist in rural school districts and in southern states as of 2007.[68]

Prior to the founding of Project 10, a school-based support program for LGB students in the Los Angeles public schools, informal discussions with LGB students revealed that they felt they were without any traditional support systems, sympathetic adults to talk to, or peers like themselves with whom to socialize. In 1985, after Project 10 had been in place for a full school year at Fairfax High School in Los Angeles, a study of the general student population was conducted. Of the 342 (out of 500) surveys that were returned, 56 percent of the respondents said they knew an LBG person and felt that there should be outreach to such students on every campus. Fifty-one percent felt that the effect of Project 10 on Fairfax High School had been positive. Only 11 percent felt that the effect had been negative and that it had given the school a bad name; 38 percent were unsure as to the effect. Seventy-nine percent of students surveyed felt that "the greatest benefit of Project 10 was that it provided all students with a place to get accurate information" on LGB-related issues.[69] Portions of the Project 10 model have since been replicated in schools across the country.

In 2007, the New York City Department of Education began implementing its Respect for All initiative, a safe schools program designed "to combat bullying and harassment based on ethnicity, national origin, religion, gender, sexual orientation, disability, and other factors."[70] Overall, the initiative "requires schools to develop annual plans to convey appropriate standards of behavior to students and staff, to track and monitor all bias incidents, to investigate complaints properly, and to take follow-up steps to ensure that schools maintain safe and respectful learning environments."[71] The initiative began with a formal training program that prepares teachers, guidance counselors, and other staff members to address bullying, harassment, and intimidation of students (for more on the training component of the initiative, see the section on staff development and training earlier in this chapter).[72] Developed in collaboration with GLSEN, the Anti-Defamation League, Morningside Center for Teaching Social Responsibility, Operation Respect, and Youth Enrichment Services (YES) of the New York City LGBT Community Center, the goals of the initiative are to:

1. Build the capacity of school personnel to actively promote a community of inclusion in each school so that all students feel both safe and respected
2. Increase the likelihood that school personnel will intervene when witnessing anti-LGBTQ language, harassment, and/or bullying
3. Build the capacity of school personnel to serve as a resource and support for students who may be lesbian, gay, bisexual, transgender, or questioning
4. Build the capacity of school personnel to serve as a resource for other school personnel regarding issues faced by lesbian, gay, bisexual, transgender, and questioning students
5. Decrease hurtful, offensive, or exclusionary language and/or practices[73]

In addition to training teachers and school staff, the Respect for All initiative was expanded in 2008 to include mandated reporting and investigation guidelines for incidents of bullying and harassment. In 2009, the number of school staff required to attend trainings was increased, and principals were required to develop antibullying plans for their schools. Evaluation of schools' efforts to prevent and respond to bullying were also included in their overall quality review.[74] In 2010, the initiative was expanded again to include an annual Respect for All Week (March 8–12), which is designed to focus schools' attention on creating safe and supportive environments for all students. The Department of Education provided a variety of resources and lesson plans to help teachers develop activities for the week.[75] At the press conference launching Respect for All Week, the Speaker of the New York City Council, Christine Quinn, summarized the ultimate goal of the Respect for All initiative.

We have a responsibility to provide every student in New York City with a safe and inclusive learning environment. Teaching our students to embrace diversity is essential to preventing hate among future generations. For the past two years, we've been working with advocates and community members to expand our Respect for All program. This week is part of our long-term effort to make this subject matter part of our school culture. We will use this opportunity to build awareness of this issue and the tools that are available to educators, students, and parents as they seek to eliminate bias-based harassment in our schools.[76]

Gay-Straight Alliances

Gay-straight alliances are in-school, extracurricular groups that support LGBT students, those questioning their sexual orientation or gender identity, and their straight friends and allies. They are an important part of an overall strategy to insure that schools provide education in a safe and welcoming environment.[77] GSAs bring together students and school staff to end anti-LGBT bias and homophobia or transphobia in their schools,[78] and they are the most visible and widely adopted component of safe schools programs.[79] As of 2008, there were more than four thousand GSAs in U.S. schools registered with GLSEN.[80]

The Gay-Straight Alliance Network, a youth leadership organization that connects GSAs to each other and to community resources through peer support, leadership development, and training, helps students start, support, and maintain GSAs in their schools. Founded in 1998, the organization initially worked with forty GSAs in the San Francisco Bay Area. Today, the GSA Network supports over eight hundred GSAs across the state of California. Through its National Association of GSA Networks program, launched in 2005, the organization has also established GSA networks in twenty-six states, with a goal of fifty states by 2020.[81] While there has been significant progress in growing the number of GSAs available to support LGBT students, there is still significant need: only one-third of students report having a GSA in their school.[82]

GSAs are often the only school-based place where LGBT youth can safely discuss issues associated with their sexual orientation or gender identity, and GSAs foster communication with others who understand what they are going through.[83] Students are able to make friends without hiding their sexual orientation or gender identity, helping them develop social skills and self-esteem.[84] Among LGBT students and their allies, GSAs also increase interest in learning about cultural and social issues related to sexual orientation or gender identity.[85] A teacher in Connecticut and GSA coadviser told *Education World* magazine,

> I have seen changes in students who come to the GSA. Kids with support move away from risk behaviors and experience school success. You can't pretend these kids don't exist. Even kids who won't step foot in the room benefit. At least they know there is a safe place; someone is acknowledging them and the issues they face.[86]

A study of the Massachusetts Safe Schools Program published in 2001 found that the presence of GSAs made a positive difference. In those schools with a GSA, 52 percent of the students indicated that there were members of the faculty, staff, or administration who supported LGB students, in contrast to only 37 percent of students in schools without a GSA. Students in schools with a GSA were also more comfortable referring a friend with questions about sexual orientation to a counselor, and staff in schools with a GSA were more comfortable assisting students with questions about sexual orientation.[87]

Guidance for Students, Parents, and Staff Who Want to Create a GSA

In *Gay-Straight Alliances: A Handbook for Students, Educators, and Parents*, Ian Macgillivray offers the following guidance to students, teachers and counselors, principals and superintendents, school boards, and parents in dealing with LGBT students and GSAs:

For students wanting to start GSAs:
- You must be absolutely certain you want to do this. This may put you in the spotlight.
- Find a teacher or counselor whom you trust to be an advisor for the GSA.
- Get the required form from the office for starting a new student club.
- Make a list of objectives and goals.
- Decide on a mission statement that reflects your objectives.
- Decide if you will have a president, vice president, secretary, and treasurer, or alternative leadership, such as rotating facilitators or a steering committee, and choose a name for your club.
- Prepare information on GSAs and the 1984 Equal Access Act for your principal.
- Submit the New Student Club form and meet with the principal.
- Be patient. It's not going to happen overnight.
- Protect yourself if things get ugly.

For teachers and counselors working with LGBT students and GSAs:
- The club's advisor should ensure that straight allies feel comfortable attending the meetings and also that the concerns of lesbian, gay, and bisexual students, transgender students, disabled students, and students of color are taken into consideration.

- Understand that for students with same-sex attractions, their primary identity may not be their sexual orientation.
- Some transgender students and students with same-sex attractions will not be comfortable joining the GSA and they should not be antagonized by students in the GSA for choosing not to attend meetings.
- Sometimes educators feel a stronger need for a GSA than do students. While it's okay to inspire students and let them know you will support them, there is a fine line between that and pushing your own agenda on them. Ultimately, it must be the students who initiate and run the GSA.

For principals and superintendents seeking information on their responsibilities regarding GSAs:
- The 1984 Equal Access Act states that if a school district allows non-curricular clubs then they cannot prohibit a GSA.
- Some school districts try to finagle their way around the law, but this often results in costly lawsuits. A better use of time and money is to honor the students' right to form the GSA and educate the school and community members who oppose it.
- The freedom of speech and assembly clauses of the First Amendment to the U.S. Constitution support the provision of safe spaces (such as GSAs) in which groups of students can assemble and speak about topics of importance to them.
- The equal protection clause of the Fourteenth Amendment has been cited in court cases where school administrators did not stop antigay abuse directed at students. School districts risk losing their Title IX funds if they do not stop peer sexual harassment of all students, including LGBT students.

For school boards managing debates that may arise regarding GSAs:
- Listen to the opposition's concerns.
- Get advocates and opponents to talk with one another.
- Draw on the expertise of organizations, religious establishments, or individuals in the community.
- Build support for the GSA by showing how it can help enhance school safety.
- Invite students to speak at school board meetings.

For parents seeking information about LGBT youth and GSAs:
- Parents and community members may not regularly attend or participate in meetings of student clubs, including GSAs.

- Parents who support students' right to form GSAs should make their voices heard. Often it is the minority of religious fundamentalist parents who get noticed because they are better organized and protest the loudest.
- Students who start GSAs need the support of parents and caring adults who respect their rights and can help teach them important lessons about democracy.
- Don't presume your child has same-sex attractions just because he or she is involved with a GSA. Many students involved in GSAs are heterosexual allies.
- School districts have substantial discretion to set their own policies and curricula. Under a state's opt-out provisions and for religious reasons, parents often have the right to pull their children from educational activities that are part of the mandated curriculum.[88]

Research on GSAs published in 2002 found that they have a positive impact on the academic performance of students and enhanced their sense of belonging to the school community. Students' sense of physical safety improved as well, and they reported that they attended school more often and worked harder when they were at school. They also improved their relationships with their families, developed a higher comfort level with their own sexual orientation, learned strategies for dealing with others' presumptions about their sexuality, and felt better about their ability to contribute to society.[89]

A 2003 study of GSAs in twenty-two schools describes four key roles that they can play in the school environment:

1. Counseling and support: Two of the GSAs in the study served as places where students could meet as a group or individually with the GSA advisor. These GSAs focused on assisting students with issues about sexual orientation or gender identity issues.
2. Creating "safe" space: Six of the GSAs became highly visible throughout the school through announcements over the school's public-address system and posters advertising their meetings. Their goal was to provide a place where students could socialize and talk about common interests and experiences. Typical activities included watching movies, eating pizza, listening to an invited speaker, and discussing school safety issues. (Students of color or students who were not openly gay were underrepresented in these GSAs. The authors of the study

consequently used the word *safe* in quotation marks to underscore that not all students felt safe and included there.)

3. Raising awareness, educating, and increasing visibility: Nine of the GSAs had regularly scheduled meetings that included both social and educational or political activities. These groups not only were visible through announcements and posters but also played a lead role in calling attention to safety issues affecting LGBT students. These GSAs initiated LGBT-supportive school programming and lobbied for staff training; students planned schoolwide assemblies that addressed LGBT issues and visited classrooms to talk to their peers.

4. Becoming part of broader efforts: Five of the GSAs partnered with other schools, community members, or groups addressing LGBT issues. School-based safe schools task forces comprised of staff members, parents, and students took on a primary role and sponsored community-wide and school-based projects, such as administering school climate surveys to students. In partnership with the GSAs, these organizations also developed mandatory staff development programs on LGBT issues and facilitated the inclusion of LGBT curricula in the classroom. The staff in these schools also created intervention strategies for ending anti-LGBT harassment and fought for the inclusion of domestic partnership benefits for LGBT staff.[90]

A review of studies of GSAs by GLSEN further confirmed that they can have a significant effect on school climate. Compared to students in schools without a GSA, students in schools with GSAs are

- less likely to hear homophobic remarks in school on a daily basis;
- less likely to report feeling unsafe at school because of their sexual orientation or the way they express their gender;
- less likely to miss school because they feel unsafe;
- two times more likely to say they hear teachers make supportive or positive remarks about lesbian and gay people;
- more likely to be aware of a supportive adult at school;
- more likely to feel a sense of belonging to their school community.[91]

The positive effects of GSAs may also save lives. A study of 142 LGBT youth ages fourteen to twenty-one in Denver, Colorado, found that those who attended a school with a GSA were significantly less likely to report that they attempted suicide.[92]

GSA in Utah Fights for Its Right to Meet at School

A Profile of Kelli Peterson

A struggling student and out lesbian, Kelli Peterson had been beaten up on occasion. She also battled depression, isolation, and thoughts of suicide. "I hated high school," she recalls, "I didn't feel like I had anything there."[93] In the autumn of 1995, her senior year at Salt Lake City's East High School, Kelli began talking with a friend about the difficulties LGBT students faced. "Wouldn't it be great," they wondered as they compared stories, "to have a place where we could meet regularly and talk about stuff . . . a place where we could feel safe and just be ourselves?"[94] Kelli found inspiration for action in the activism of Candace Gingrich, the openly gay half sister of former House Speaker and archconservative Newt Gingrich. After attending a November 1995 speech by Candace, Kelli and twenty-five other students formed the East High Gay-Straight Alliance.

In February 1996, the Salt Lake City School District Board of Education banned all extracurricular clubs rather than allow the alliance to meet.[95] Although the alliance's mission was initially approved, resistance arose once some religious conservatives got involved, and on February 20, the school board voted four to three to discontinue all clubs rather than permit the existence of the GSA.[96] On February 23, students of both East High School and West High School walked out of school in protest, marched to the Utah State Capitol Building, and held a rally.

While protests against the ban continued, the school board began a reclassification project, which allowed selected clubs defined as "curricular" to continue their meetings. In a special session, the state legislature passed a law that allowed schools to deny a free meeting space to any group that they believed encouraged criminal conduct, promoted bigotry, or involved human sexuality. As a result, the school board began charging the GSA rent for its meeting space at the school. In addition, the school denied the alliance official standing, and it was not allowed to announce meetings or post notices of its activities, nor was it represented in the high school yearbook, as other clubs were.

Two years after Kelli and her friends inadvertently caused a statewide controversy simply because they wanted a safe space for LGBT students to meet, three civil rights groups joined forces to file a lawsuit against the school board.[97] In 1999, the U.S. District Court for the District of Utah ruled that the school board had violated the Equal Access Act by banning some extracurricular clubs while allowing others to meet.[98]

Despite a senior year filled with hate mail, scorn from her relatives, and a death threat, Kelli finished high school on a high note. Her grades and her relationship with her friends improved. Kelli graduated with no regrets, believing that "people should not always take the middle ground, because you definitely need to take sides on issues."[99] Standing up for the right of LGBT students to meet on school grounds ultimately led to positive changes in Kelli's personal life. For Kelli, a life of depression, isolation, and thoughts of suicide turned into a life full of friendship and support.

The Harvey Milk High School

New York City's Harvey Milk High School, named for a slain civil rights leader, was established to create "a public school where some of the city's most at-risk youth—those who are gay, lesbian, bisexual, transgender, and questioning (LGBTQ)—could learn without the threat of physical violence and emotional harm they faced in a traditional educational environment."[100] The only school of its kind, it provides a place for LGBT youth to go to high school in a safe and supportive environment. It was established in 1984 as an accredited program of the New York City Department of Education's Career Education Center, in partnership with the Hetrick-Martin Institute, a social service agency serving LGBT youth since 1979.[101]

Employing the same curricula and teachers and requiring the same regents exams and graduation standards as any other New York City public high school, it is similar to other specialized public schools, including the Frederick Douglass Academy in Harlem, which serves primarily African American students; the Young Women's Leadership School for Girls in East Harlem; and the Urban Academy Laboratory School, a multicultural, multiracial, 120-student school on Manhattan's

East Side. Admissions standards are the same as those for other New York City public schools.[102]

The majority of students at Harvey Milk High School belong to racial minorities: nearly three-quarters of the seventy-one enrollees in 2002–3 were either African American or Latino. Forty percent reported a family income below twenty thousand dollars. Although the school is located in Manhattan's Greenwich Village, 60 percent of its students come from Brooklyn, the Bronx, and Queens. A significant number of its students are either homeless or living in group homes with a guardian because they have been thrown out of their own homes by their parents.[103] In the 2008 school year, 96 students were enrolled in grades nine through twelve, and nearly 90 percent of seniors graduated, well above average in New York City.[104] More than 60 percent of Harvey Milk High School students go on to attend advanced programs or college.[105] Given that, according to Hetrick-Martin, LGB adolescents drop out of school at a rate three times the national average, such success is extraordinary.[106]

From Group Home to Harvey Milk High

A Profile of Luis A.

Luis A. does not believe that Harvey Milk High School in New York City is successful because it is a "gay high school."[107] He thinks it is successful because the teachers and staff actually care about the students and view all races, sexual orientations, and gender identities as legitimate. A recent graduate, Luis feels that Harvey Milk High School provides a safe and supportive environment for all students—gay or straight. This level of support was not present in his home life.

Early in his adolescence, Luis felt the need to verbalize and understand his attraction to men, and he began exploring the Internet for a community. As he searched Web sites and visited chat rooms, his identity as a young gay man slowly began to solidify. However, he was forced to come out to his family prematurely when his mother checked the computer's Internet history and saw the Web sites he had visited.

Luis characterizes his mother as "old school," to explain why she reacted negatively and blamed herself for his sexual orientation. As a result, Luis became depressed, and his relationship with his mother suffered greatly. Due to their tumultuous relationship, in addition to other factors, Luis ended up in a group home when he was fifteen.

Going through the New York City Administration for Children's Services was not a pleasant experience for Luis. However, it did lead him to a group residence in Harlem run by Green Chimneys Children Services, which uniquely provides a homelike environment for LGBT young people outside of the traditional foster care system. During his stay at Green Chimneys, Luis began attending Harvey Milk High School, which allowed him to create an even stronger connection to the LGBT community in New York City. The lure of the "big city" and its thriving queer community caused Luis to act out and break certain rules set up by the group home. As a result, he was transferred to another Green Chimneys group home in upstate New York when he was sixteen.

While upstate, Luis was enveloped in a whole new world. He was free from the congested streets and smog of the city and began adjusting to the small community. He enjoyed the simple pleasures of rural high school life, like homecoming and other school functions that brought the small community together. Although this upstate life did not provide him with a supportive LGBT community, he still enjoyed the two years he spent there. Luis initially wanted to transition to the independent living program through Green Chimneys upstate, but when he turned eighteen, he decided to drop out of school and restart his life in New York City.

Although Luis's mother was not initially supportive of his sexual orientation, she never closed her doors to him, and he moved back in with her in Harlem. This time, his home life was good, and he felt like he was on the right track. He reenrolled at Harvey Milk High School and graduated a year and half later. Luis then explored his interest in theater by writing short plays and performing them with his friends in small theaters. Many of his plays discussed his coming-out process, allowing him to express himself in a new way.

An only child, Luis was frequently alone after school and on the weekends while his mother worked numerous jobs. As a result, he became extremely passionate about creating and implementing a successful after-school program. His ultimate goal is to help create after-school programming that provides a safe, supportive space for youth to engage with each other while also participating in the arts.

For Luis, acting and writing plays allowed him to work through a number of his own struggles, while showcasing his talents at the same time. He believes all youth should have a similar opportunity to explore their potential, and he wants to do what he can to make those opportunities a reality for youth who, like him, may have a lot of obstacles to overcome but even more talent to offer.

In June 2002, the New York City Board of Education approved $3.2 million in funds for the renovation and expansion of the Harvey Milk High School, and in September 2003, the school opened its doors as a full-fledged public high school. The allocation of those funds led to intense media and community scrutiny. Acknowledging the good intentions behind the Harvey Milk High School and supporting its basic aim, the *New York Times* nonetheless could not "condone the concept of establishing a special school specifically for students based on their sexual orientation."[108] The *Wall Street Journal* accused the school system of creating an institution for an "education elite" in response to pressure from a "politically influential group." Ignoring the economic background of much of Harvey Milk High School's student body, it concluded, "Only in America's big-city public schools do you get better treatment if you're gay than if you're poor."[109]

Of the major newspapers in New York City, only the *Daily News* called the concern over the school's expansion overblown, noting that many of the students at the school had been ostracized by their families or their former schools. The paper wrote, "[A] lot of people reasonably contend it would be better if New York didn't have dozens of differently themed schools—that students should adjust to their surroundings, as they one day will have to do when they are adults. . . . But since the goal of education is not just to teach students, but to enable them to learn, policies that help that process along are worth trying."[110]

Democratic state senator Ruben Diaz, a politician with a long record of antagonism toward the LGBT community, even sued to block the school's opening, with the help of attorneys from the Florida-based Liberty Counsel, a group that defends "traditional families, sanctity of life and religious liberty." Cloaked in the language of civil rights and decrying the school as a "separate but equal" institution, Senator Diaz accused the school of "taking from the poor and giving to the rich," segregation, and "leaving my Spanish children, my black children behind."[111]

Even segments of the LGBT community were ambivalent. Michael

Bronski, a prominent journalist, activist, and academic, writing in the *Boston Phoenix*, commented,

> [S]egregating these students for their own protection also patronizes them, and that's why [the Harvey Milk School]—as helpful as it may be for a few queer kids at the moment—is not really a solution.... The Harvey Milk School made sense in the 1980s, when the prevailing politics on GLBT youth favored carving out private spaces to protect them. But the gay-rights movement has grown since then, and the politics of privacy has given way to a more forceful politics of public intervention.... At this point the public-school system should mandate a series of measures that will make all schools safe for all students."[112]

In fact, a separate school is not the best solution. It is available only to a small percentage of youth who need it: those whose parents have either abandoned them or who will allow them to go. Making sure that *all* schools are safe for LGBT youth is, of course, a better and necessarily long-term goal. But that goal for future LGBT youth should not come at the expense of the mental and physical well-being of today's students. Given the dismal statistics on the treatment of these youth in American schools, LGBT-supportive institutions like the Harvey Milk High School are an important interim solution to the epidemic of violence and harassment against LGBT students in America's public schools.

Only one other such school has ever existed. Founded in 1997, the Walt Whitman School in Dallas, a private school with a sliding-scale tuition, closed its doors in 2003, having repeatedly failed to win accreditation from the Southern Association of Colleges and Schools.[113]

5 | The No Child Left Behind Act and LGBT Students

There's no greater challenge than to make sure that every child . . . not just a few children, every single child, regardless of where they live, how they're raised, the income level of their family, every child receive[s] a first-class education in America.

President George W. Bush[1]

President George W. Bush signed the No Child Left Behind Act (NCLB Act) in front of a cheering crowd of high school students in Hamilton, Ohio, on January 8, 2002.[2] A complex and comprehensive package of policies reauthorizing the Elementary and Secondary Education Act of 1965, the NCLB Act codified his administration's campaign promise to improve public education for every child in the United States.[3] The law focused on creating accountability for student performance through federally mandated standardized testing, allowing parents to choose their children's schools through vouchers and the creation of charter schools, and giving greater control of federally funded education programs to local governments.[4] It received bipartisan support in Congress, including from liberal senator Edward Kennedy (D-MA), and both houses symbolically assigned the bill the number "1" to illustrate that education policy was its top priority.

Given the historic changes in education policy included in the NCLB Act and President Bush's public promise of helping every student, this chapter offers a unique examination of how the NCLB Act affects LGBT youth in schools. It summarizes certain provisions that may specifically affect LGBT students—concerning school vouchers, single-sex education, standardized testing, Internet filtering, violence prevention, and parental rights—and amendments to the bill that have been passed by Congress to specifically address anti-LGBT policies supported by the Boy Scouts of America and the U.S. military. This chapter analyzes how those provisions and amendments address issues already discussed, in previous chapters, as affecting LGBT students.

Vouchers and School Choice

> [W]e trust parents to make the right decisions for their children. Any
> school that doesn't perform, any school that cannot catch up and do its
> job, a parent will have these options: a better public school, a tutor, or a
> charter school.[5]
>
> —President George W. Bush

Beginning with the 2003–4 school year, the NCLB Act allowed parents of children attending "schools identified for improvement, corrective action, or restructuring" to send their children to a different public school or charter school within the same school district. Low-income students attending schools that failed to meet state standards for at least three of the four preceding years must be allowed to use federal funds to pay for "supplemental education services from the public- or private-sector provider selected by the students and their parents."[6] The NCLB Act also requires school districts to spend up to 20 percent of their federal funding to provide school choice and supplemental educational services to eligible students.[7] Given the effect of antigay harassment and violence on academic achievement, does this provision help parents of LGBT students who qualify as "low-income"? The answer is complicated and requires more detailed explanation of how charter schools and school vouchers work. For example, parents of LGBT students may have no real "choice" in school districts where religious charter or private schools are the only alternative to public schools.

School vouchers allow public tax dollars to be used to pay for private, religious schooling, which had historically been a losing proposition for social conservatives. However, in *Zelman v. Simmons-Harris* (2002), the U.S. Supreme Court ruled five to four that a school voucher program in Cleveland was constitutional because it was "entirely neutral with respect to religion" and "provide[d] benefits directly to a wide spectrum of individuals, defined only by financial need and residence in a particular school district."[8] Referring to a 1947 case in which the Court had ruled that "[n]o tax in any amount, large or small, can be levied to support any religious activities or institutions, whatever they may be called, or whatever form they may adopt to teach or practice religion,"[9] Justice John Paul Stevens, in his dissent, called the *Zelman v. Simmons-Harris* decision "profoundly misguided."[10]

The Court's ruling paved the way for the school vouchers provision in the NCLB Act, which allows federal dollars to support private schools, which may not be mandated to follow state or local education policies that protect youth from harassment or discrimination based on sexual orientation and gender identity. Many of these private schools are religiously affiliated and have policies and practices that are discriminatory toward LGBT teachers, parents, and youth.[11] In 2000, more than 80 percent of the private schools included in Cleveland's voucher program were affiliated with a specific religion. As a result, $8 million in public funds were distributed to schools in Cleveland that taught religious doctrine to thirty-seven hundred economically disadvantaged children in the 1999–2000 school year.[12] Nonetheless, there is at least some anecdotal evidence that religious schools may, in some cases, provide a haven of sorts for LGBT students harassed in public schools. For example, Jamie Nabozny, a gay student subjected to significant antigay harassment and violence in Wisconsin public schools (see profile in chapter 2), reported that he experienced less harassment and violence in a religious school to which he was temporarily transferred than in public school.

Charter Schools

Beginning with a single school in Minnesota in 1992, the charter school movement has burgeoned into a nationwide phenomenon with more than three thousand schools in 2004–5 serving more than seven hundred thousand students in thirty-nine states and the District of Columbia.[13] Publicly funded but granted relative autonomy with regard to structure, curriculum, and educational focus, charter schools function more or less independently of the public school system. Proponents argue that a charter school's freedom from the regulations and bureaucracy of a public school system allows for greater innovations that can ultimately better meet students' needs.

The types and quality of charter schools vary dramatically, as do the state laws and regulations that govern them. Arizona, one of the states with the most charter schools, imposes almost no restrictions on them at all. In Rhode Island, charter schools' curricula and teacher certification standards are highly regulated. Some charter schools have been created by groups of parents and teachers seeking an alternative to the neighborhood public school. Others have been established by private, for-profit enterprises. Some are even former public schools that have converted to charter status, in the hopes of having greater freedom with which to provide innovative education.[14]

School choice is "not just about making opportunities for people to create new, potentially more effective public schools [but also] represents a dramatic change in the way states offer public education."[15] The same can be said about the charter school movement itself. Both have become controversial issues that have forged unusual political alliances (e.g., between conservative white members of Congress and black urban parents) and caused friction between other long-standing political allies, like the national teachers unions and their local affiliates.[16] Some advocate for vouchers and school choice programs because they use tax dollars to provide affordable alternatives to low-income, mostly black and Latino students in urban areas. In some urban school districts, students may indeed get a better education at charter schools than at struggling public schools. But many educators and elected officials denounce such programs for draining scarce public funds from already struggling public school systems and for funneling the brightest students to private and parochial schools, all the while meeting the educational needs of a very small number of students.

Lesbian Youth Takes Control of Her Life with the Help of the Harvey Milk High School

A Profile of Tenaja Jordan

Tenaja's high school career began well.[17] As a freshman at Staten Island Technical High School, she felt loved by her parents and accepted at school. She knew she was a lesbian, but she was not out to anyone. During her sophomore year, Tenaja started seeing her sexual orientation in a social and political context and began her coming-out process. By her junior year, everyone at school knew that she was gay. She never felt in physical danger, but she did experience verbal harassment. Female students would say, "At least I'm not a lesbian like *her*," while male students taunted her by calling out, "Come with me, I'll make you straight." Generally speaking, Tenaja felt that students viewed her lesbianism as "disgusting." The other students' reactions to her sexual orientation quickly took a toll on Tenaja's well-being; she began to skip school, and her grades started to slip. During the middle of her junior year, she went to a guidance counselor for help.

Unfortunately, the guidance counselor was not equipped to help Tenaja deal with the harassment she was experiencing. At a loss, the counselor called Tenaja's parents, even though Tenaja was afraid to tell them about her lesbianism: her parents are Jehovah's Witnesses, and Tenaja knew they would have a difficult time accepting her sexual orientation. In a meeting with her parents, Tenaja was backed into a corner by the counselor, who kept pushing her to tell her parents what was bothering her. Feeling that she had no choice, Tenaja came out to her parents. Her mother refused to accept that she was gay, while her father refused to deal with it at all. Her mother believed it was the result of the bad influence of other students and forbid Tenaja from attending any extracurricular school activities. As Tenaja put it, "All I had was school and home." Neither environment offered her much in the way of support.

The situation went from bad to worse when her Jehovah's Witnesses congregation excommunicated her. Even so, Tenaja's mother continued to take her to church, where she was forbidden to speak to anyone and others were prohibited from speaking to her. By the end of the school year, Tenaja had made the decision to move out and live on her own. She got into an independent living program in Brooklyn during the summer and was determined to graduate from Staten Island Tech and prove to her parents that she could make it on her own. However, Tenaja found it difficult to return to her old school life and be constantly reminded that she was not accepted.

Worse still, she was identified as a "troubled teen" and an "underprivileged kid" by the city's Department of Youth Services, which was trying to make decisions for her at a time when Tenaja felt it was important to make decisions for herself. She fell into a deep depression, slept a lot, and rarely went to school. When she did go, she was regularly harassed. Fortunately, while searching the Internet for LGBT youth resources, Tenaja discovered the Hetrick-Martin Institute, home of the Harvey Milk High School.

During the middle of her senior year, Tenaja transferred to Harvey Milk, and the world became a brighter place. She went from a school where she was one of eight black students and the only lesbian to a school where LGBT youth of color were the majority. From an environment where she was taught, she recalls, that "everything that is white is beautiful and everything that is beautiful is white," she moved to a place that embraces diversity. Tenaja was surprised when other students asked her to identify as aggressive or femme. She responded by declaring herself a "nondenominational lesbian." She made friends with other lesbians for the first time. "It was great," Tenaja explains. "It felt very, very positive to me." She also loved the teachers at the Harvey Milk High School, whom she describes as "really, really nice people" who gave her the freedom to make her own choices and create a plan for her life.

Tenaja went on to Hunter College, with plans to go to graduate school. She remained actively involved with the Hetrick-Martin Institute, becoming the chairperson of its youth advisory board. She even reestablished contact with her parents, hoping that they could all reconcile their differences. In response to the criticism that the publicly funded Harvey Milk High School is a return to segregated schools, Tenaja argues, "Separation of at-risk students is not segregation. It is a temporary solution to a problem. It stabilizes young people so that they can get an education. [In extreme cases,] it saves a life. The Department of Education owes kids a safe space." The Harvey Milk High School provided support and guidance for Tenaja and enabled her to draw on her own strength and follow her own path. She says she shares her experiences because "if my story helps another queer minority youth, I'm all for that."

The National Education Association supports "public charter schools that have the same standards of accountability and access as other public schools,"[18] but, as the American Federation of Teachers point out, very few can claim to.[19] Charter schools are also problematic because they often pay their teachers far less than public schools (which are often unionized), may be more racially segregated than public schools, and are often unable to meet the needs of students with disabilities.[20] The jury is still out on whether the quality of the education they provide is better than or even equal to public schools.

The school choice movement will continue to be a presence in the debate on improving public education in the United States. Ideally, all youth, gay and straight, would be able to receive a first-rate education by attending a public school that is free of any type of violence and harassment. Nonetheless, it would be wrong to ask today's youth to bear the burden of creating the public schools of tomorrow by not acknowledging that some of today's public schools are substandard, unsafe, and educationally unsound. For LGBT youth experiencing harassment, progressive charter schools with explicit values of acceptance may provide a much-needed alternative to their public schools. The charter school option might also provide an opportunity to replicate successful LGBT-supportive schools like New York City's Harvey Milk High School. But the decentralized nature of charter school governance may leave charter schools susceptible to homophobic policies. Given the increasing popularity of the charter school movement, it is important to advocate for the inclusion of LGBT-friendly curricula and policies at all such schools.

Administrators of charter or private schools may simply be unwilling to implement LGBT-inclusive safe schools initiatives, creating hostile environments for LGBT youth and the children of LGBT families. Even in states with nondiscrimination laws protecting LGBT people, such legislation often exempts private or religious institutions.[21] Because of these serious limitations, the Gay, Lesbian, and Straight Education Network warns of the negative impact that school voucher programs and other privatization programs can have on LGBT youth.

> Public money should be spent on improving the nation's public schools rather than diverted to private institutions that may not be accountable to local educational policies and may not provide equal access or treatment for all students.[22]

Single-Sex Education

The NCLB Act allows federal education funds to be used for "programs to provide same-gender schools and classrooms" as long as they comply with applicable civil rights laws, including Title IX, which guarantees equal educational opportunities for all students regardless of sex.[23] That may be easier said than done. In 1996, the Supreme Court declared that single-sex programs must have "an exceedingly persuasive justification" in order to be constitutional under the Equal Protection Clause of the Fourteenth Amendment. Though it ruled out programs that "perpetuate the legal, social, and economic inferiority of women," the Court decided that single-sex education would be permissible if it were used to "compensate women for particular economic disabilities they have suffered, to promote equal employment opportunity, [and] to advance full development of the talent and capacities of our nation's people."[24] In 2002, the U.S. Department of Education issued a report supporting the amendment of Title IX "to provide more flexibility to educators to establish single-sex classes and schools at the elementary and secondary levels."[25] Given the research indicating that students who do not conform to gender-role stereotypes are more likely to be targeted in schools, it is important to explore the proposed benefits and costs of single-sex education, as well its potential impact on LGBT students.

Civil rights groups opposed to single-sex education cite *Brown v. Board of Education,* the historic 1954 U.S. Supreme Court ruling that declared a separate public education system for black children to be inherently unequal. "Separate but equal" single-sex education could potentially result not only in inequities but also in the reinforcement of harmful gender-role stereotypes.[26] Opponents of single-sex education argue that, at best, it is a cheap solution to educational problems in urban schools that would be better addressed by improving the quality of education for all students.

Proponents of single-sex education argue that it is merely a response to what they view as the failure of schools to increase academic achievement "even after allocating significant dollars," particularly for urban schools.[27] They also claim that there is no comparison between today's single-sex schools and the segregated schools of the past, because today's parents and children are actively choosing a separate education. According to the *Christian Science Monitor,*

> We have scores of books and articles on how disadvantaged boys just don't identify with academic achievement. They gain their self-esteem from sports. . . . even disadvantaged girls too often seek validation in early motherhood. . . . Equal doesn't necessarily mean the same kinds of services have to be provided. Sometimes to achieve equal educational opportunity, we have to provide different kinds of opportunity to students.[28]

Similar arguments, focusing on LGBT students' safety and well-being, have been made about the need for the Harvey Milk High School.

Organizations like the ACLU and the American Association of University Women (AAUW) strongly disagree and have even disputed the ability of single-sex schools to meet the needs of female students. According to Maggie Ford, president of the AAUW Educational Foundation, "[S]eparating by sex is not the solution to gender inequity in education. . . . When elements of good education are present, girls and boys succeed."[29] These elements include small classes, a rigorous curriculum, high standards, discipline, good teachers, and attention to eliminating gender bias. Strategies that help to achieve an equitable learning environment for all students regardless of gender include staff development for all teachers focusing on gender equity, the recruitment of female and minority administrators who can act as role models, the adoption and dissemination of school nondiscrimination policies, sexual harassment prevention programs, and equal opportunities for female students in athletic programs.[30]

Brown v. Board of Education overturned a government-enforced policy of racial segregation that sanctioned an inherently inferior education system for blacks that was indeed separate but unequal to the education offered to white students. Today's generation of single-sex schools, the Harvey Milk High School, and schools for students with disabilities were created, in part, to respond to the failure of mainstream public schools to serve certain populations of students, not out of a desire to exclude them. Dealing with the gender inequality that girls experience in coeducational institutions is obviously the best long-term goal. But while the necessity for such schools might not exist in a perfect world, it is hard to argue either with parents who want the best for their children today and cannot find it in the public school system as it exists or with youth who merely want to go to school without being harassed, threatened, and assaulted.

Do single-sex schools reinforce gender-role stereotypes or free their students from them? Proponents of single-sex education believe the latter and cite complex reasons rooted in both sociology and biology. According to the National Association for Single Sex Public Education, "At every age, girls in girls-only classroom[s] are more likely to explore 'non-traditional' subjects such as computer science, math, physics, woodworking, etc." But are single-sex institutions better? A comprehensive report by the AAUW that analyzed existing research on single-sex education found that girls in single-sex education programs did have higher indicators of self-esteem than those in coeducation institutions, a difference attributed to a learning environment in which girls were less critical of their own behavior. However, a ten-year study of student attitudes and achievements in one all-boys and one all-girls high school in Australia reported conflicting results. After each school made the transition from single-sex to coeducational, indicators of both girls' and boys' self-esteem dropped slightly. However, after five years, their self-esteem increased to a higher level than when students were in single-sex classrooms. Research on academic achievement differences is also contradictory, with no definitive answer to whether single-sex education is better than coeducation.[31]

Because many of the LGBT youth who are harassed are gender nonconforming, would single-sex school environments be better for them? Or would they fare better in coeducational environments, because they may be more likely to have friendship networks that include members of the opposite sex? No one knows for sure. Very little has been written about the impact of single-sex education programs on gender and sexuality development or on anti-LGBT harassment and violence. Despite the need for more research, there is preliminary evidence and a historical context that indicates single-sex schools could affect gender equality and the gender development of all students, particularly those that are gender nonconforming and transgender. According to one education expert, "The underlying message of these schools is that girls are less capable, and that the only way to control boys' behavior is to separate them from girls."[32] A 2001 report on California's pilot program for single-gender schooling expressed similar concerns.

> Our interviews and observations of the single-gender academies often revealed definitions of gender that were either limited, as was the case with masculinity, or unrealistic, as was heard in messages about femininity. Gender was constructed as a dichotomous entity within the single gender academies, promoting a paradigm of girls as good, boys as bad.[33]

Such environments raise other questions as well. Would a transgender student who was born male but identifies as female be welcome at an all-female school? Would gender-nonconforming boys be further stigmatized in a boys-only elementary school? Further research into the effect of single-sex education is needed to specifically assess how these schools would affect LGBT youth.

Standardized Testing and Multicultural Education

> [The] first principle is accountability. . . . in return for federal dollars, we are asking states to design accountability systems to show parents and teachers whether or not children can read and write and add and subtract in grades three through eight. . . . I understand taking tests aren't [*sic*] fun. Too bad.[34]
>
> —President George W. Bush

The NCLB Act requires school districts to administer annual exams in reading and math to students in the third through eighth grades. Data from those exams become part of annual report cards on school performance, which give parents information about the quality of their children's schools. Statewide reports also include performance data specific to the race and gender of students, "to demonstrate progress in closing the achievement gap between disadvantaged students and other groups of students" largely along economic, racial, and ethnic lines.[35] Some educators argue, however, that relying almost exclusively on standardized testing to measure school performance undermines efforts to close that gap.[36] Innovative studies in improving education policy and bridging the achievement gap have focused on multicultural education, which centers on curricula that validate and explore the diverse experiences of students, including LGBT students.

> Multicultural education is a philosophical concept built on the ideals of freedom, justice, equality, equity, and human dignity. . . . It recognizes the role schools can play in developing the attitudes and values necessary for a democratic society. It values cultural differences and affirms the pluralism that students, their communities, and teachers reflect. It challenges all forms of discrimination in schools and society . . . [and] helps students develop a positive self-concept by providing knowledge about the histories, cultures, and contributions of diverse groups.[37]

According to one researcher, textbooks designed to help students achieve high scores on standardized tests give students "predigested knowledge presented as indisputable fact . . . written to be as non-controversial as possible . . . and are still based largely around the worldview and sensibilities of the white male middle and professional class."[38] Thus the highly prescriptive curricula required to meet objectives determined solely by standardized testing may be incompatible with the goals of multicultural education, as well as the policy changes required to close the achievement gap. Another researcher adds,

> Texts still completely ignore the idea that social classes exist in this country. . . . Americans all appear to be happy, middle-class, well-treated members of society enjoying equal access to success. One wonders how those images fit with the experiences of many of the children who read those texts. . . . When someone with the authority of a teacher, say, describes the world and you are not in it, there is a moment of psychic disequilibrium, as if you looked into a mirror and saw nothing.[39]

This is particularly salient for LGBT students. The inclusion of test questions on LGBT literature, history, and the arts would be essential to ensuring that LGBT issues are covered in curricula. However, the school environment in many school districts is hostile to even the mention of homosexuality in the classroom, let alone the creation of LGBT-inclusive curricula and textbooks.

Standardized testing operates on the assumption that all students have an equal opportunity to learn. Given that much of the variation in student performance on these tests may be attributable to factors outside of the classroom—such as school funding levels, class size, and other socioeconomic issues—the playing field may be anything but level.[40] Standardized tests that are culturally biased can adversely affect students from many cultural groups and contribute to lower expectations of student performance, negative attitudes toward low-performing students, and decreased self-esteem.[41] This is especially likely for the proportion of LGBT students who miss school because of harassment and violence and score lower on other indicators of school performance, including grade point average.[42]

It is highly unlikely that standardized testing mandated by the NCLB Act will include LGBT history and issues. This more exclusive focus on measuring educational achievement marginalizes not only LGBT youth and the children of LGBT parents but also other groups largely ignored by school curricula and textbooks. Addressing the violence and harassment faced by LGBT students does not end with nondiscrimination policies and the creation of gay-straight alliances. A school curriculum that accurately portrays the contributions made by all people is more likely to address the root causes of racism, sexism, homophobia, and other forms of intolerance at the heart of social inequality. From the writings of Walt Whitman,[43] Gertrude Stein,[44] and Audre Lorde[45] to the activism of Emma Goldman,[46] Magnus Hirschfeld,[47] and Bayard Rustin,[48] there is a rich history of LGBT people who have made important contributions to American and world culture. The education and school experience of LGBT students could also improve if curricula and standardized testing included the contributions of LGBT people.

Internet Filtering

The NCLB Act allows school districts to apply for federal funds to purchase computers and other Internet-related technology. Schools receiving these funds must have a "policy of Internet safety for minors that includes the operation of a technology protection measure with respect to any of its computers with Internet access that protects against access . . . to visual depictions that are obscene; child pornography; or harmful to minors."[49] The technology protection measure most readily available to public schools is Internet filtering software. But the federal definitions of "obscene" and "harmful to minors" are unclear, and studies have shown that filtering software routinely prevents students from accessing information about sex education, sexually transmitted diseases, sexual orientation, and gender identity.[50] This is particularly problematic for LGBT students, who may feel uncomfortable accessing age-appropriate information from the Internet on these issues at home even if they are able to do so.

According to the American Civil Liberties Union, "There is no universal definition of obscenity that a blocking software company can employ."[51] In fact, creating a definition for "obscene" has plagued U.S. courts for more than fifty years. In 1964, Supreme Court justice Potter Stewart tried to explain his definition for obscene: "I shall not today attempt further to define the kinds of materials I understand to be embraced . . . [b]ut I know it when I see it." The spirit of Justice Stewart's definition is not too far from the standard still used by courts today, which was explained by Chief Justice Warren Burger in 1973:

(a) whether the 'average person applying contemporary community standards' would find that the work, taken as a whole, appeals to the prurient interest,
(b) whether the work depicts or describes, in a patently offensive way, sexual conduct specifically defined by the applicable state law, and
(c) whether the work, taken as a whole, lacks serious literary, artistic, political, or scientific value.[52]

According to these guidelines, the determination of obscenity is relative to individual community standards. One local school board might decide that information about a LGBT youth group or local LGBT community center is obscene, while another deems such material completely appropriate.

Because Internet filtering software is developed for a national audience, tailoring it to individual community standards is difficult, which, according to the ACLU, makes the software both ineffective and constitutionally suspect. The ACLU also argues that a community's definition of obscenity cannot be legally determined by government entities, such as school boards or public libraries. Only a judge or a jury can make that decision, requiring a lengthy and costly court hearing.[53] Similar problems arise when applying the "harmful to minors" standard established by the NCLB Act. Information that is inappropriate for a five-year-old may be lifesaving for a seventeen-year-old gay student facing harassment in school and rejection at home because of his sexual orientation.

The U.S. Supreme Court ruled in 1997 that a single "harmful to minors" standard is not applicable to the Internet, as it would limit some minors from accessing constitutionally protected speech.[54] The case arose out of challenges to the Communications Decency Act, signed by President Bill Clinton in 1996. It sought to protect minors from harmful material on the Internet by criminalizing the transmission of obscene or indecent messages to any recipient under eighteen.[55] The Supreme Court's seven-to-two ruling also declared that Internet content should enjoy the same First Amendment protections as print media. This decision was influenced by the wide range of socially valuable speech censored by the law, including speech about safe-sex practices and many other sexually related topics of importance to both youth and adults.[56] Supreme Court justice John Paul Stevens summarized the majority opinion as follows:

> As a matter of constitutional tradition, in the absence of evidence to the contrary, we presume that governmental regulation of the content of speech is more likely to interfere with the free exchange of ideas than to encourage it. The interest in encouraging freedom of expression in a democratic society outweighs any theoretical but unproven benefit of censorship.[57]

One year after that ruling, in October 1998, Congress passed the Childhood Online Protection Act (COPA). Designed with the unconstitutionality of its predecessor in mind, COPA criminalized the communication for commercial purposes of any material deemed harmful to minors by community standards. Despite the change in language, the ACLU argued that COPA was still unconstitutional, because it "effectively suppresse[d] a large amount of speech on the World Wide Web that adults are entitled to communicate and receive," even if that speech was deemed harmful to minors by some communities' standards.[58] Examples of Web sites that would have been censored under COPA include Beacon Press, an independent publisher of a wide variety of books, including titles about gay, lesbian, and gender studies,[59] and the Sexual Health Network, which provides educational material to disabled persons about how they can express their sexuality despite their disability.[60]

COPA was ruled unconstitutional by multiple federal courts. According to the National Academy of Sciences, education is more likely than restrictive laws like COPA to protect youth from harmful content on the Internet. Still, Congress opted to introduce a new Internet censorship law, the Children's Internet Protection Act (CIPA), which was signed into law by President Clinton in 2000.[61] Like its forebears, CIPA restricts access to obscene or harmful material on the Internet among minors using computers and related equipment purchased with federal funds in public schools and libraries. However, it also includes a provision that allows any Internet filtering software or device to be turned off at the request of any student or library patron age seventeen or older.[62]

In 2002, the American Library Association challenged only the provision that restricted Internet access in libraries. But the Supreme Court ruled in 2003 that CIPA was constitutional, because library patrons can turn off the filters at any time without having to give a reason or revealing what information they are trying to access.[63] Consequently, both libraries and public schools must either have implemented Internet filtering software by July 1, 2004, or have chosen to forfeit federal funds.

How Internet Filtering Works

Despite the legislative focus on filtering as the solution for protecting youth from harmful Internet content, many experts, Internet monitoring organizations, and civil liberties groups warn that filtering software is not only ineffective but also allows software companies to censor Internet content based on their political beliefs and religious ideologies.[64] In testimony in a Senate committee hearing on the legislation, one expert summarized the flaws inherent to filtering the Internet as follows:

The word "filter" is much too kind to these programs. It conjures up inaccurate gee-whiz images of sophisticated, discerning choice. When these products are examined in detail, they usually turn out to be the crudest of blacklists, long tables of hapless material which has run afoul of a stupid computer program or person, perhaps offended by the word "breast" (as in possibly breast cancer).[65]

Keyword filtering is the least sophisticated method used by filtering software to block access to various Web sites. It compares the text of a Web page to a list of restricted words or phrases. The software then removes the words from the Web page, or blocks the site altogether. There are inherent flaws to this method. While blocking access to Web pages that include the text string *s-e-x* may prevent youth from accessing some, but not all, pornographic sites, it may also block sites with information about, for example, musical sextets; Essex, England; the poet Anne Sexton; and the Catholic Church's position on same-sex marriage.[66]

Address- or URL-based filters block access to specific Web sites. Companies that produce such software typically employ automated programs that search the Internet for content deemed objectionable. Reviewers then look at each site and rate it according to a corporate standard. Internet filtering software can also use systems that require Web site publishers to rate their own pages or that rely on third-party ratings of Internet sites. Given the number of new Web pages available on the Internet every year, this method is humanly impossible to maintain properly.[67]

Internet Filtering and LGBT Students

In 2001, as debate over the Childhood Internet Protection Act intensified, GLSEN tested the home version of Bess, filtering software whose manufacturer, N2H2, claimed it was installed on "over 40 percent of all schools in the U.S. that have chosen to filter Internet access" and was "trusted to protect over 16 million students."[68] (N2H2 was eventually acquired by McAfee in 2008.) GLSEN found that the software blocked approximately 20 percent of LGBT youth advocacy sites it attempted to access.[69] This finding was consistent with a study published the same year by *Consumer Reports*, which found that several Internet filtering programs blocked one in five sites that contained "serious content on controversial subjects."[70]

In 2003, the Frontier Foundation and the Online Policy Group conducted a study on Internet blocking in public schools, which tested Bess and SurfControl, another popular Internet filtering tool, by attempting to access almost one million Web pages. The goal of the study was "to measure the extent to which blocking software impedes the educational process by restricting access to Web pages relevant to the required curriculum."[71] The study found that "schools that implement Internet blocking software even with the least restrictive setting will block at a minimum tens of thousands of Web pages inappropriately."[72] In fact, when researchers elected to use all of the block codes suggested by the software manufacturers for compliance with CIPA guidelines, the software blocked and miscategorized up to 85 percent of the one million Web pages in the sample.

The same study also found that schools using Internet filtering software's most restrictive settings block 70 percent or more of the Web sites listed in search results based on state-mandated curriculum topics. The study concluded that Internet filtering software cannot help schools comply with CIPA: while failing to block many sites deemed obscene or harmful to minors by some community standards, they restrict access to many others protected by the First Amendment.[73] In 2005, *Consumer Reports* published a follow-up analysis of eleven popular Internet filtering programs and found that sites about health issues, sex education, civil rights, and politics were still blocked and that "[m]ost unwarranted blocking occurred with sites featuring sex education or gender-related issues."[74]

In *United States v. American Library Association,* the Supreme Court upheld CIPA, which the NCLB Act references directly in its provision requiring schools to protect students from material that is "obscene" or "offensive." Despite the inherent flaws of using Internet filtering software to protect minors from harmful content, schools must either develop ways of providing students access to Internet resources while employing such software or refuse federal funding for computers and related Internet technology.

Filtering software may significantly affect the educational experiences of both LGBT and straight youth, who are forced to view the Internet through a lens meant to keep out material that may be an important part of their education, health, and safety. Denying LGBT youth access to age-appropriate information on the Internet may reinforce their isolation and put them at greater risk. This makes their ability to access such materials from schools and libraries all the more vital. Toward that end, GLSEN has developed alternative recommendations for protecting minors from pornographic or other harmful content on the

Internet while still maintaining access to educational and sometimes lifesaving information:

- Develop an Acceptable-Use Policy for the Internet. School administrators should create policies on Internet usage, in partnership with students and teachers, allowing access to valuable educational information while restricting access to pornography and other inappropriate material.
- Conduct trainings on Internet usage. Schools should make instruction in this policy a prerequisite for Internet access, along with instruction on how to use the Internet as an educational resource. Students should be made aware of the privilege they exercise, and taught to respect its power and inherent dangers.
- Enforce policies. If students are informed of their responsibilities and the tentative nature of their connection to the Internet, they will use it more responsibly. If Internet access is used inappropriately, the student should be held responsible, in accordance with the school's acceptable-use policy.
- Increase teacher presence. A $40 software program will never replace an experienced teacher. The supervision of trained teachers is much likelier to protect children from accessing inappropriate Internet sites than any filtering program. But the debate over Internet filtering software has largely ignored the shortage of teachers and resultant large class size at many American schools.[75]

Violence Prevention and Unsafe Schools

The NCLB Act reauthorizes the Safe and Drug-Free Schools and Communities Act of 1986, which grants federal funds for the creation of programs that "prevent and reduce violence in and around schools . . . and foster a safe and drug-free learning environment that supports academic achievement."[76] The NCLB Act specifically defines "violence prevention" as

the promotion of school safety, such that students and school personnel are free from violent and disruptive acts, including sexual harassment and abuse, and victimization associated with prejudice and intolerance, on school premises, going to and from school, and at school-sponsored activities, through the creation and maintenance of a school environment that . . . fosters individual responsibility and respect for the rights of others.[77]

This provision of the NCLB Act could be interpreted to address the need for programs that both protect LGBT students and educate teachers and students about tolerance and violence prevention. For example, the provision not only calls for programs to "assist localities most directly affected by hate crimes" in developing educational and training programs to prevent them; it also uses the definition of "hate crime" from the Hate Crimes Statistics Act of 1990: "[a] crime against a person or property motivated by bias toward race, religion, ethnicity/national origin, disability, or sexual orientation."[78]

This provision could also be interpreted to address bias-motivated harassment and violence against LGBT youth, as such harassment and violence is motivated by "prejudice and intolerance." However, it does not specifically mention such characteristics as race, ethnicity, religion, sexual orientation, or gender identity, which are often the basis of bias-motivated harassment or violence. Because sexual orientation and gender identity are not specifically enumerated categories, some school administrators and teachers may claim that the law does not specifically require them to protect LGBT youth. This concern is supported by the Supreme Court's decision in *Romer v. Evans,* in which Justice Anthony Kennedy wrote, "Enumeration [i.e., specifically including the phrase *sexual orientation* in nondiscrimination laws] is the essential device used to make the duty not to discriminate concrete and to provide guidance for those who must comply."[79] Specific inclusion of sexual orientation and gender identity (as well as race, religion, and ethnicity) in this provision of the NCLB Act would have provided clearer direction about its scope and impact and given teachers and school administrators the backing they need to feel confident in their response to harassment and violence against LGBT students.[80]

Despite this shortcoming, the law does provide opportunities for an LGBT student in an unsafe school to go to a different, hopefully safer school. Under the Unsafe School Choice Option of the NCLB Act, every state that receives federal funds under the act must establish and implement a statewide policy that allows a student who is attending a persistently dangerous public school or is a victim of a violent criminal offense while on school grounds to attend a different, safer school, including a public charter school.[81] While this school choice option establishes the right of LGBT youth to attend school in a safe environment, there are few school districts that have alternative public or charter schools that are any safer. It also places the burden of going to a safe school on students and parents, who must arrange, on their own, to travel to a different school.

Parental Rights Provisions

The NCLB Act kept a provision from its predecessor, the Elementary and Secondary Education Act of 1965, which gives parents the right to inspect "any instructional material used as part of the educational curriculum for the student," as well as student surveys that ask questions about political affiliations, mental illness, sexual behavior, illegal or antisocial behavior, family members, religious beliefs, or family income. This provision only applies to surveys that students are "required, as part of an applicable program, to submit to."[82] An additional provision requires school districts to develop written policies and procedures, in consultation with parents, regarding any student survey. At a minimum, these policies must specify how parents will be notified about surveys and how they will be given the opportunity to excuse their children from participating. School districts are required to notify parents of these rights annually.[83]

As written, this provision does not dramatically inhibit researchers' ability to collect information. Many schools regularly choose to notify parents about surveys administered to students, allowing them to request that their child not participate. In practice, however, few parents exercise their opt-out option, and it has had no substantial impact on survey results. But any policy requiring that parents actively opt in by sending prior written consent for their child's participation makes collecting reliable data extremely difficult. The danger inherent in the parental rights provision of the NCLB Act is that conservative activists may attempt to modify it in the future or may use it to pressure their state legislatures or local school boards to adopt active permission or opt-in requirements for surveys. Once in place, such active parental consent regulations would make it virtually impossible to collect data on large representative samples of students, including information about their sexual orientation or gender identity. This has already occurred in three states—Alaska, New Jersey, and Utah—which require the prior written informed consent of a parent before any survey, even one that is voluntary, can be administered to a student.[84] Alaska's opt-in law actually prevented the state from obtaining a high enough response rate for it to participate in the national 2001 Youth Risk Behavior Survey.[85]

Additionally, if a school uses federal Safe and Drug-Free Schools money to fund education programs to prevent illegal drug use, sexual harassment, and "victimization associated with prejudice and intolerance," as well as programs that foster "respect for the rights of others," the school must make "reasonable efforts" to inform parents about such programs. If parents disagree with the content in these programs, they can excuse their child from participating.[86] Fortunately, very few programs designed to prevent such victimization are actually funded through the Safe and Drug-Free Schools program, but school districts should be aware of the potential repercussions of paying for them with that program's money.

Preventing the Promotion of "Sexual Activity, Whether Homosexual or Heterosexual"

According to the NCLB Act, federal education funds cannot be used "to develop or distribute materials, or operate programs or courses of instruction directed at youth, which are designed to promote or encourage sexual activity, whether homosexual or heterosexual."[87] This is significantly different from and, in fact, somewhat preferable to some existing state laws that only prohibit positive discussion of homosexuality (see chapter 3).

The NCLB Act provision prevents schools from directly promoting sexual activity of any kind—gay or straight—with federal education money. But schools can still develop and implement curricula or programs designed to provide age-appropriate and comprehensive sex education, because such curricula and programs focus on enhancing the physical and emotional health of all students and are not designed to encourage or promote sexual activity of any kind. They must treat homosexuality no differently than heterosexuality and "include the health benefits of abstinence."[88] The NCLB Act also explicitly states that the federal government has no right "to mandate, direct, review, or control a State, local educational agency, or school's instructional content, curriculum, and related activities," nor does it have a right to "require the distribution of scientifically or medically false or inaccurate materials."[89]

None of the provisions in the NCLB Act restricts the ability of schools to implement programs designed to prevent anti-LGBT harassment or discrimination. Indeed, school districts have both a legal responsibility and an ethical obligation to ensure that LGBT students, like any other students, can receive the benefits of education without being subjected to harassment or discrimination.

The Boy Scout Equal Access Act and the Vitter Amendment

Included in the family protections section of the NCLB Act are the Boy Scouts of America Equal Access Act (Boy Scouts Act) and the Vitter Amendment. These provisions threaten public schools with the loss of federal funding if they prevent the Boy Scouts or the U.S. military from using public school facilities for meetings or recruitment. Both additions to the NCLB Act were crafted in response to the increasing number of school districts that limited the Boy Scouts' access to school grounds, in response to a U.S. Supreme Court ruling affirming the Boy Scouts' right to discriminate against gay scouts and scoutmasters.[90] To legally prevent the Boy Scouts from using school facilities, school districts would have had to prohibit *all* outside organizations from using them, and the few that only limited the Boy Scouts' access eventually garnered the attention of Congress.

Specifically, the Boy Scouts Act states,

> [N]o public elementary school, public secondary school, local educational agency, or State educational agency that has a designated open forum or a limited public forum and that receives funds made available through the Department [of Education] shall deny equal access or a fair opportunity to meet to, or discriminate against, any group officially affiliated with the Boy Scouts of America, or any other youth group listed in Title 36 of the United States Code (as a patriotic society), that wishes to conduct a meeting within that designated open forum or limited public forum, including denying such access or opportunity or discriminating for reasons based on the membership or leadership criteria or oath of allegiance to God and country of the Boy Scouts of America or of the youth group listed in Title 36 of the United States Code.[91]

The seventy-four organizations listed as patriotic societies in the U.S. Code include a number of national organizations that regularly provide services to youth, like Big Brothers Big Sisters of America, Boys and Girls

Clubs of America, the Girl Scouts, and Little League Baseball.[92] The Boy Scouts Act redundantly affirms the legal right for any and all of the seventy-four private organizations to access the resources of public schools whose policies prohibit anti-LGBT discrimination while openly discriminating against LGBT youth and adults. (Except for the Boy Scouts, none of the seventy-four currently does so.) The act does not require schools to officially sponsor any of the organizations.

In *Boy Scouts of America v. Dale,* the U.S. Supreme Court upheld the Scouts' right to prohibit openly gay scoutmasters from participating in scouting. Under the First Amendment, Boy Scouts have the right to both exclude gays and still have access to public school facilities regardless of state and local nondiscrimination laws.

House sponsor Van Hilleary (R-TN) and Senate sponsor Jesse Helms (R-NC) introduced the Boy Scouts Act because "the Boy Scouts are under attack and being thrown out of public facilities that are open to other similarly situated groups . . . as retribution for the Supreme Courts' ruling. . . . This amendment is designed to stop this wasteful cycle in litigation and harassment."[93] Those in favor of the amendment argued that protecting the Boy Scouts from unequal treatment was necessary to ensure that America's children could continue to embrace the "timeless values" of the Boy Scouts as "a model of integrity, strong ethics, devotion to God and the public good."[94]

Those opposed to the Boy Scouts Act, however, rejected the notion that it was the Boy Scouts of America that was being treated inequitably. According to Representative Bill Delahunt (D-MA),

> The reality is that this amendment is not about the Boy Scouts. It is about a conservative social agenda that holds passionate views about sexual orientation. The Boy Scouts' policy on sexual orientation is well known. That is fine. [Representative Hilleary] is entitled to his views, and the Boy Scouts are entitled to their views. But they ought not to be entitled to use the Congress of the United States to make a political statement that promotes intolerance and discrimination.[95]

Holding a letter of support signed by twenty-two organizations, including the National Parent Teacher Association, the National School Boards Association, and the National Association of Secondary School Principals, Representative Lynn Woolsey (D-CA) summarized her arguments against the Boy Scouts Act as follows: "[W]e should vote against this because it is not necessary in the first place. . . . [A] vote against this amendment would be a vote telling our children that all children are important, not just some children."[96]

In a May 2001 letter to the Senate, the ACLU argued that the amendment represented an unconstitutional endorsement of a specific point of view: "By punishing schools for excluding the Boy Scouts and other youth groups for their discriminatory membership criteria, the [Boy Scouts Act] would provide protection for the Boy Scouts' discriminatory viewpoint that no other viewpoint receives. Such unequal treatment of different viewpoints is unconstitutional."[97] Its opponents did not prevail, and the Boy Scouts Act passed by a voice vote.

The U.S. Department of Education office responsible for enforcing the Boy Scouts Act is the Office for Civil Rights. On March 25, 2002, that office sent a letter to every school district in the United States, explaining the Boy Scouts Act and warning, "If a public school or agency does not comply with the requirement of the Boy Scout Act, it would be subject to enforcement action by the Department [of Education]." The letter also encouraged school districts to file complaints against other districts that were not in compliance with the policy. Signed by the assistant secretary for civil rights, the letter ends, "I look forward to working with you to insure equal access to education and to promote educational excellence throughout the nation."[98]

The Vitter Amendment forces public schools to allow the military to actively recruit on their campuses, regardless of school nondiscrimination policies, by threatening to cut off federal funds if they refuse. In support of the amendment, Congress members claimed that the victim of discrimination was the military, not the 13,500 gay men, lesbians, and bisexuals who have been investigated and discharged as of fiscal year 2009 because of its "Don't Ask, Don't Tell" policy.[99] According to the amendment's lead sponsor, Representative David Vitter (R-LA), "This amendment will prevent discrimination against armed services recruiters and will simply offer them fair access to secondary schools that accept Federal funding."[100] In 2002, the U.S. Defense Department reported that two thousand of more than twenty-one thousand high schools did not allow the military to actively recruit on campus.[101] Representative Vitter claimed this was "because of school administrators' own personal antimilitary bias. . . . [W]hat is clearly going on is pure, old-fashioned bad political correctness and antimilitary ideology being shoved down the throats of our young people."[102] There was no significant opposition to the Vitter Amendment in Congress, and it passed by a voice vote.

6 | Sex Education, Abstinence-Only Programs, and HIV Prevention

Closely linked to political struggles over how to treat lesbian, gay, bisexual, and transgender youth in schools are controversies related to sex education and HIV prevention. From the early 1980s until 2009, the federal government funded abstinence-only programs, many of which taught that only abstinence could protect young people against unwanted pregnancy, HIV, and other sexually transmitted infections (STIs). Advocates for sex education, women's health, and LGBT youth oppose abstinence-only programs, not only because most studies found them ineffective, but also because many abstinence-only curricula exhibit a pervasive antigay bias, regressive gender roles, and widespread misinformation about contraception and prevention of STIs. Congress and President Obama finally ended federal funding for abstinence-only sex education in December 2009 by signing the Consolidated Appropriations Act of 2010. In so doing, Obama fulfilled a campaign promise and ended federal funding for a program that has received nearly $1.5 billion over three decades.[1]

Background

LGBT youth advocates and others oppose abstinence-only-until-marriage (AOUM) programs as counterproductive and harmful to America's youth. They do not include accurate and scientifically sound evidence about contraception and instead promote an ideological agenda. These programs have been found ineffective in preventing youth from becoming sexually active. In fact, many youth who have experienced AOUM education are less likely to use protection when they start having sex, and they are less likely to get tested for STIs.[2]

There are three main streams of funding for AOUM programs: the Adolescent Family Life Act (AFLA), the Title V abstinence-only program, and Community-Based Abstinence Education (CBAE). In addition to providing support for pregnant and parenting teens, AFLA was established to promote "chastity" and "self-discipline." Since 1981, $125 million of AOUM funding has been funneled through AFLA.[3]

Title V of the 1996 Temporary Assistance for Needy Families Act allocated fifty million dollars from the U.S. Department of Health and Human Services to various states throughout the country for AOUM funding.[4] Title V AOUM was originally authorized for five years. This program was started in 1996 and was reauthorized in July 2008, receiving fifty million dollars in federal funds in fiscal year 2009. The current authorization expired at the end of June 2009. However, Title V abstinence-only funding was reauthorized by the Patient Protection and Affordable Care Act in March 2010 at $50 million per year over five years.[5]

The other funding stream, known originally as Special Projects of Regional and National Significance and now as Community-Based Abstinence Education, allows the federal government to award grants directly to organizations across the country. This funding has given the government more authority over which organizations receive funding and how much each organization receives from CBAE. Funding for CBAE, which was created in 2001 by the Bush-Cheney administration, began in fiscal year 2001 at $20 million dollars. By fiscal year 2006, CBAE funding increased over 450 percent, to $113 million.[6] On March 10, 2009, Congress passed the 2009 Omnibus Appropriations Act, which cut funding for CBAE by $14.2 million for the current fiscal year. Total funding for the program dropped to $99 million from $113 million in fiscal year 2008.[7] The budget for fiscal year 2010 completely eliminated funding for this program.

The Sexuality Information and Education Council of the United States reports the following statistics for fiscal year 2008:

- Texas received the highest amount of federal funding: $14,289,087
- The majority of AOUM funding continued to be concentrated in southern states, with more than half of all federal funding ($82,267,900) directed into 16 southern states
- Crisis pregnancy centers in 20 states received federal AOUM funding in the amount of at least $19,102,209. Illinois distributes the most funds ($1,944,620) to crisis pregnancy centers.
- Forty-nine hospitals and local health departments continue to participate in federally-funded AOUM programs, despite years of evidence showing that these programs have no value in promoting positive public health outcomes.[8]

What Is Wrong with Abstinence-Only Funding?

Research shows that AOUM programs are ineffective.[9] A study commissioned by the U.S. Department of Health and Human Services in April 2007 found that these programs were not effective in increasing teen abstinence rates. This study found that half of the youth became sexually active before marriage whether or not they had taken a "virginity pledge,"[10] and the National Campaign to Prevent Teen and Unplanned Pregnancy found the same results.[11] Additionally, youth who receive AOUM "education" show no significant differences in terms of pregnancy rates or STIs.[12] A medical journal review of the most recently available data found that AOUM programs do not lower HIV infection rates.[13] Youth in communities where high numbers of students have taken "virginity pledges" are one-third less likely than students in other communities to use contraception. These students have similar rates of STIs yet are less likely to seek medical attention about suspected sexually transmitted infections.[14] These programs damage public health and demonstrate a misuse of resources; a wiser investment should include a more comprehensive sex education curriculum—one that teaches abstinence *and* the necessary practices to prevent STIs and unwanted pregnancies, given that, according to the 2009 National Youth Risk Behavior Survey, nearly half of youth in high school (46 percent) choose to engage in sexual intercourse.[15]

Abstinence-only programs promote regressive, sexist gender stereotypes; spread dangerous misinformation about the efficacy of contraception and how to prevent HIV infection; and demonstrate pervasive antigay bias and ignorance about people living with AIDS. As such, they are not only ineffective and a waste of public dollars; they are also harmful to young people.

Regressive, Sexist Gender Stereotypes

In many texts used in abstinence-only programs, boys are presented as sex-crazed, girls as less interested in sex than in finding love. Girls are given the primary responsibility of managing the sexual predations of boys. Consider the following examples involving regressive, sexist gender stereotypes:[16]

> Watch what you wear. If you don't aim to please, don't aim to tease. (*Sex Respect*)

Woman gauge their happiness and judge their success by their relationships. Men's happiness and success hinge on their accomplishments. (*Why kNOw*, 122)

Guys are able to focus better on one activity at a time and may not connect feelings with actions. Girls access both sides of the brain at once, so they often experience feelings and emotions as part of every situation. (*Choosing the Best Life, Leader Guide*, 7)

[T]he bride price is actually an honor to the bride. It says she is valuable to the groom and he is willing to give something valuable for her. (*Why kNOw*, 59)

The father gives the bride to the groom because he is the one man who has had the responsibility of protecting her throughout her life. He is now giving his daughter to the only other man who will take over this protective role. (*Why kNOw*, 61)

Men sexually are like microwaves and women sexually are like crockpots . . . a woman is stimulated more by touch and romantic words. She is far more attracted by a man's personality while a man is stimulated by sight. (*WAIT Training*, Workshop Manual, 37)

Lesbian Youth Killed in Newark

A Profile of Sakia Gunn

Fifteen-year-old African American lesbian Sakia Gunn was stabbed to death while waiting at a bus stop in Newark, New Jersey, during the early morning hours of Sunday, May 11, 2003. A sophomore at West Side High School in Newark, Sakia had just spent Saturday night with her friends in Manhattan's Greenwich Village. The Christopher Street Pier is a popular area for LGBT youth of color to hang out, and Sakia and her friends had spent the evening there and on the promenade along West Street. "The pier is somewhere we go to feel open about ourselves and have fun," explains Victoria Dingle, a sixteen-year-old lesbian friend and fellow West Side student who was with Sakia on the night of her murder. "Me and Sakia and some friends were just chilling and having fun and feeling good about being together."[17] They all returned to Newark via the PATH train. Victoria took a cab home from there, while Sakia waited at a bus stop with four other friends.

While awaiting the bus, a car with two men in it pulled up to the curb. Valencia Bailey, a friend of Sakia, recalls what happened next. "Yo, shorty, come here," one of them said. We told them, "No, we're OK. We're not like that. We're gay."[18] After refusing the men's sexual advances, Sakia's killer, later identified as twenty-nine-year-old Richard McCullough, got out of the car, and a fight ensued. During the fight, McCullough grabbed Sakia by the throat and thrust a knife into her chest. Rushed to the hospital by a Good Samaritan, Sakia died in the emergency room in the arms of her friend Valencia.

Sakia had always been candid about her sexual orientation. She spoke openly about it, publicly showed affection for her girlfriend, and wore boyish clothing that marked her within the black community as "AG" (aggressive lesbian).[19] Her murder deeply affected the LGBT youth of Newark, who turned out en masse for Sakia's funeral on May 16, 2003. The turnout was extraordinary, predominately black high school students and mostly lesbians.[20] Local lesbian youth also played a prominent role in planning and participating in the vigils and marches immediately following Sakia's death, as well as initiating memorials and shrines at both the site of the murder and West Side High School. Citing a lack of school-sponsored support, Sakia's friends Valencia Bailey and Jamon Marsh founded the Sakia Gunn Aggressive and Fem Organization as a support group for young lesbians.[21]

School officials were not as supportive. After the murder, West Side High School principal Fernand Williams instructed his receptionist to inform the media that all inquires were to go through the school district's spokesperson, Michelle Baldwin. Five days later, Baldwin still had not responded to at least one journalist's calls.[22] Meanwhile, Baldwin claimed that she had referred requests for interviews to Williams and other school officials, none of whom responded.[23] Principal Williams further angered students and journalists when he refused a request by students for a moment of silence to honor Sakia's life. Williams also reportedly refused requests for a memorial and threatened students with suspension if they wore rainbow colors to school.[24] However, his most horrifying response came in the form of a remark he allegedly made to students, reported in a local gay newspaper: "If someone chooses to live a certain lifestyle, they must pay a certain price."[25]

It is hard to accept Williams's response in the wake of Sakia's death, yet homophobia often knows no bounds. Fortunately, neither does love. As activist Keith Boykin stated, "The only antidote to fear is love. No matter how much some people choose to hate, we can still live our lives with dignity and create a world where love is rewarded over fear. That won't bring Sakia Gunn back to life, but it will ensure that her death was not in vain."[26] In the wake of this homophobic murder, it is the love expressed by Sakia's friends and thousands of LGBT youth, as well as their sorrow and anger, that must always be remembered.

Dangerous Lies about HIV/AIDS and Contraception

Abstinence-only curricula teach inaccurate information about how HIV is transmitted, promote stigma against people living with HIV, and misrepresent safer sex techniques (such as condom use) as ineffective in preventing sexually transmitted diseases and pregnancy.

At the least, the chances of getting pregnant with a condom are 1 out of 6. (*Me, My World, My Future*) [In fact, when used correctly, condoms are 98 percent effective in contraception.]

Condoms provide no proven reduction in protection against Chlamydia, the most common bacterial STD. (*Choosing the Best PATH, Leader Guide*)

In heterosexual sex, condoms fail to prevent HIV approximately 31 percent of the time. (*Why kNOw*) [In fact, when used consistently and correctly, condoms reduce the risk of STIs, including chlamydia.]

Touching another person's genitals "can result in pregnancy" (*Sexual Health Today*).

"[T]ears" and "sweat" are included in a column titled "at risk" for HIV transmission (*WAIT Training*). [In fact, the CDC states, "contact with saliva, tears, or sweat has never been shown to result in transmission of HIV."][27]

Antigay Bigotry

While many abstinence-only curricula ignore homosexuality, some abstinence-only curricula confirm antigay stereotypes.

> Many homosexual activists are frustrated and desperate over their own situation and those of loved ones. Many are dying, in part, due to ignorance. Educators who struggle to overcome ignorance and instill self mastery in their students will inevitably lead them to recognize that some people with AIDS are now suffering because of the choices they made. (*Facing Reality*, Parent/Teacher Guide)

> Among Kinsey's most outrageous and damaging claims are the beliefs that pedophilia, homosexuality, incest, and adult-child sex are normal. [In fact, research has shown that there is no connection between pedophilia and homosexuality. See "Social Science Research Finds No Link between Sexual Orientation and Child Sexual Abuse" in chapter 3.][28]

Discrimination

In addition to being ineffective and counterproductive, AOUM programs are discriminatory. Section 510(b) of Title V of the Social Security Act, which defines "abstinence education," includes many clauses that continuously refer to sex within heterosexual marriage only—a right that gay citizens have yet to federally secure. In addition, beginning in 2006, CBAE-funded programs are informed that "throughout the entire curriculum, the term 'marriage' must be defined 'only as a legal union between one man and one woman as a husband or a wife.'" This language comes directly from the Defense of Marriage Act.[29]

The Demise of Abstinence-Only Programs under the 111th Congress and President Obama

In recent years, significant political will built up against continuing wasteful spending on ineffective and harmful abstinence-only programs. As of March 2009, twenty-two states and the District of Columbia had rejected federal funding for AOUM programs.[30] Although these states are not receiving Title V funds, each may receive funding for AOUM programs through another avenue, such as CBAE.

Several attempts were made in Congress to extend the Title V AOUM program, but this program expired June 30, 2009. Despite the program's termination, organizations that previously received Title V funding for AOUM programming have two years from the date in which the funding was received to spend the money. This means that some organizations may be using Title V money well into 2011.

President Obama's budget for fiscal year 2010 included the following changes:

- ending funding for CBAE and Title V programs;
- providing $178 million for evidence-based comprehensive sex education programs;
- providing an increase of $10 million in the Title X family planning program, to a total of $317 million; and
- extending access to basic health care through the Medicaid State Option Family Planning Waiver.[31]

Despite attempts by some conservatives to restore abstinence-only funding in the Senate, the final 2010 spending bill put on President Obama's desk eliminated all abstinence-only funding, and it was signed into law in December 2009.

Young Gay and Bisexual Men and HIV

Sex education is very important to LGBT youth. Fifty-seven percent of new HIV diagnoses in the United States in 2006 occurred among men who have sex with men (MSM).[32] About half of these MSM are black or Latino. The bulk of new infections among black and Latino MSM occur among teens and young men in their twenties. Among white MSM, most new infections occur among men in their thirties and forties. In New York City, young black and Latino gay and bisexual men are disproportionately affected. There, new infections among gay and bisexual men ages thirteen to twenty-nine are up 33 percent since 2001.[33]

A lack of science-based prevention and comprehensive sex education puts youth in danger. According to the National Youth Risk Behavior Survey, almost half (46 percent) of high school students in the United States report that they have had sexual intercourse.[34] That youth are not receiving adequate information about protecting themselves when they choose to engage in sexual activity significantly contributes to the fact that approximately nine million young people (15–24) in the United States contract sexually transmitted diseases each year.[35] The New York Department of Education does not mandate sex education in public schools, meaning that school principals decide whether or not to include sex education in their school's curriculum, and the information shared within each school can vary by school and class.[36]

There is also a need for LGBT-affirmative interventions in schools. In the 2007 National School Climate Survey conducted by the Gay, Lesbian, and Straight Education Network, 64 percent of LGBT high school students reported that they had been verbally harassed in the past year because of their sexual orientation, and 46 percent reported harassment because of their gender expression.[37] Studies show that an unsafe educational atmosphere can push students out of school and into high-risk behavior. A study by the Massachusetts Department of Education found that young gay and bisexual men in schools with gay-straight alliances and other gay-affirming interventions were less likely to engage in HIV-related risk behavior than their counterparts in schools without these interventions.[38] The New York City Department of Education has put together a curriculum called Respect for All that addresses issues of bias in school, but only one in seven New York City high schools has a gay-straight alliance.

While education and programs geared toward LGBT populations are important in promoting healthy choice and overall well-being, factors like family acceptance also play a critical role. A study published in *Pediatrics* in 2009 found that family rejection of lesbian, gay, and bisexual youth correlates with poor health outcomes.[39] LGB youth who are rejected by their families are 3.4 times more likely to report having engaged in unprotected sexual intercourse compared with peers from families who accept them as gay children.[40]

Sex education, LGBT-affirming programs, and family acceptance all correlate with lower rates of HIV-related risk behavior among young gay and bisexual men. Schools and other institutions serving youth should train staff and promote acceptance of LGBT youth among mostly heterosexual student bodies. Public health departments should develop and fund campaigns to promote family acceptance of LGBT youth as a public health strategy.

SECTION 3 | A Research Agenda to Guide and Inform Future Policy

7 | Political and Methodological Issues Affecting Research on LGBT Youth

The collection and analysis of data on the lives and experiences of lesbian, gay, bisexual, and transgender youth have enabled researchers and policymakers to begin addressing the needs of this diverse population. Questions about sexual identity, behavior, and attraction have been added to population-based surveys like the Youth Risk Behavior Survey and the National Longitudinal Study of Adolescent Health. This has enabled researchers to collect information from large samples of lesbian, gay, and bisexual youth and to analyze the correlations between sexual orientation, sexual identity, and the health and educational experiences of these youth.[1]

As a result, we know that LGB youth not only have an increased risk for suicide and substance abuse but also exhibit remarkable strength and resiliency despite facing prolonged periods of adversity at school and at home. This information has provided the foundation for advocates and policymakers to develop interventions like gay-straight alliances and antiharassment policies at the local and state levels, which support LGBT youth and the children of LGBT parents. These studies and the new public policies they support further the cause of equal protection for LGBT youth; the demographic information they provide is one of their most important contributions.

This book provides a comprehensive summary of the research and literature available on LGBT youth, their experiences in public schools, and the public policies that have been developed and implemented to intervene on their behalf. This chapter more clearly identifies gaps in research and knowledge about this population. For example, the overwhelming majority of academic social science research cited in this book does not specifically include or identify transgender youth as a cohort within the population from which data were collected (see chapter 1 for a brief summary of methodological barriers to research on LGBT youth). This chapter is a more pointed narrative designed to inspire graduate students, professors, government-based researchers, and community activists to overcome those obstacles and help fill the research gaps these obstacles create.

The majority of the subheadings in this chapter were inspired by research questions developed during a meeting held in Minneapolis in October 2002, sponsored by the Kevin J. Mossier Foundation and attended by more than a dozen researchers and policymakers with expertise on LGBT issues in primary and secondary education.[2] Also participating were four LGBT youth advocacy groups, the National School Boards Association, the American Federation of Teachers, and the American Psychological Association. Where possible, these questions are wreathed in additional information and citations that may aid in the development of future research. Some questions, however, stand on their own, highlighting the areas of greatest need within the growing body of research and knowledge about the educational experiences of LGBT youth.

Politics and Research on LGBT Youth

The intersection of politics and social science forces researchers to break through multiple barriers that threaten the quality and scientific integrity of their work. That much of this research is supported by federal funding through agencies like the National Institutes of Health (NIH) requires researchers to be accountable to elected officials and bureaucrats often biased by their political or religious ideologies. This became readily apparent in the spring of 2003, when the journal *Science* reported that program staff at the NIH had warned researchers not to include terms such as "condom effectiveness," "transgender," and "men who have sex with men" in federal grant proposals if they wished to avoid extra scrutiny.[3] This was followed by a close vote in the U.S. House of Representatives narrowly defeating an amendment to a bill funding NIH research grants in the 2004 fiscal year. The amendment would have forbidden the NIH from funding four proposals that focused on sexuality and the prevention of sexually transmitted diseases, including

- $237,000 for a study on mood arousal and sexual risk-taking by the Kinsey Institute;
- $500,000 for a study of LGBT and two-spirit Native Americans and Alaskan Natives by researchers at the University of Washington in Seattle;
- $69,000 for a study on the sexual habits of older men who have sex

with men, conducted by the New England Research Institutes, Inc.;
- $641,000 for a study conducted by the University of California-San Francisco's Department of Medicine on drug use and HIV-related behaviors in Asian prostitutes in San Francisco.[4]

Representative Pat Toomey (R-PA), the congressman who sponsored the amendment, questioned the scientific value of this research: "I ask my colleagues, who thinks this stuff up[?] . . . These are not worthy of tax-payer funds."[5] According to Representative Toomey, "There are far more important, very real diseases that are affecting real people" that NIH funding should be used for.[6]

Murdered in the Classroom

A Profile of Lawrence King

In February 2008, after publicly announcing that he was gay, fifteen-year-old Lawrence King faced harassment from a group of schoolmates that led to his untimely death. As an eighth grader at E. O. Green Junior High School in Oxnard, California, Lawrence "Larry" King wore his favorite high-heeled boots most days, riding the bus to school from Casa Pacifica, a center for abused and neglected children in the foster care system, where he had been living since the previous fall. On some days, he would slick up his curly hair in a bouffant, imitating the music artist Prince. Sometimes he would paint his fingernails hot pink and dab glitter or white foundation on his cheeks. "He wore makeup better than I did," said thirteen-year-old Marissa Moreno, one of his classmates. He had bought a pair of stilettos at Target and was more proud to wear them than a varsity football jersey. He thought nothing of chasing the boys around the school in them, teetering as he ran. These expressions and actions prompted a group of male students to bully him.

On the morning of February 12, 2008, King came to school dressed as any other boy. He seemed upset and told one school employee that he did not sleep the night before and had thrown up his breakfast. One student noticed that as Larry walked across the quad, he kept looking back nervously over his shoulder before he slipped into his first-period English class. There, the teacher, Dawn Boldrin, had the students collect their belongings so they could go to the computer lab to work on their papers about World War II. Brandon McInerny, a fellow classmate of King's, who told the teacher he had finished his paper, pulled up a chair behind King and began to read from a history textbook. Other students saw McInerny frequently looking at King. Around 8:30 a.m., McInerny withdrew a .22 caliber pistol from his backpack and shot King in the head. Boldrin, who was helping another student with a paper, turned around and exclaimed, "Brandon, what the hell are you doing!" With no reply, McInerny fired the gun a second time at King's head. He then calmly put the gun down and left the school. King was rushed to the hospital, where he was declared brain dead. He was kept on life support for two days so that his organs could be donated.

McInerny, who was arrested blocks from the school minutes after the shooting, initially refused to speak to police about the killing. However, their investigation found that he had attempted to recruit other students to participate in the murder. When no one agreed, he decided to kill Larry himself. Just two days before the shooting, King had asked McInerny to be his Valentine. As a result McInerny was the subject of ridicule from some of his school friends. He told a classmate the day before the shooting to "say goodbye to your friend Larry because you're never going to see him again." The murder of Larry King sent shockwaves throughout the nation, with *Newsweek* calling it "the most prominent gay-bias crime since the 1998 murder of Matthew Shepard."[7]

While Representative Toomey may believe that LGBT Native Americans are not real people experiencing real health risks, research indicates that Native American LGBT youth are among the most understudied and underserved populations. Groundbreaking research by Dr. David Barney at the University of Oklahoma on health risk factors for gay American Indian and Alaskan Native adolescent males revealed that prior to his analysis of data from the Indian Adolescent Health Survey, only two studies had been published that provided any information about this population.[8] Dr. Barney's analysis found statistically significant differences between gay male Native American and Alaska Native adolescents and their heterosexual peers: they were nearly twice as likely to be physically abused and were almost six times as likely to be sexually abused by a family member. They were also twice as likely to have thought of or attempted suicide.[9] If Congressman Toomey had read

Dr. Barney's study, perhaps he would have realized that although LGBT Native American and Alaska Native youth are a small population often hidden from view on reservations or in urban indigenous communities, they are nonetheless real people in need of real programs and social service interventions to protect and support them.

Representative David Obey (D-WI) spoke out against Representative Toomey's amendment and the politicization of scientific, peer-reviewed research.

> [T]he day we politicize NIH research, the day we decide which grants are going to be approved on the basis of a ten-minute horseback debate in the House of Representatives with 434 of the 435 Members in this place who do not even know what the grant is, that is the day we will ruin science research in this country. . . . We have the NIH for a reason. . . . I would rather trust the judgment of ten doctors sitting around a table than I would ten politicians sitting around a table when we decide how to allocate taxpayer money for those grants.[10]

The politicalization of scientific research has a profound impact for one simple reason: without funding, there is no research. Studies based on the research questions that follow would help to provide critical data on the experiences of LGBT youth. But it is equally as important to lay a foundation for successful research in the future. Creating partnerships with political and bureaucratic allies who are capable of supporting the changes necessary for collecting population-based data is essential to identifying the most effective policy interventions. Collaboration between researchers and LGBT rights advocates may even succeed in convincing the Centers for Disease Control to include mandatory questions about sexual orientation and gender identity on the Youth Risk Behavior Survey and similar, national population-based studies where questions about sexual orientation and behavior are optional.

The Need for Standardized Definitions

There are many ways of asking about or conceptualizing sexuality. Researchers have variously measured sexual orientation or attraction, behavior, and self-identity. Among other factors, the political barriers to research on LGBT youth and the lack of coordination of federally funded research on LGBT people in general have prevented the creation of standardized definitions and measures of sexual orientation, such as those created for determining race and ethnicity for the 2000 U.S. Census.[11] Even less work has been done to develop a measure for gender identity or expression. This is particularly problematic for youth, as the formation of sexual orientation and gender identity is central to adolescence. Consequently, the need for the development, testing, and selection of standard definitions and measures of sexual orientation and gender identity based on sound methodological research is paramount.[12] Imprecision in the measurement of sexual orientation has resulted in inadequately specified population parameters and differing criteria for research and analysis. Survey instruments that use differing criteria for measuring sexual orientation prevent the comparison of data, because portions of population parameters may either overlap or be mutually exclusive.[13]

Studies that use measures of attraction as the basis for research do not measure the same thing as studies that ask about sexual behavior. For example, the National Longitudinal Study of Adolescent Health found that 6 percent of participants between the ages of thirteen and eighteen reported same-sex attraction, with 1 percent reporting that they were only attracted to members of their own sex and 5 percent reporting attraction to both sexes.[14] A 1999 report by the Safe Schools Coalition of Washington found that in eight population-based studies administered over ten years to 83,042 youth, 4 to 5 percent of teens in secondary schools either identified themselves as gay, lesbian, or bisexual; had engaged in same-sex sexual activity; or had experienced same-sex attractions.[15] Which percentage should be used to most accurately identify LGBT youth?

There is little consensus on how sexual orientation and gender identity should be measured in social science research. Sell and Becker recommend that the U.S. Department of Health and Human Services (HHS) take a leadership role in both the development of standardized measures of sexual orientation and the collection of these data, by

- creating working groups within the Data Council and National Committee on Vital Health Statistics to examine the collection of sexual orientation data and reporting;
- creating a set of guiding principles to govern the process of selecting standard definitions and measures of sexual orientations;
- recognizing that race, ethnicity, immigration status, age, and socioeconomic and geographic differences must be taken into ac-

count when selecting standard measures and assessing the validity and reliability of these measures;
- selecting a minimum set of standard sexual orientation measures for use in HHS databases and information systems;
- developing a long-range strategic plan for the collection of sexual orientation data.[16]

The development and use of standard measurements and definitions of sexual orientation and gender identity in government surveys, such as the Sell Assessment of Sexual Orientation[17] and the Friedman Measure of Adolescent Sexual Orientation,[18] is perhaps most hampered by the political context of publicly funded research. While many researchers may not include political lobbying in their curricula vitae, increased collaboration between academics and LGBT advocacy organizations may hasten the bureaucratic decisions necessary to meet this objective.

Specific Methodological Issues

The gaps in research on LGBT people widen to chasms for LGBT youth.[19] Many are due to the methodological difficulties associated with research on small, often hidden populations. Of course, methodological problems afflict and impede social science research regardless of the population being studied, but they do not negate the need for it. An awareness of the problems common in research on LGBT youth is a critical step toward the development of strategies to overcome these limitations.

Quantitative versus Qualitative Research Methodologies

Data on LGBT youth and their lives are often difficult to gather or simply not available.[20] The belief that research is worthwhile only when it involves the analysis of quantitative data is common among researchers, regardless of the population being studied. While there is an important role for empirical, quantitative research that permits the study of correlations or causal relationships, there is also an important role for data collection and analysis that employs qualitative methods.[21] These methods allow for an in-depth understanding of beliefs, behaviors, and experiences, particularly when studying LGBT youth. Qualitative methods can facilitate the collection of valuable information, especially on hard-to-reach segments of LGBT youth, such as youth of color. Qualitative approaches can be valuable for preliminary research about a specific population, which can be a guiding force in the development of future, more representative research projects. However, the value of qualitative research can also stand on its own. Qualitative techniques can provide contextual information that cannot be captured via statistical analysis. A number of studies on LGBT and questioning youth have employed interviews, ethnographies, surveys, and case studies.[22] However, few studies have employed mixed-method approaches, and none has employed participatory action research.

Participatory Action Research

An innovative approach to gathering information about LGBT youth is participatory action research, a method in which the people being studied are given control over the purpose and procedures of the research.[23] There are five major guidelines for conducting participatory action research:

1. The community's interests are identified and defined as a starting point.
2. The process of doing research is connected to the potential for community action.
3. The researcher stands with the community, not outside of it as an objective observer.
4. The researcher maintains flexibility in research methods and focus, changing them as necessary; the outcome is intended to benefit the community, with risks acknowledged and shared between the researcher and the community.
5. Differences between participants from the community and the researcher are acknowledged, negotiated at the outset, or resolved through a fair and open process.[24]

Participatory action research is typically used with historically disadvantaged populations. Because it allows them to define their own problems, the remedies they desire, and the direction of the research that will help them realize their goals, it is seen as more socially conscientious and less exploitative than other kinds of social science research.[25] Participatory action research could be particularly relevant to the study of LGBT youth, giving them a voice while allowing researchers to learn in-depth information about their lives and unique experiences.

Sampling and Bias

Sampling methods, such as probability sampling, can be powerful tools for understanding large or hidden populations. Probability sampling offers an opportunity to make generalizations about individuals who were not studied directly. To gather these data, appropriate questions can be added to existing population-based surveys. Although researchers are beginning to identify LGB youth by including questions about sexual orientation and/or same-sex behavior or attraction on these surveys, most research still relies on convenience sampling.

While convenience sampling is often the only viable solution for research limited by population, financial, or time constraints, it hinders researchers from making generalizations about the larger population. Unfortunately, until sexuality and gender identity are no longer stigmatized, so that LGBT and questioning youth no longer face harassment and violence, only some will be willing to discuss their sexual orientation or gender identity, forcing researchers to employ convenience sampling methodologies. Selective disclosure of sexual orientation and gender identity can have adverse affects on samples, as well as on the results of a study. Any sample that only includes youth who are openly gay is not necessarily generalizable to the greater LGBT youth population.

Longitudinal Research

One of the continuing challenges to understanding the lives of LGBT youth is the lack of longitudinal data. Longitudinal research would enhance understanding of the evolution of sexual orientation, behavior, and identity from adolescence to adulthood. While some representative surveys, such as the Youth Risk Behavior Survey and the National Adolescent Health Survey, are collecting time-series data, none is collecting enough data to analyze all segments of the LGB youth population— whether by race, ethnicity, specific age cohorts, or geography—to make statistically significant comparisons. These surveys do not collect any data on gender identity.

More important than collecting data over time is the need to collect longitudinal data on the same population of youth about their identity, attraction, and sexual behavior. The longitudinal data currently collected on LGB youth are trend data. Trend studies collect similar data over time but use different samples. Unlike trend studies, panel studies collect information over time from the same sample. Panel data would improve our understanding of how sexuality and gender identity develop.

This lack of longitudinal studies is not surprising. The inherently small size of the LGBT youth population makes it difficult to study the same adolescents over time. Most samples of LGBT youth number between one and five hundred, which falls short of the magnitude required for panel studies. Representative studies from Vermont, Massachusetts, and Washington indicate that about 1 to 4 percent of youth identify as lesbian, gay, or bisexual.[26] In the Gay, Lesbian, and Straight Education Network's 2007 National School Climate Survey of 6,209 LGBT students, 5 percent (297) identified as transgender, and 4 percent (248) identified as having an "other gender identity" (e.g., genderqueer, androgynous).[27] Given that longitudinal studies typically suffer from attrition, such a study could only be conducted with appropriate oversampling of LGBT youth. Even then, there is a chance that the people who drop out of the study may differ from people who remain, and such differences could distort the ultimate results.

Ethical Issues Involved in Research on LGBT Youth

While any research involving human subjects involves weighty ethical considerations, these become even more acute when the subjects are children and adolescents. Federal law requires the informed consent of parents or legal guardians when minors are involved in research.[28] However, parental consent may be waived if securing parental consent would jeopardize the participant's welfare or violate a teenager's privacy.[29] Because of the physical and psychological risks LGBT teens often face if their parents find out the teens' sexual orientation, institutional review boards should consider granting such a waiver when considering proposed research on LGBT youth.[30] Researchers should always obtain written assent from participants under the age of consent.[31]

8 | The Need for Research on Understudied LGBT Populations

The lack of research on the school experiences of a number of under-studied populations—including lesbian and transgender youth of color; immigrant lesbian, gay, bisexual, and transgender youth; LGBT youth who live in rural school districts; and transgender and gender-nonconforming youth—raises a number of critical questions:

- What are the differences among the experiences of LGBT youth of color from different racial and ethnic groups?
- How are LGBT issues currently talked about? Is it through predominantly white models? Are these models effective? How can they become more inclusive of the experiences of LGBT youth and families of color?
- How do LGBT youth of color integrate their racial and ethnic identities with their sexual or gender identities? What interventions can be used or altered to better facilitate this process?
- How can the issues of LGBT youth of color and AIDS be addressed without further stigmatizing and pathologizing them?
- Are immigrants, particularly undocumented immigrants, less likely to report anti-LGBT harassment and violence due to a desire to minimize their interactions with governmental authorities?
- Does the reliance of immigrant LGBT youth and the children of immigrant LGBT parents on their ethnic communities make them or their parents less likely to self-identify as LGBT or to be out?
- How does culture influence identity and disclosure of sexual orientation and gender identity?
- What interventions help transgender and gender-nonconforming youth to deal effectively with harassment and violence while remaining in school?
- What is the impact of single-sex education on transgender and gender-nonconforming youth?

A review of the academic literature on LGBT youth that was published in 2000 found that of 166 publications addressing health, mental health, and identity development among lesbian, gay and/or bisexual youth from 1972–99, only nine publications focused on the particular issues affecting youth of color. None focused on the particular issues affecting lesbian or transgender youth of color.[1] Of the fourteen primary and secondary journals most widely read among key school practitioners, such as teachers, guidance counselors, and social workers, only twenty-five of approximately twenty-five hundred articles published in these journals during a twenty-seven-year period (1 percent) addressed the health concerns of lesbian, gay, and bisexual youth. Of those twenty-five articles, only 4 percent focused on LGB youth of color, and none addressed transgender youth of color.[2]

A follow-up review of the literature on LGBT youth, published in 2002 by the National Youth Advocacy Coalition, identified the need for in-depth qualitative studies of how sexuality and gender identity are experienced in ethnic minority communities, both by LGBT youth of color and by the predominantly heterosexual majority within each ethnic community. The study called for research on "the life trajectories and health outcomes of LGB youth of color in the context of coming out."[3] The review also highlighted the impact of gendered notions of homosexuality in some communities of color, as well as the impact of various forms of cultural oppression (racism, homophobia, poverty, xenophobia) on HIV-related risk behavior and other health risks.[4]

In her 2002 review of the professional literature and research needs of LGBT youth of color, Dr. Caitlin Ryan describes the particularly complex forces that shape identity, attraction, and behavior among immigrant youth.

> Many youth are reared in immigrant families and are themselves immigrants who are adjusting to a new mainstream culture with different social and gender roles, and media representations of sexuality. Values and beliefs from their countries of origin also inform behavior, collectively through the influence of their family and ethnic community, and individually, through internalized representations that shape attraction and desire.[5]

The experiences of immigrant LGBT youth, especially the children of undocumented immigrant parents, in negotiating a homophobic school environment also warrant inquiry. While immigrant youth of color share experiences different from white immigrant youth, it is important to understand the cultural specificities of each group's experiences. Southeast Asian immigrants' experiences differ greatly from those of East Asian or South Asian immigrants. Similarly, Eastern European immigrants' experiences differ from those of immigrants from Latin America or West Africa.

There is no literature on the issues specific to LGBT youth growing up in rural areas. The Gay, Lesbian, and Straight Education Network's School Climate Survey differentiates among students in rural, suburban, and urban areas and has revealed significant variations in availability and access to educational and informational resources about LGBT issues between youth in rural communities and youth in suburban or urban communities:

- only 9 percent of rural students reported that LGBT issues were taught in class, compared with 14 percent of suburban students and 15 percent of urban students;
- 20 percent of rural students reported that LGBT issues were represented in their textbooks, compared with more than 43 percent of suburban students and 37 percent of urban students;
- 24 percent of rural students reported that LGBT resources were available in their school libraries, compared with 45 percent of suburban students and 32 percent of urban students;
- 22 percent of rural students had access to LGBT resources via Internet connections at school, compared to 42 percent of suburban students and 32 percent of urban students.[6]

Future research should attempt to correlate these differences among rural, suburban, and urban LGBT youth with educational achievement measures, as well as with measures of psychological and social well-being. For example, do LGBT youth in suburban areas who have greater access to LGBT resources in their school libraries report fewer incidents of depression or suicidal ideation? Do they have higher grade point averages than youth in rural areas?

Correlations between access to resources and education and measures of mental and physical health can be a powerful tool for influencing public policy. For example, LGBT youth in rural areas may be more dependent on the Internet to access LGBT resources than youth in metropolitan areas who can, for example, take the subway or drive downtown to visit the local community center or an LGBT youth program.

Consequently, Internet filtering software may disproportionately impact LGBT youth in rural areas. The role of the Internet in LGBT identity and community development, particularly among rural and ethnic minority youth, warrants further research.

Researchers may benefit from partnerships with the growing number of national transgender rights organizations, such as the National Center for Transgender Equality, the National Transgender Advocacy Coalition, and the Transgender Law Center. These organizations may, in turn, further advance their missions by seeking funding for the sponsorship of research that could provide valid and reliable data on the diverse experiences of transgender youth.

The Prevalence and Demographics of LGBT Youth

- How many LGBT youth are there?

Data from population-based studies allow for estimates of the prevalence of homosexuality and bisexuality among adolescents. The National Longitudinal Study of Adolescent Health, a comprehensive study of more than twelve thousand youth in grades seven through twelve, found that 6 percent of participants between the ages of thirteen and eighteen reported same-sex attraction, with 1 percent reporting that they were only attracted to members of their own sex and with 5 percent reporting attraction to both sexes.[7] Similarly, a 1999 report by the Safe Schools Coalition of Washington found that in eight population-based studies administered over ten years to 83,042 youth, 4 to 5 percent of teens in secondary schools either identified themselves as gay, lesbian, or bisexual; had engaged in same-sex sexual activity; or had experienced same-sex attractions.[8] More recent population-based studies have similar results:

- The 2001 Massachusetts Youth Risk Behavior Survey reported that 5 percent of respondents either self-identified as gay or bisexual or reported same-sex sexual experiences.[9]
- The 2001 Vermont Youth Risk Behavior Survey reported that 3 percent of students had engaged in same-sex sexual relations.[10]

To estimate the number of LGBT youth in public schools in the United States, researchers could focus on students in grades seven through twelve (ages thirteen to eighteen), who are likely to be more aware of their sexual orientation. For the 2007–8 school year, the U.S. Department of Education estimated that there were 22.4 million students in this grade range.[11] Given the studies indicating that 4 to 6 percent of the U.S. population is homosexual or bisexual, we estimate that between 896,000 and 1.34 million students in grades 7 through 12 may identify as LGB.

LGBT Parenting

- How many school-age youth have LGBT parents?
- What are the similarities and differences between the experiences of LGBT-identified youth and children of LGBT parents? Do they experience harassment and discrimination differently?
- Where are the policy gaps that fail to protect or account for the children of LGBT parents?
- What are the school experiences of LGBT parents who adopt children of other races, and what are the experiences of these youth in school?
- How can we utilize the information gathered from a small sample of parents in same-sex relationships in the National Adolescent Health Survey?
- Does the degree to which their LGBT parents are out affect the way children experience harassment and violence?
- What are the particular experiences of the children of transgender parents?

According to the 2000 U.S. Census, female and male same-sex couples parent at, respectively, about three-quarters and about half the rate of opposite-sex married couples. Black and Latina same-sex female couples parent at higher rates than white female same-sex couples; these data in particular offer new research opportunities that could alter the stereotypical picture of gay parenthood: well-off, white, and urban, with adopted or artificially conceived children.[12] Where do African American and Latina lesbians with children tend to live? What percentage are raising their children by themselves? Are these children adopted or the result of a previous heterosexual relationship? This question is particularly important given the legislative focus on sex education using abstinence-only-until-marriage programs and on initiatives promoting marriage and fatherhood: do cultural, religious, and other social factors specific to lesbian and bisexual women of color make them more likely to have heterosexual relationships prior to coming out? What impacts are initiatives promoting heterosexual marriage and fatherhood having on lesbian and bisexual mothers who first parented in a heterosexual context?

Primary School Experiences

• What are the elementary school experiences of LGBT youth, the children of LGBT parents, and youth who are perceived to be LGBT; and what successful interventions, if any, have worked at those grade levels?

The experiences of harassment and violence reported by the parents of children in elementary schools in the five-year study sponsored by the Safe Schools Coalition of Washington, described in chapter 2, is among the largest bodies of research available on this age-group. GLSEN's National School Climate Survey focuses primarily on students in high school, with more than 86 percent of participants from the 2007 survey in grades nine, ten, eleven, and twelve. In fact, only 4 percent of the participants ($N = 267$) were in sixth or seventh grade.[13] The qualitative research presented in Human Rights Watch's report *Hatred in the Hallways* included retrospective accounts of violence and harassment in elementary school by LGBT students who were in high school, but it provided no direct accounts by elementary school students. Given this lack of data on the prevalence of harassment and violence in elementary schools, it is not surprising that there is little information on specific interventions that would help to prevent it.

The data cited by the Safe Schools Coalition of Washington, Human Rights Watch, and LGBT youth who discuss their past experiences underscore the need for a coordinated effort on behalf of researchers and LGBT activists to conduct research on harassment and violence in elementary schools. Researchers will have to be innovative in their approaches to collecting this information. The Safe Schools Coalition of Washington was able to successfully involve parents in the process by creating a hotline for them to call if their children were being harassed or abused at school. Another approach could ask participants in population-based surveys, such as the Youth Risk Behavior Survey, to report their experiences of anti-LGBT harassment and violence prior to sixth grade.

Life Outside of School

- What are the experiences of LGBT youth outside of schools, and how can research that produces information representative of their whole lives be conducted?

The quality and magnitude of research on the experiences of LGBT youth in schools, the harassment and violence they face, and its impact on their educational, physical, and mental health outcomes has grown significantly during the past decade. However, researchers need to be wary of creating an incomplete picture of the lives of LGBT youth. What are their experiences outside of school? Do they face discrimination in their part-time jobs? Do the activities they participate in outside of school differ from the activities of their heterosexual peers? How do they find support networks to counterbalance harassment and bias they experience in school? There is little research available to shed light on these questions. Again, the most effective method of collecting data on these issues may be to add questions to existing population-based surveys administered in schools, such as the Youth Risk Behavior Survey, which can assess the broader context in which LGBT students live their lives.

Teachers and School Staff

- What are the attitudes of school personnel (teachers, school staff, parents, school board members, etc.) toward LGBT issues in education?
- How are teachers and other school staff trained on LGBT-related issues? Are they incorporated into teacher education, staff training, and recredentialing? How can this be institutionalized as an ongoing process? What types of training are effective?
- How is multicultural education conceptualized, and is it inclusive of LGBT issues?
- How can LGBT issues be integrated into school curricula?
- What is the role of LGBT-related nondiscrimination language in union contracts? Does it protect school personnel? Does it encourage school personnel to be out as LGBT or as allies? Does it help to support LGBT youth and youth who are targeted by anti-LGBT harassment?

Pohan and Bailey highlight some common goals cited in implementing a multicultural approach to education, which are also applicable to LGBT issues:

- combating a narrow and/or monodimensional curriculum; affirming and legitimizing the presence and contributions of diverse groups;
- creating a climate that promotes an appreciation of diverse peoples, values, perspectives, and ways of life;
- reducing prejudice and working toward the elimination of discrimination in teaching and in society;
- working toward equality and justice for all;
- respecting the rights and the dignity of all individuals;
- supporting pluralism within the educational system;
- broadening and/or diversifying the values schools promote.[14]

Schools are, however, reluctant to support these common goals when they are applied to the prohibition of discrimination on the basis of sexual orientation and gender identity or the development of curriculum and a school environment that is more inclusive and representative of LGBT students. Pohan and Bailey call on teachers and administrators who support multicultural education to confront this reluctance and incorporate LGBT issues into multicultural curricula.[15] Future research could collect data from elementary and secondary education programs in colleges and universities to assess whether and how LGBT issues are raised within the context of multicultural education courses offered to future teachers. These data could provide the foundation for the development of a more uniform curriculum that could be disseminated to teacher training programs around the United States.

A Cry for Help on Deaf Ears

A Profile of Jayron Martin

In November 2009, Jayron Martin, a ninth-grader at Langham Creek High School in Houston, Texas, felt so threatened by a group of classmates at school that he asked two assistant principals and his bus driver for help. The assistant principals said they would call the students down to their offices for further information and assistance. But that call never came.

At the end of the school day on November 12, 2009, Martin rode the bus home along with the group that had been threatening him. Martin approached the bus driver but again received no assistance. When he got off the bus, the group of students ran after him. "You don't understand, I was just running for my life and nobody was like there at all. Nobody was doing anything for me," said Martin. Martin then ran into a neighbor's home, where one of the boys in the group beat him for approximately seven minutes with a metal pipe while yelling antigay slurs. The other students stood around and watched. "All they kept saying was, 'We going to get you. We going to fight you,' and all that and so when they started coming after me, they were like, 'You're not going to be gay anymore.' They just kept hitting me," he said. Luckily, the neighbor who lived in the home came downstairs and told the boy to stop beating him. When he would not stop, the neighbor threatened him with a shotgun, prompting the boy and those watching to run away.[16]

Martin suffered a concussion, as well as cuts and bruises on his arms and hands. Subsequent to the investigation, a sixteen-year-old classmate was charged with aggravated assault, and the bus driver was fired.[17] "I'm disgusted," said Martin's mother, Lakenya. "[Saying] I'm sorry after the fact doesn't do it. The school district let us down. I mean, let all of us down because it could have been anyone's kid."[18]

Rofes's survey of eight of his former middle school students found that having an openly gay teacher in the 1970s had a number of positive effects. Respondents said that this experience served to "normalize" lesbians and gay men for them, and it made the respondents believe that they themselves were "less xenophobic."[19] None said that having an openly gay teacher made them question their own sexual orientation (all eight are heterosexual adults), and they reported a number of positive impacts. One said that she was "more comfortable with my entire sexuality probably" because of Rofes's honesty about being gay. "I also respected him. This is all-important because it all, coupled with his seeming security in his sexuality and his self-respect, was a definite influence in shaping my opinion of the entire spectrum of sexuality." Other students "felt that witnessing a teacher who was politically active as a gay liberationist affected their views about political activism and discrimination against gay people."[20]

Rofes's study provides a good model for research examining the impact of openly LGBT teachers, guidance counselors, and administrative staff on students. Diaz and Ayala found that having an openly gay adult role model while growing up is a resiliency factor for gay and bisexual Latino men at risk for HIV.[21] Are there other ways the presence of openly gay role models among school staffers benefits LGBT youth?

The impact of the political activism of openly LGBT students on the school community would also make for an interesting inquiry. Are schools with active gay-straight alliances or legal battles over LGBT youth sites of greater civic engagement in general? Rofes suggested provocatively,

> [T]he greatest influence of openly lesbian, gay and bisexual teachers may be on students' relationship to political activism and social movements. By witnessing up close the importance of political advocacy on a teacher's job security and social position, children's understanding of the importance of activism and its relevance to their lives might be enhanced.[22]

GLSEN's 2007 survey found that eight out of ten students could identify at least one school staff member supportive of LGBT students at their school, and more than a third could identify six or more supportive school staff.[23] Both GLSEN and Human Rights Watch have documented the positive effect supportive teachers and staff have on a school's climate. Diaz and Ayala found openly gay role models to be a resiliency factor for gay and bisexual Latino youth.[24] Future studies could ask questions about the impact of openly LGBT teachers and staff members on school environments and the lives of LGBT youth in those schools.

There is little research on the prevalence or impact of nondiscrimination language that includes sexual orientation and gender identity in teachers' union contracts, a fact that warrants further research. The following are a few examples of contracts with language that included sexual orientation as an enumerated category:

• City Union of Baltimore (FY 2002–3): "All provisions of this Agreement shall be applied equally to all employees in the bargaining units for which CUB is the certified representative without discrimination as to age, sex, marital status, race, color, creed, national origin, political affiliation, disability or sexual orientation."

- Local 4200-AFT/CSFT, AFL-CIO, Connecticut (July 1, 1999–June 30, 2003): "The parties agree that neither shall discriminate against any employee, because of the individual's race, color, religious creed, age, sex, marital status, national origin, ancestry, physical or mental disability, sexual orientation, history of mental disorder or mental retardation, except on the basis of bona fide occupational qualifications."
- Albuquerque, New Mexico, Teachers Federation, Local 1420 of the American Federation of Teachers (August 2002): "The Board shall not discriminate against any teacher in the bargaining unit on the basis of race, color, religion, gender, age, national origin, marital status, sexual orientation, place of residence, disability, membership or non-membership in any teacher organization, except when the District determines there is a bona fide occupational qualification."[25]

A comprehensive data set of similar contracts would allow for the testing of a wide variety of questions about their impact on teachers and students. For example, it would be interesting to locate for comparison two school districts with similar socioeconomic demographics, one with a contract inclusive of sexual orientation and one without. The experiences of both students and teachers in those districts could then be compared, perhaps using existing data from the Youth Risk Behavior Survey or GLSEN's National School Climate Survey, to assess whether there are statistically significant differences in the incidence of anti-LGBT harassment and violence, whether teacher interventions occur to challenge such harassment, and the number of students who know an openly gay teacher. The expansion of enumerated categories to include "gender identity and expression" would protect the rights of transgender teachers and could benefit transgender youth in particular.

Gay-Straight Alliances and Other School-Based Organizations

- How many gay-straight alliances or similar school-based student organizations are there? How do they differ demographically and geographically?
- How are these organizations changing? How are GSA models being adapted for rural and urban communities? How are organiza-

tions purposefully diversifying their membership and leadership?
- What is the impact of student activists using GSA models to build social change organizations?
- How do GSAs function as sites of civic engagement and leadership development? What is their impact on school environment, personal development, and the community at large?
- What is the development process of the straight allies of LGBT students (other students, teachers, school personnel, etc.)? How do student clubs impact this process?
- How do community-based LGBT groups support youth and school communities? What are the connections and distinctions between school-based and community-based groups?

Griffin and Ouellett's analysis of the Massachusetts Safe Schools Program found that "clear policy statements (both statewide and local) backed up by technical, legal, and financial resources, along with improvement from key administrators (e.g., building principals, district superintendents and school committees), educators, community leaders, and student leaders are at least as important as GSAs in creating lasting school safety."[26] Unfortunately, as we noted in chapter 4, former Massachusetts governor Jane Swift vetoed an appropriation of funds for the Safe Schools Program in 2002. This followed nearly a decade of opposition by local and national antigay religious extremists. Although Governor Swift and her supporters vowed to redirect other funds to make up for the defunding of the eight-hundred-thousand-dollar program, it never happened. It is unlikely that Massachusetts's model program will be as effective without the significant resources for staff training and support it had enjoyed for the previous decade. A follow-up study to Griffin and Ouellett's analysis could document the impact of defunding the program on youth, teachers, and administrators and make the case for restoring funding. This could be useful in other states considering public funding for safe schools programs.

Evaluation of Safe Schools Programs and Interventions

- How are safe schools programs and other interventions being evaluated? How do they differ across social, class, and racial differences?
- How are interventions and policies implemented and enforced?

How aware of them are members of the school community, and how are they perceived? How do different community members (students, teachers, members of the board of education, etc.) access and evaluate them?

• What is the impact of zero-tolerance policies? Are they effective in preventing anti-LGBT harassment and violence, or do they reinforce oppression?

• How can such interventions be woven into policies and programs addressing other issues, such as racism and sexism? What different outcomes are facilitated when these links are made?

Szalacha's survey of seventeen hundred students at thirty-three schools in Massachusetts documented a statistically significant, more positive "sexual diversity climate" in schools with "higher levels of implementation of the Safe Schools Program." More specifically, students in schools that had implemented staff training, nondiscrimination policies, or gay-straight alliances reported "less homophobic school climates" and "higher levels of personal safety for sexual minority students."[27]

Future research in this area could examine the relative impact of nondiscrimination laws, antiharassment laws, and state education regulations on school climate. As discussed in more detail in chapter 3, forty-six states and the District of Columbia have either passed a law or issued a school regulation or ethical code that addresses bullying in schools. Some explicitly enumerate sexual orientation and gender identity as protected categories. Others prohibit bullying or harassment without listing protected categories. Do laws have a greater impact than regulations? Are laws that do not explicitly protect students based on sexual orientation and gender identity implemented the same as those that do? Because harassment is a form of discrimination that violates the Fourteenth Amendment's equal protection clause, are antiharassment laws as effective as nondiscrimination laws, or is one category of laws preferable to the other?[28] Research examining the implementation of such laws and regulations and evaluations of their effectiveness would enable policymakers to adopt the most effective interventions.

The Economic Costs of Not Protecting LGBT Youth

• What is the impact of the lawsuits brought against school districts and school administrators who fail to protect LGBT youth?

Chapter 3 highlights a report that summarizes fifteen lawsuits against school districts that failed to protect students from pervasive anti-LGBT harassment and violence at school. Settlements in these cases ranged from forty thousand to almost one million dollars, and the combined total of the known settlements for these lawsuits was more than $2.3 million.[29] Future research should focus on how they affected policy change at the local or state level. What happened after these school districts lost these lawsuits or settled out of court? Did they implement policies that include sexual orientation and gender identity? If they did not, why not? Given the precedent-setting nature of these lawsuits, data on their impact on school districts could be a valuable lobbying tool in states and school districts that lack LGBT-inclusive antiharassment and nondiscrimination policies.

Resiliency

Some researchers attempt to balance the attention given to at-risk LGBT youth with a better understanding of those who are resilient in the face of adversity.[30] According to Dr. Stephen Russell, director of the Frances McClelland Institute at the University of Arizona, "As researchers, we must be diligent that research does not serve to marginalize or label individual sexual minority youth as unavoidably at risk."[31] This research on resiliency "seeks to identify protective, nurturing factors in the lives of LGBT youth" that "frame the preeminent health and human services delivery question. . . . [T]o what extent and under what circumstances can protective factors be transplanted into the lives of young people who have been socialized in a stressful climate of uncertainty and fear?"[32] Factors that have been found to support resiliency in the general adolescent population include connectedness with parents and family members, perceived social connectedness, and associations with caring adults outside the family.[33]

For example, Diaz and Ayala found that resilience factors for Latino gay men include family acceptance and the presence of an openly gay role model while growing up. Latino gay men whose immediate families included someone they could "talk openly with about . . . homosexuality/bisexuality" were less likely to have low self-esteem or engage in unsafe sex. Latino gay men who had an openly gay adult role model while they were children or adolescents also had higher self-esteem and lower health-related risk behaviors as adults than Latino gay men who did not.[34]

Research on LGB youth using National Adolescent Health Survey data correlated similar factors with reduced likelihood to attempt suicide, including

- perceived parent and family connectedness;
- emotional well-being;
- high parental expectations for school achievement;
- actual school achievement;
- more people living in the household;
- religiosity.[35]

This list of variables that affect resiliency may be incomplete, and each may affect the experiences of LGBT youth uniquely. For example, LGBT youth are likely to experience barriers to feeling connected with their parents and families differently than heterosexual youth.[36] More research is needed to further explore how these variables specifically help or hinder resiliency in LGBT youth.

More than Just the Gay Football Team Captain

A Profile of Corey Johnson

> "I'd keep so much in all day long. Then at night, when I'd be by myself in bed, I'd just cry and cry because of everything I kept in during the day, all the pain."[37] That was Corey Johnson's life before he came out—first to a school counselor, then to a teacher, then to his parents, and finally to the varsity football team. At the time, Corey was a junior at Masconomet Regional High School in Topsfield, Massachusetts, and the elected cocaptain and starting linebacker of his school's football team.
>
> Corey had been hiding his sexual orientation since the sixth grade. It was during his sophomore year that his coming-out process began—appropriately enough, as a result of a football game. At a 1998 Super Bowl party, a few of his uncles made disparaging remarks about gay people. The remarks infuriated him but also caused him to retreat to the bathroom to cry.[38] Corey knew then that he had to speak out. His burdens lightened with each person he told. He received unconditional support from his teachers and unconditional love from his parents. But how would his teammates respond? They often engaged in rowdy sexual ban-

ter and ridiculed gays. Moreover, his coach repeatedly told the players, "Don't be a bunch of fairies/fags."[39]

Despite such remarks, his coach turned out to be supportive and arranged a team meeting where Corey stood in front of his teammates and announced, "Guys, I called this meeting because I have something to tell all of you. . . . I'm coming out as an openly gay man." When he noticed the wide eyes and dropped jaws, Corey quickly added, "I'm still the same person . . . I didn't come on to you in the locker room last year. I'm not going to do it this year. Who says you guys are cute enough anyway?" Corey's honesty and sense of humor defused the tension, and his teammates rallied behind him with comments like "I'd like to be supportive in any way possible" and "Even if others on the team don't agree with you being gay, in order to be a cohesive team, they just have to accept it and put it aside."[40]

The team joined together in support of Corey. Their cohesiveness not only led them to a 25–0 victory over a vocally homophobic opposing team but also prompted the Gay, Lesbian, and Straight Education Network to honor Corey and his teammates with their Visionary Award. "I want to get beyond being the gay football captain, but for now I need to get out there and show these machismo athletes who run high schools that you don't have to do drama or be a drum major to be gay," Corey said.[41]

Corey did move beyond football: he became a successful radio personality, cohosting the McMullen and Johnson Show on OutQ, a gay and lesbian radio station on the Sirius Satellite Radio network. Broadcasting live from Rockefeller Center, he conducted high-profile interviews and initiated issues-oriented dialogue. Even after Corey moved beyond his role as "the gay football captain," the significance of his actions remained. Corey not only effectively challenged dominant stereotypes of male gay identity, but his experience also serves as a reminder that coming out as a gay youth can have a happy ending. Amid the epidemic of violence, harassment, and discrimination against LGBT youth, Corey's story provides hope of how things should be.

Another researcher focusing on LGBT youth resilience is Dr. Ritch Savin-Williams, the chair of human development at Cornell University, who has examined the experiences of LGBT youth who have performed particularly well in the classroom social space and in their everyday lives. Research emphasizing self-harming practices among LGBT youth is limited, he argues. These "studies include only those willing to identify themselves as gay or at least acknowledge same-sex attraction." These samples, Savin-Williams argues, are "significantly smaller than the total number who will eventually turn out to be gay, lesbian, bisexual, or transgender. Many teenagers in the larger group may be adjusting very well but simply prefer to keep their sexual orientations to themselves even on anonymous surveys."[42]

The implications of Savin-Williams's research and observations are significant and part of a relatively new effort to publish data that further identify and explain resilience factors in LGBT youth. The *Journal of Gay and Lesbian Issues in Education* has published an issue addressing this topic, titled "Beyond Risk: Resilience in the Lives of Sexual Minority Youth."[43] It was edited by Stephen Russell and advocates for research on the "paradox of adolescent resilience and risk."[44] In a call for submissions for the issue, Russell asked for research or reflection articles that address some important questions:

- How do LGBT youth develop and exhibit resilience in light of their origins in cultures characterized by sexual prejudice?
- How can schools and educators work to prevent risk outcomes while fostering resilience?
- With regard to educational policy, what purpose has the historic focus on risk among LGBT youth served, and at what cost?[45]

Articles in the issue include a study of the impact of religion on the mental health of LGBT youth.

[T]hose who left Christianity because of its institutional heterosexism, which might be interpreted as a coping response and thus as a protective factor, had both higher internalized homophobia and poorer mental health. One might conclude that religious faith and participation are as important for the mental health of sexual minority youth as they are for many other youth. These results also raise the question: Do youth who leave institutional religion feel they have failed or believe it is their religion that has failed them?[46]

Another subject Russell highlights is innovative programming that creates a safer and more supportive environment for all students, including GSAs, which are " bridging risk and resilience in the lives of many real students in schools across the country."[47] He concludes,

> [W]e need to know more about basic developmental processes and milestones in education and how they are affected (or not) by sexual minority status. Studies of resilience are an important next step to help us understand basic development in the context of education. What are the specific issues, challenges, or opportunities that define same-sex sexuality in relation to education, such as success in negotiating relationships with peers and teachers, the development of academic motivation and achievement, or the development of future goals and aspirations? Moving beyond risk will help us see the many ways that sexual minority youth are unique, as well as the ways they are no different from other young people.[48]

Additional research on LGBT youth who thrive despite bias, harassment, and violence is critical to preventing any pathologizing effect that may result from a disproportionate emphasis on drug abuse, unsafe sexual behavior, and suicide.[49]

9 | Conclusion and Policy Recommendations: Making It Better for LGBT Students

[An education is] about giving each and every one of us the chance to fulfill our promise; to be the best version of ourselves we can be. And part of what that means is treating others the way we want to be treated—with kindness and respect.

Now, I know that doesn't always happen. Especially not in middle or high school. Being a teenager isn't easy. It's a time when we're wrestling with a lot of things. When I was your age, I was wrestling with questions about who I was; about what it meant to be the son of a white mother and a black father, and not having that father in my life. Some of you may be working through your own questions right now, and coming to terms with what makes you different.

And I know that figuring all that out can be even more difficult when you've got bullies in class who try to use those differences to pick on you or poke fun at you; to make you feel bad about yourself. . . .

So, what I want to say to you today—what I want all of you to take away from my speech—is that life is precious, and part of its beauty lies in its diversity. We shouldn't be embarrassed by the things that make us different. We should be proud of them. Because it's the things that make us different that make us who we are. And the strength and character of this country have always come from our ability to recognize ourselves in one another, no matter who we are, or where we come from, what we look like, or what abilities or disabilities we have.

—President Barack Obama[1]

President Barack Obama delivered his 2010 back-to-school speech to a crowd of cheering students at the Julia R. Masterman Laboratory and Demonstration School in Philadelphia on September 14. Less than a week earlier, fifteen-year-old Billy Lucas took his own life after being suspended from school for fighting back against bullies who, according to friends, would "call him gay and tell him to go kill himself."[2] For several weeks following the speech, the attention of the United States would continue to be captured by a series of tragic suicides completed by several more teenagers who were bullied at school because of their real or perceived sexual orientation.[3] In that context, the president's message to students that "life is precious, and part of its beauty lies in its diversity" is more poignant than perhaps even he thought it would be.

One month later, the president would revisit his attention to bullying and diversity in schools in a video he created for the It Gets Better Project, an online social media movement started by syndicated columnist and gay activist Dan Savage in response to LGBT youth suicide, "to show young LGBT people the levels of happiness, potential, and positivity their lives will reach—if they can just get through their teen years."[4] In his video, President Obama said,

> Like all of you, I was shocked and saddened by the deaths of several young people who were bullied and taunted for being gay, and who ultimately took their own lives. As a parent of two daughters, it breaks my heart. It's something that just shouldn't happen in this country.
>
> We've got to dispel the myth that bullying is just a normal rite of passage—that it's some inevitable part of growing up. It's not. We have an obligation to ensure that our schools are safe for all of our kids. . . .
>
> . . . As a nation we're founded on the belief that all of us are equal and each of us deserves the freedom to pursue our own version of happiness; to make the most of our talents; to speak our minds; to not fit in; most of all, to be true to ourselves. That's the freedom that enriches all of us. That's what America is all about. And every day, it gets better.[5]

What needs to happen to meet the obligation to "ensure that our schools are safe for all of our kids," including those who are LGBT? In addition to telling them that it gets better when they are older, what can be done to make it better now for LGBT youth in America's schools? The social science research and policy analysis included in this book supports a comprehensive policy agenda that promotes strength and resiliency among LGBT youth and ensures that schools are supportive, affirming places where young people can reach their full potential.

Federal Policy Recommendations

As discussed in detail in chapter 3, there is significant opportunity and need for the federal government to lead efforts to protect students through the enforcement of existing laws and the creation of new laws and policies that explicitly include sexual orientation and gender identity as enumerated categories of protection. The following recommendations would decrease anti-LGBT bullying and enhance LGBT youths' ability to access an education free of violence and discrimination. These changes would also improve health outcomes and decrease young gay men's disproportionate vulnerability to HIV and other sexually transmitted infections. The addition of behavioral and demographic questions to federal surveys will also provide a better understanding of the experiences of LGBT youth as compared with their heterosexual and non-gender-variant peers.

- We encourage Congress to pass and the president to sign the Student Nondiscrimination Act, which would outlaw harassment, bullying, and violence against students based on real or perceived sexual orientation or gender identity, and the Safe Schools Improvement Act, which would require schools to adopt codes of conduct that specifically prohibit bullying and harassment and to collect and report data on bullying and harassment to the Department of Education.
- The U.S. Department of Education should work closely with state and local partners to expand nondiscrimination and antiharassment policies in schools and to educate school districts about existing federal laws that require them to protect students from discrimination, harassment, and bullying.
- The president, members of Congress, and other influential political leaders should continue to show leadership acknowledging the impact of homophobia and anti-LGBT prejudice on students and the moral and ethical obligation to ensure that all youth have access to a safe and quality education.
- Elected representatives and the leadership of anti-LGBT advocacy groups should be held accountable for their efforts to prevent the passage of legislation and policy that protects students from anti-LGBT harassment and violence.
- Comprehensive sex education that includes age-appropriate infor-

mation about safer sex practices for same and opposite-sex partners should be mandatory for all public schools.
- Questions that assess sexual orientation and gender identity
  should be mandatory for federal surveys like the Youth Risk Behavior Survey, so that valuable data about LGBT youth can be collected. Federal agencies should also be equipped with expertise to
  analyze these data and make appropriate recommendations.
- Qualified LGBT people should be appointed to federal advisory
  boards and committees that guide the implementation and enforcement of existing federal laws and policies related to schools
  and school safety.

State Policy Recommendations

In addition to federal leadership, states must be equal partners in ensuring not only that LGBT youth have equal access to a quality and safe education but also that LGBT educators and administrators are protected
and encouraged to serve as role models and mentors for youth (see chapter 3). The following recommendations cover the range of opportunities
schools have to fundamentally change and prevent anti-LGBT school climates.

- Existing laws and policies that protect students from discrimination and harassment should be enforced and, if necessary,
  amended to include real or perceived sexual orientation and gender identity as enumerated categories of protection.
- States without school nondiscrimination and antiharassment laws
  should pass comprehensive legislation with enumerated categories
  of protection, as New York State did in September 2010 when Governor David Paterson signed into law the Dignity for All Students
  Act.[6] New Jersey also has a model antibullying law, with tough reporting requirements and real consequences for students who bully
  and for teachers/administrators who fail to intervene and report.
- Charter and private schools should be required to abide by state
  nondiscrimination and antibullying laws and regulations.
- In addition to making public schools safe for LGBT youth, appropriate schools and programs like the Harvey Milk High School in
  New York City, which specifically reach out to LGBT youth who
  are struggling in the school system because of issues related to

their sexual orientation or gender identity, should be created. While such schools are not a long-term solution, they may be the best option in larger school systems where broadscale change is not possible in a short period of time.

- "No promo homo" laws and policies, which prevent educators from including age-appropriate information about LGBT people in health classes and other school courses, should be repealed.
- School curricula and textbooks should include the contributions to history and culture made by LGBT people.
- States should reject funding for abstinence-only-until-marriage programs in favor of programs that include comprehensive, age-appropriate information about how to prevent the transmission of HIV and other sexually transmitted diseases. Health and family planning curricula should include positive and accurate information about LGBT people and same-sex couples.
- In addition to federal efforts, state boards of education and school districts should ensure that teachers and school administrators are educated about legal requirements to protect LGBT students from discrimination and harassment. State political leaders should learn from the model policies and actions in Massachusetts to create commissions that examine the challenges faced by LGBT youth and identify policy solutions.
- Boards of education should create and support comprehensive safe schools programs modeled after successful programs in Massachusetts, California, and New York City.
- States should include optional questions about sexual orientation and gender identity on the Center for Disease Control's Youth Risk Behavior Survey and other federal surveys that collect data on the sexual orientation and gender identity of students.

School-based Policy Recommendations

While the ability of schools to protect LGBT students is affected by federal and state policy, there is significant opportunity to adopt regulations, policies, and curricula that bridge legal gaps and ensure that the daily experiences of students and teachers occur in an environment that not only has zero tolerance for harassment and bullying but also facilitates diversity and acceptance. The following recommendations are summarized from the research and analysis in chapter 4.

- School districts should adopt regulations that prohibit discrimination against students, teachers, and staff based on real or perceived sexual orientation and gender identity.
- Teachers and school administrators should enforce existing school safety and antibullying laws and policies.
- School districts should conduct trainings to ensure that teachers and other staff are culturally competent in serving LGBT youth and confronting bullying and harassment. This training should address particular issues affecting LGBT youth of color and children with LGBT parents.
- School administrators should create safe spaces for LGBT teachers to work openly and honestly about themselves and their families and should encourage them to be role models for students and staff.
- Schools should conduct periodic surveys that measure incidence of anti-LGBT harassment and bullying in school, similar to the GLSEN National School Climate Survey.
- Principals should support the creation and maintenance of gay-straight alliances and should support teachers/administrators who choose to sponsor such groups (see "Guidance for Students, Parents, and Staff Who Want to Create a GSA" in chapter 4).
- School boards and administrators should support programs that create community and safe spaces for LGBT and questioning students, such as GLSEN's Safe Space campaign and New York City's Respect for All Week.
- School libraries should include age-appropriate books about LGBT people, history, and culture.
- Internet filters on school computers should not prevent students from accessing age-appropriate information about LGBT issues.

Making it Better for Transgender Youth in Schools

Throughout this book, we frequently noted the need for more research on transgender youth. Advocacy organizations like GLSEN have made significant contributions to this need through the inclusion of transgender youth and their experiences in surveys and school outreach programs. Research findings indicating that the school experiences of transgender youth are even more harmful and dangerous than those of their LGB peers highlight a critical need for attention to this population of students. To reduce the harm currently experienced by transgender youth, a number of key actions are required.

- Educators and school administrators must acknowledge that transgender youth exist in schools and that they have a legal obligation to support and protect transgender youth regardless of how they choose to express their gender identity.
- Educators and school administrators must intervene to reduce the risks experienced by transgender youth in schools because of discrimination and marginalization.
- Steps must be undertaken to reduce the vulnerability of transgender students by providing them access to resources that meet their specific needs, including sensitive and effective care by school health staff and guidance counselors.
- Education about transgender people should be included in the professional preparation and in-service training programs for all teachers and school administrators.
- Youth who identify as transgender must be educated about society's gender constructs and how these contribute to their vulnerability and devalue their health status. Strategies to enhance emotional, social, and physical development must be established to assist transgender youth in building the resiliency they need to live in a culture that tenaciously maintains a binary concept of gender.[7]

Beyond Policy to Social Change

Implementation of these policy recommendations will significantly help and protect LGBT students. Alone, however, they are not enough to ensure that schools are safe and supportive learning environments. Homophobia and anti-LGBT discrimination in schools is deeply rooted in sociocultural history and beliefs about gender stereotypes and how young people should be educated. Beyond policy, there are several ways in which the American ethos needs to change in order to comprehensively prevent anti-LGBT harassment and violence in schools.

Family acceptance and support are integral to the positive development and overall wellness of all children, including young LGBT people. Parents who reject LGBT children cause immeasurable harm. We must send a clear message to families that they play a critical role in promoting positive health and wellness outcomes of LGBT youth. Families who embrace their LGBT children should be visible in their communities in order to set positive examples, and LGBT youth who feel supported in their families should share their stories. Such publicity will promote the strengths and resiliency of families and encourage others to follow their lead.

State and local community organizations should implement interventions to disseminate and reinforce these messages, such as Gay Men's Health Crisis's 2008 My Son Is My Life campaign, which presented the importance of parental support in the lives of black young gay men. The informational palm cards and ads on bus shelters and phone kiosks created for this campaign, aimed at both young men and their fathers, acknowledge the many reactions parents can have upon learning that their son is gay, and they illustrate the steps parents can take to continue to provide support and love to their children.[8]

To achieve fundamental change, we must also expose and challenge the myth of the "normal" family in America. We must counsel families to let go of the heterosexist notion that all children will automatically be heterosexual, so that couples who plan to have children will consider the possibility of having a gay or transgender son or daughter. We must encourage families to let go of stigma and silence around homosexuality, so that parents who believe their child may be gay can find other families like theirs. Groups that advocate for acceptance of LGBT youth, such as Parents, Families, and Friends of Lesbians and Gays, serve extremely important functions in this regard.

The active support of religious leaders, who have enormous impact on family values, is also critical for helping not only families with LGBT children but also all parents who influence the worldview of their children, gay or straight. While some religious leaders and organizations promote positive messages about LGBT people, many send messages of intolerance that influence family reactions to LGBT youth. We should also enlist the business sector, organized labor, the nonprofit philanthropic sector, and other parts of society in support of these efforts. Shifting to messages of love, acceptance, and support and ending the political exploitation of anti-LGBT sentiment will better not only the lives of LGBT students but also society as a whole.

Notes

INTRODUCTION

1. McKinley 2010. Additional news outlets reported that at least six of the youth who completed suicide were gay. See Burford 2010.

2. See Troiden 1989; Herdt and Boxer 1996; Grov et al. 2006; Ryan et al. 2009.

3. A study of twenty-four transgender youth found that, on average, they were just over ten years old when they first realized that their gender identity did not correspond to their biological sex. Other people began to label these youth transgender at a mean age of 13.5. They first labeled themselves transgender at a mean age of 14.3. See Grossman and D'Augelli 2006. In another study of transgender youth, Grossman and D'Augelli briefly review developmental milestones in children's understanding of their birth sex, gender, and gender role expectations, which begin a early as age two. Children also respond negatively at an early age to others who are gender nonconforming. Some of the transgender youth in this study reported suicide attempts as early as age ten, indicating both awareness of and significant distress related to their different gender identities. See Grossman and D'Augelli 2007.

4. Ryan and Futterman 1998.

5. Kosciw, Diaz, and Greytak 2008.

6. A more comprehensive summary of available data on anti-LGBT harassment and violence in schools is included in chapter 2.

7. Lewin 2003.

8. Ibid.

9. *Mclaughlin v. Bd. of Educ. of Pulaski County Special Sch. Dist.*, No. 4:03-CV-00244GTE, 2003 WL 21182283 (E.D. Ark. April 22, 2003).

10. Lewin 2003.

11. American Civil Liberties Union 2003b.

12. American Civil Liberties Union 2003a.

13. Ibid.

14. A study published in 1987 found that 50 percent of gay male adolescents reported being rejected by their parents because of their sexual orientation. Ten years later, another survey of LGB youth ages fourteen to twenty-one found that 26 percent of fathers and 10 percent of mothers rejected their LGB children after disclosure of their sexual orientation. In 2009, a study published in the journal of the American Academy of Pediatrics found that LGB youth continue to experience significant family rejection. See Savin-Williams and Dube 1998; Remafedi 1987; D'Augelli, Hershberger, and Pilkington 1998; Ryan et al. 2009.

15. Cited in Kitts 2005.
16. Grossman and D'Augelli 2007.
17. Cochran et al. 2002. See also Ray 2007.
18. Ryan and Futterman 1998.
19. Varney 2001.
20. Kosciw and Diaz 2008.

CHAPTER 1

1. *Protection of Pupils Rights Amendment, U.S. Code* 20 (2003), § 1232h.
2. *Alaska Stat.* § 14.03.110 (Michie 2002).; *N.J. Stat. Ann.* § 18A: 36-34 (West 2001); *Utah Code Ann.* § 53A-13-302 (1999).
3. State of Alaska Department of Health and Social Services 2010.
4. Savin-Williams 2006.
5. See, for example, Savin-Williams 2001a.
6. Savin-Williams and Lenhart 1990.
7. Information included in this profile is from a personal interview conducted with Louie Garay in August 2010.
8. For more information, see http://www.nonamecallingweek.org.
9. For more information on the House ad Ball culture in New York City, see http://en.wikipedia.org/wiki/Ball_culture.
10. For example, see Mosher, Chandra, and Jones 2005; Gates 2010.
11. Russell, Seif, and Truong 2001.
12. Reis and Saewyc 1999.
13. Massachusetts Department of Education 2002.
14. Vermont Department of Health Office of Alcohol and Drug Abuse Programs 2002.
15. Mosher, Chandra, and Jones 2005.
16. Ibid.
17. Villarroel et al. 2006.
18. Cloud 1998.
19. American Psychiatric Association 1997.
20. Noel and Sable 2009.
21. Currah and Minter 2001.
22. Ibid. Transsexual youth may or may not be diagnosed with gender dysphoria or gender identity disorder, diagnoses listed in the Diagnostic and Statistical Manual of Mental Disorders (*DSM-IV*).
23. Grossman and D'Augelli 2006.
24. Bochenek and Brown 2001; Leach 2002; Leck 2000.
25. Greytak, Kosciw, and Diaz 2009. See also Kosciw, Diaz, and Greytak 2008.
26. Gender PAC 2002.
27. Mottet 2004.
28. Kosciw, Diaz, and Greytak 2008.
29. Greytak, Kosciw, and Diaz 2009.
30. Di Ceglie et al. 2002.
31. Ibid.

32. Mallon 1999.

33. *Doe v. Yunits*, No. 001060A, 2000 WL 33162199 (Mass. Super. Ct. 2000), *aff'd, Doe v. Brockton Sch. Comm.*, No. 2000-J-638, 2000 WL 33342399 (Mass. App. Ct. 2000).

34. PlanetOut 2000.

35. Ibid.

36. *Doe v. Yunits.*

37. Meek 2000.

38. Scanlan-Stefanakos 2001.

39. Intersex Society of North America, n.d.

40. Blackless et al. 2000.

41. Intersex Society of North America 2003.

42. D'Augelli and Patterson 2001.

43. Bochenek and Brown 2001.

44. Fontaine 1998.

45. Russell et al. 2010.

46. D'Augelli, Grossman, and Starks 2006.

47. Ibid.

48. Kosciw, Diaz, and Greytak 2008.

49. Varney 2001.

50. Diaz and Kosciw 2009.

51. Hunter and Mallon 2000.

52. Russell, Clarke, and Laub 2009.

53. Dube and Savin-Williams 1999.

54. Newman and Muzzonigro 1993.

55. Grov et al. 2006.

56. Ryan and Futterman 2001; Dube and Savin-Williams 1999.

57. Greene 1997.

58. Varney 2001.

59. Ibid.

60. Ryan and Futterman 2001.

61. Battle et al. 2001.

62. Dube and Savin-Williams 1999.

63. Edwards 1996.

64. Dube and Savin-Williams 1999.

65. Pilkington and D'Augelli 1995.

66. Russell and Truong 2001.

67. Pharr 1997; Leck 2000.

68. Irvine 2001.

69. McCready 2001.

70. Uribe 1994.

71. McCready 2001.

72. Russell and Truong 2001.

73. Stacey and Biblarz 2001; Johnson and O'Conner 2002.

74. Cited in Gartrell and Bos 2010.

75. Casper and Schultz 1999.

76. Simmons and O'Connell 2003.

77. Ibid.
78. Dang and Frazer 2004.
79. Cianciotto 2006.
80. Data from the 1990 census showed that women of color in same-sex couple households were more likely to have given birth. Sixty percent of black, 50 percent of Native American, 43 percent of Hispanic, and 30 percent of Asian/Pacific Islander women in same-sex couples had given birth to at least one child, compared with just 23 percent of their white non-Hispanic peers. Multiracial same-sex couple households accounted for 13 percent of female couples and 12 percent of male couples in the 1990 census. See, in this book's list for further reading, Bradford, Barrett, and Honnold 2002.
81. Battle et al. 2001.
82. Mays et al. 1998.
83. Telingator and Patterson 2008.
84. Perrin and Committee on Psychosocial Aspects of Child and Family Health 2002.
85. Cited in Ferrero, Freker, and Foster 2002.
86. Cited in Patterson 1995.
87. Ibid.
88. Because many studies do not ask people to self-identify by sexual orientation, there are no conclusive findings on bisexual parents. For more information on bisexuality, see, in this book's list for further reading, Miller et al. 2007 and Hutchins and Kaahumanu 1991.
89. Patterson 2009. See also Patterson 2000 (in this book's list for further reading); Gartrell and Bos 2010.
90. Biblarz and Stacey 2010; Tasker 2010.
91. Stacey and Biblarz 2001.
92. Patterson 2006.
93. Wainright and Patterson 2006.
94. Wainright and Patterson 2008.
95. Patterson 2009.
96. Bos et al. 2008.
97. Garner 2002.
98. Fontaine 1998.
99. Russell, McGuire, et al. 2009.
100. Perrotti and Westheimer 2001.
101. Gartrell et al. 2005.
102. Ibid.
103. Kosciw and Diaz 2008.
104. Green 1998.
105. Ibid.
106. Sears 1994.
107. Rubin 1995; Kissen 1999.
108. Ryan and Martin 2000.
109. Rubin 1995.
110. Lambda Legal Defense and Education Fund 2001.
111. Ibid.

112. Feinstein et al. 2001.
113. Mallon 1998. This study examined the experiences of fifty-four gay and lesbian youth in the New York City foster care system.
114. Cited in Dylan 2004 (see this book's list for further reading).
115. Feinstein et al. 2001.
116. Clatts et al. 2005.
117. Cochran et al. 2002.
118. Reis and Saewyc 1999.
119. Cochran et al. 2002.
120. Ibid.
121. D'Augelli 1996.
122. Rosario, Rotheram-Borus, and Reid 1996.
123. Savin-Williams 1998.
124. D'Augelli, Grossman, and Starks 2006.
125. Remafedi 1987.
126. Telljohann and Price 1993.
127. D'Augelli 1996.
128. Grossman and D'Augelli 2007.
129. Ryan et al. 2009.
130. Savin-Williams 2001a.
131. Safe Schools Coalition of Washington State 1999.
132. Lipkin 1994.
133. Munoz-Plaza, Quinn, and Rounds 2002.
134. Bochenek and Brown 2001.
135. Gilliam 2002; Ginsberg 1999.
136. Lee 2002.
137. Russell and Joyner 2001.
138. Proctor and Groze 1994.
139. Bauermeister et al. 2010.
140. Russell 2005.
141. Ibid.
142. Bennett 1997.

CHAPTER 2

1. Safe Schools Coalition of Washington State 1999.
2. Letts and Sears 1999.
3. Carter 1997 (see this book's list for further reading), cited in Callahan 2001.
4. D'Augelli, Grossman, and Starks 2006.
5. Kosciw, Diaz, and Greytak 2008.
6. Bochenek and Brown 2001.
7. Faulkner and Cranston 1998.
8. Kosciw, Diaz, and Greytak 2008.
9. D'Augelli, Grossman, and Starks 2006.
10. Safe Schools Coalition of Washington State 1999.

11. Perrotti and Westheimer 2001.
12. Safe Schools Coalition of Washington State 1999.
13. Bochenek and Brown 2001.
14. Gay, Lesbian, and Straight Education Network 2009a.
15. Ibid.
16. McGuire, Dixon, and Russell 2009.
17. James 2009.
18. Wilson 2009.
19. Thurlow 2001.
20. Ibid.
21. Russell, Franz, and Driscoll 2001.
22. J. Walsh 1996.
23. *Nabozny v. Podlesny*, 92 F.3d 446 (7th Cir. 1996).
24. Lambda Legal Defense and Education Fund 1996a.
25. J. Walsh 1996.
26. Ibid.
27. Lambda Legal Defense and Education Fund 1996a.
28. Ibid.
29. J. Walsh 1996.
30. Kosciw, Diaz, and Greytak 2008.
31. D'Augelli, Pilkington, and Hershberger 2002.
32. Smith et al. 2007.
33. Cited in Online Safety and Technology Working Group 2010.
34. Ibid.
35. Rideout, Foehr, and Roberts 2010.
36. Ibid.
37. Greytak, Kosciw, and Diaz 2009.
38. Kosciw, Diaz, and Greytak 2008.
39. Finerman 2002.
40. Ibid.
41. American Association of University Women Educational Foundation 1993.
42. Finerman and Bennett 1998.
43. Finerman 2001.
44. Ibid.
45. Bochenek and Brown 2001.
46. Ibid.
47. *Seamons v. Snow*, 864 F. Supp 1111 (D. Utah 1994).
48. Stein 1999.
49. Ibid.
50. Ibid.
51. Hunter and Schaecher 1987.
52. D'Augelli 1998.
53. Kosciw, Diaz, and Greytak 2008.
54. Greytak, Kosciw, and Diaz 2009.
55. Faulkner and Cranston 1998.
56. Garofalo et al. 1998.

57. Massachusetts Department of Education 1999.
58. Russell, McGuire, et al. 2006.
59. Russell, Talmage, et al. 2009.
60. Russell, Seif, and Truong 2001.
61. Ibid.
62. Gardner 2002.
63. Kosciw, Diaz, and Greytak 2008.
64. Ibid.
65. Garofalo et al. 1998.
66. DuRant, Krowchuk, and Sinal 1998.
67. Russell, Franz, and Driscoll 2001.
68. D'Augelli, Grossman, and Starks 2006.
69. Bontempo and D'Augelli 2002.
70. Jordan 2000.
71. Faulkner and Cranston 1998.
72. Bontempo and D'Augelli 2002.
73. Russell, Truong, and Driscoll 2002.
74. Corliss et al. 2008.
75. Bochenek and Brown 2001.
76. Remafedi 1994.
77. Lemp et al. 1994.
78. Moon et al. 2000.
79. Kitts 2005.
80. Gibson 1989.
81. Garofalo et al. 1999.
82. Massachusetts Department of Education 2000.
83. Silenzio et al. 2007.
84. Rosario, Schrimshaw, and Hunter 2005.
85. Savin-Williams 2001b.
86. D'Augelli et al. 2005.

CHAPTER 3

1. Sheldon 2001.
2. Family Research Council 2003.
3. *E. High Gay/Straight Alliance v. Bd. of Educ.*, No. CIV. 2:98-CV-193J, 1999 WL 1390255 (D. Utah 1999).
4. Schneider and Owens 2000.
5. Griffin and Ouellett 2002.
6. *Nabozny v. Podlesny,* 92 F.3d 446 (7th Cir.1996); *Flores v. Morgan Hill Unified Sch. Dist.,* 324 F.3d 1130 (9th Cir. 2003). Although Flores and Nabozny involved lesbian and gay students, the same rationale would likely be applied if a school failed to protect a transgender student from harassment or discrimination.
7. Stader and Graca 2007.
8. National Center for Lesbian Rights 2002.
9. California Safe Schools Coalition, n.d.a.

10. American Civil Liberties Union of Northern California 2003.

11. SpeakTruth.com., n.d.

12. American Civil Liberties Union of Northern California 2003.

13. Clair, n.d.

14. American Civil Liberties Union of Northern California 2003.

15. Clair, n.d.

16. Ibid.

17. *Flores v. Morgan Hill Unified Sch. Dist.*

18. American Civil Liberties Union of Northern California 2003.

19. Ibid.

20. Clair, n.d.

21. *U.S. Code* 20 (2003), §§ 1681–88 (2003).

22. Cited in Bedell 2003.

23. Stader and Graca 2007.

24. U.S. Department of Education 2001.

25. Stader and Graca, 2007.

26. U.S. Department of Education 2001.

27. M. Walsh 1994.

28. Stader and Graca 2007.

29. Cited in Meyer 2010.

30. *U.S. Code* 20 (2003), §§ 4071–74.

31. *Boyd County High Sch. Gay Straight Alliance v. Bd. of Educ. of Boyd County, Ky.*, 258 F. Supp. 667 (E.D. Ky. 2003).

32. *U.S. Code* 20 (2003), § 4071(a).

33. *Colin v. Orange Unified Sch. Dist.*, 83 F. Supp. 2d 1135 (C.D. Calif. 2000).

34. Ibid.

35. National Safe Schools Partnership 2007.

36. Ibid.

37. *Safe Schools Improvement Act of 2007*, H.R. 3132, 110th Cong., 1st sess.

38. Human Rights Campaign 2010a.

39. *Safe Schools Improvement Act of 2009*, H.R. 2262, 111th Cong., 1st sess.

40. *Safe Schools Improvement Act of 2010*, S. 3739, 111th Cong., 2nd sess.

41. Gay, Lesbian, and Straight Education Network 2009b.

42. *Student Nondiscrimination Act of 2010*, H.R. 4530, 111th Cong., 2nd sess.

43. *Student Nondiscrimination Act of 2010*, S. 3390, 111th Cong., 2nd sess.

44. Human Rights Campaign 2010c.

45. American Civil Liberties Union 2010.

46. Joyner 2010.

47. Ibid.

48. Gay, Lesbian, and Straight Education Network 2004b; Lambda Legal Defense and Education Fund and Gay, Lesbian, and Straight Education Network 2001; D'Augelli 1996; Lipkin 1994.

49. Lambda Legal Defense and Education Fund 1996b.

50. *Romer v. Evans*, 517 U.S. 620 (1996).

51. *Ark. Code Ann.* § 6-18-514, available at http://www.lexisnexis.com/hot topics/arcode/Default.asp.

52. *Cal. Educ. Code* § 220–221.1, retrieved November 13, 2010, from http://www.leginfo.ca.gov/cgi-bin/displaycode?section=edc&group=00001-01000&file=220-221.1; *Cal. Educ. Code* § 234–234.3, retrieved November 13, 2010, from http://www.leginfo.ca.gov/cgi-bin/displaycode?section=edc&group=00001-01000&file=234-234.3.

53. *C.R.S.* § 22-32-109, retrieved November 13, 2010, from http://www.michie.com/colorado/lpext.dll/cocode/1/350da/36951/37328/373f5?f=templates&fn=document-frame.htm&2.0#JD_22-32-109; *C.R.S.* § 24-34-301, retrieved November 13, 2010, from http://www.michie.com/colorado/lpext.dll/cocode/1/3bdef/3d7e8/3f2db/3f5d5/3f5db?f=templates&fn=document-frame.htm&2.0#JD_24-34-301.

54. See *Conn. Gen. Stat.* § 10-15(c), retrieved November 7, 2010, from http://www.cga.ct.gov/2009/pub/chap164.htm#sec10-15c.htm; *Conn. Gen. Stat.* § 46a-51(21), retrieved September 14, 2011, from http://www.cga.ct.gov/2011/ACT/PA/2011PA-00055-R00HB-06599-PA.htm.

55. *D.C. Code* §§ 2-1402.41 and 2-1401.02, available at http://government.westlaw.com/linkedslice/default.asp?SP=DCC-1000.

56. § 105 *Ill. Comp. Stat.* 5/27-23.7, retrieved November 13, 2010, from http://www.ilga.gov/legislation/ilcs/fulltext.asp?DocName=010500050K27-23.7.

57. *Iowa Code* § 280.28, retrieved November 13, 2010, from http://coolice.legis.state.ia.us/Cool-ICE/default.asp?category=billinfo&service=IowaCode&ga=82&input=280.28.

58. 20-A *M.R.S.A.* § 1001(15)(H), retrieved November 13, 2010, from http://www.mainelegislature.org/legis/statutes/20-A/title20-Asec1001.html.

59. *Md. Code Ann., Educ.* §§ 7-421 and 7-421.1, available at http://michie.lexisnexis.com/maryland/lpext.dll?f=templates&fn=main-h.htm&cp=mdcode.

60. See *Minn. Stat.* § 121A.0695, retrieved November 13, 2010, from https://www.revisor.mn.gov/statutes/?id=121A.0695; *Minn. Stat.* § 363A.02(5), retrieved September 14, 2011, from https://www.revisor.mn.gov/statutes/?id=363A.02; *Minn. Stat.* § 363A.03(Subd. 44), retrieved September 14, 2011, from https://www.revisor.mn.gov/statutes/?id=363A.03.

61. *N.H. Rev. Stat.* § 193-F, retrieved November 7, 2010, from http://www.gencourt.state.nh.us/rsa/html/NHTOC/NHTOC-XV-193-F.htm.

62. *N.J. Stat.* 18A:37-13–17, retrieved November 13, 2010, from http://lis.njleg.state.nj.us/cgi-bin/om_isapi.dll?clientID=423706&Depth=2&depth=2&expandheadings=on&headingswithhits=on&hitsperheading=on&infobase=statutes.nfo&record=%7B8070%7D&softpage=Document42. In November 2010, New Jersey's governor signed a new antibullying law that requires most public school employees to attend trainings on how to identify and respond to bullying. The law also requires all school districts to form school safety teams to review bullying complaints. School superintendents are required to report bullying incidents to the state board of education, which will grade schools and districts on their efforts to respond to and prevent bullying. The law requires tougher sanctions on school officials who do not report bullying and allows for students who bully to be suspended or expelled. See Friedmann 2010.

63. *NY CLS EDN* § 2, retrieved November 7, 2010, from http://public

.leginfo.state.ny.us/LAWSSEAF.cgi?QUERYTYPE=LAWS+&QUERYDATA=@SL EDN0T1A2+&LIST=LAW+&BROWSER=BROWSER+&TOKEN=48068495+ &TARGET=VIEW. This law does not go into effect until July 1, 2012.

64. *N.C. Gen. Stat.* § 115C-407.15, retrieved November 7, 2010, from http://www.ncga.state.nc.us/EnactedLegislation/Statutes/HTML/ByArticle/Chapter_115C/Article_29C.html.

65. *Or. Rev. Stat. Ann.* § 339.351–64, retrieved November 7, 2010, from http://www.leg.state.or.us/ors/339.html.

66. 16 *V.S.A.* § 565, retrieved November 14, 2010, from http://www.leg.state.vt.us/statutes/fullsection.cfm?Title=16&Chapter=009&Section=00565; 16 *V.S.A.* § 11(a)(26), retrieved November 7, 2010, from http://www.leg.state.vt.us/statutes/fullsection.cfm?Title=16&Chapter=001&Section=00011.

67. In 2002, Washington State enacted a law that protected students from harassment and bullying based on sexual orientation. In 2006, the Anderson-Murray Antidiscrimination Law was passed, which added sexual orientation and gender identity to the categories protected by Washington's Law Against Discrimination. This law covers public accommodations, including all public schools. See *Wash. Rev. Code.* § 49.60 (2006), retrieved November 7, 2010, from http://apps.leg.wa.gov/rcw/default.aspx?cite=49.60; *RCW* § 28A.300.285, retrieved November 14, 2010, from http://apps.leg.wa.gov/RCW/default.aspx?cite=28A.300.285; *RCW* 28A.600.480, retrieved November 14, 2010, from http://apps.leg.wa.gov/RCW/default.aspx?cite=28A.600.480

68. *Mass. Ann. Laws*, ch. 76, § 5, retrieved November 7, 2010, from http://www.malegislature.gov/Laws/GeneralLaws/PartI/TitleXII/Chapter76/Section5. In 2010, the Massachusetts legislature passed and the governor signed antibullying legislation that does not include enumerated categories of protection. See *Chapter 92: An act relative to bullying in schools, approved by the governor, May 3, 2010*, retrieved November 14, 2010, from http://www.malegislature.gov/Laws/SessionLaws/Acts/2010/Chapter92.

69. *Wis. Stat.* § 118.13, retrieved November 13, 2010, from http://nxt.legis.state.wi.us/nxt/gateway.dll?f=templates&fn=default.htm&d=stats&jd=118.13.

70. *Ala. Code* § 16-1-24.1, retrieved November 13, 2010, from http://alisondb.legislature.state.al.us/acas/CodeOfAlabama/1975/16-1-24.1.htm.

71. *Alaska Stat.* § 14.33.200–250 (2006), retrieved November 13, 2010, from http://www.legis.state.ak.us/basis/folioproxy.asp?url=http://wwwjnu01.legis.state.ak.us/cgi-bin/folioisa.dll/stattx07/query=*/doc/%7Bt6443%7D.

72. *A.R.S.* § 13-2911, retrieved November 13, 2010, from http://www.azleg.state.az.us/FormatDocument.asp?inDoc=/ars/13/02911.htm&Title=13&DocType=ARS.

73. 14 *Del. Code Ann.* §§ 4112D and 4123A, retrieved November 13, 2010, from http://delcode.delaware.gov/title14/c041/index.shtml#P243_28297.

74. *Fla. Stat.* § 1006.147 (2008), retrieved November 13, 2010, from http://www.leg.state.fl.us/Statutes/index.cfm?mode=View%20Statutes&SubMenu=1&App_mode=Display_Statute&Search_String=harassment&URL=1000-1099/1006/Sections/1006.147.html.

75. *O.C.G.A.* § 20-2-751.4–5, available at http://www.lexisnexis.com/hottopics/gacode/Default.asp.

76. *I.C.* § 18-917A, retrieved November 14, 2010, from http://legislature
.idaho.gov/idstat/Title18/T18CH9SECT18-917A.htm.

77. See *IC* 20-30-5.5, retrieved November 14, 2010, from http://www.in.gov/
legislative/ic/code/title20/ar30/ch5.5.html; *IC* 20-33-8-0.2 and 20-33-8-13.5, retrieved November 14, 2010, from http://www.in.gov/legislative/ic/code/title20/
ar33/ch8.html; *IC* 5-2-10.1-2 and 5-2-10.1-11, 12, retrieved November 14, 2010,
from http://www.in.gov/legislative/ic/code/title5/ar2/ch10.1.html.

78. *KSA* § 72-8256 (2007), retrieved November 13, 2010, from http://www
.kslegislature.org/legsrv-statutes/getStatute.do?number=31187.

79. *KRS* § 158.150, retrieved November 13, 2010, from http://www.lrc.ky.gov/
KRS/158-00/150.PDF.

80. *La. R.S.* 17:7, retrieved November 13, 2010, from http://www.legis.state.la
.us/lss/lss.asp?doc=81029.

81. In 2001, Mississippi passed a non-enumerated law requiring the state
board of education to develop conflict resolution and peer mediation materials
for students. In 2010, the law was amended to specifically include bullying and harassment in public schools. See *Miss. Code* §§ 37-11-20, 37-11-54, 37-11-67, and
37-11-69.

82. *Mo. Rev. Stat.* § 160.775, retrieved November 13, 2010, from http://www
.moga.mo.gov/statutes/C100-199/1600000775.HTM.

83. *NE Rev. Stat.* 79-2, 137, retrieved November 14, 2010, from http://www
.nebraskalegislature.gov/laws/statutes.php?statute=79-2,137.

84. *Nev. Rev. Stat.*, ch. 388, §§ 122–39, retrieved November 13, 2010, from
http://www.leg.state.nv.us/NRS/NRS-388.html#NRS388Sec122.

85. See *N.D. Cent. Code* §§ 15.1-19-17 to 15.1-19-22, retrieved January 26,
2011, from http://www.legis.nd.gov/cencode/t15-1c19.pdf.

86. *Ohio Rev. Code Ann.* § 3301.22 (2007), retrieved November 13, 2010, from
http://codes.ohio.gov/orc/3301.22; *Ohio Rev. Code Ann.* § 3313.666 (2007), retrieved November 13, 2010, from http://codes.ohio.gov/orc/3313.666; *Ohio Rev.
Code Ann.* § 3313.667 (2007), retrieved November 13, 2010, from http://codes
.ohio.gov/orc/3313.667.

87. *OK St.* § 70-24-100.\3-5 (2008), retrieved November 13, 2010, from
http://webserver1.lsb.state.ok.us/OK_Statutes/completetitles/os70.rtf.

88. 24 *PS* 1303.1-A (2008), available at http://government.westlaw.com/
linkedslice/default.asp?SP=pac-1000.

89. *R.I. Gen. Laws* § 16-21-24, retrieved November 13, 2010, from http://www
.rilin.state.ri.us/statutes/title16/16-21/16-21-24.HTM; *R.I. Gen. Laws* § 16-21-26,
retrieved November 13, 2010, from http://www.rilin.state.ri.us/statutes/title16/
16-21/16-21-26.HTM.

90. *S.C. Code Ann.* § 59-63-110, 120, 130, 140, 150, retrieved November 13,
2010, from http://www.scstatehouse.gov/CODE/t59c063.htm.

91. *Tenn. Code Ann.* 49-6-1014, 1015, 1016, 1017, 1018, 1019, retrieved November 13, 2010, from http://www.michie.com/tennessee/lpext.dll/tncode/1b6fe/
1c4a8/1c609?f=templates&fn=document-frame.htm&2.0#JD_t49 ch6p10.

92. *Tex. Educ. Code Ann.* § 37.001, retrieved November 13, 2010, from http://
www.statutes.legis.state.tx.us/Docs/ED/htm/ED.37.htm#37.001; *Tex. Educ. Code
Ann.* § 25.0342, retrieved November 13, 2010, from http://www.statutes.legis

.state.tx.us/Docs/ED/htm/ED.25.htm#25.0342; *Tex. Educ. Code Ann.* § 37.217, retrieved November 13, 2010, from http://www.statutes.legis.state.tx.us/Docs/ED/htm/ ED.37.htm#37.217.

93. *Utah Code* 53A-11a, retrieved November 13, 2010, from http://www.le.utah.gov/UtahCode/section.jsp?code=53A-11a.

94. *Va Code Ann.* § 22.1-279.6, retrieved November 13, 2010, from http://leg1.state.va.us/cgi-bin/legp504.exe?000+cod+22.1-279.6.

95. *W.Va. Code Ann.* 18-2C, retrieved November 13, 2010, from http://www.legis.state.wv.us/WVCODE/code.cfm?chap=18&art=2C#02C.

96. *Wyo. Stat. Ann.* § 21-4-313, retrieved November 13, 2010, from http://legisweb.state.wy.us/statutes/statutes.aspx?file=titles/Title21/T21CH4AR3.htm.

97. *Hi. BOE Policy* 4211, retrieved November 14, 2010, from http://lilinote.k12.hi.us/STATE/BOE/POL1.NSF/85255a0a0010ae82852555340060479d/e6220 975a045ad6c0a2573 f7006cebcb?OpenDocument; *Hi. Admin. R.* 8–19, retrieved November 14, 2010, from http://lilinote.k12.hi.us/PUBLIC/ADMINR1.NSF/ 85255a0a0010ae82852555340060479d/4996c004afd7cbaf0a25675f006efbd9? OpenDocument.

98. *NMAC* 6.12.7 (2006), retrieved November 13, 2010, from http://www.nmcpr.state.nm.us/NMAC/parts/title06/06.012.0007.htm. In April 2011, a bill was signed into law creating a new section of public education code, which simply reads: "Bullying Prevention Programs—The department shall establish guidelines for bullying prevention policies to be promulgated by local school boards. Every local school board shall promulgate a bullying prevention policy by August 2012." Retrieved January 26, 2011, from http://www.sos.state.nm.us/2011Bills/SB78.pdf.

99. Pennsylvania State Bd. of Ed. Regs. §4.4(c), retrieved September 20, 2011, from http://www.pacode.com/secure/data/022/chapter4/s4.4.html. In 2010, the Georgia General Assembly made a number of modifications to the state's existing anti-bullying law (see note 75 in this section), including requiring the Georgia Department of Education to develop a model anti-bullying policy. That model policy includes sexual orientation among other enumerated categories. See Georgia Department of Education 2010.

100. Data on K-12 student enrollment by state for the 2000 school year were drawn from U.S. Department of Education, National Center for Education Statistics 2003; data for the 2004–5 school year were drawn from Sable and Hill 2006. Because 2010 enrollment estimates by state were not available, we instead used 2009 data from Keaton 2010; data on state laws, including the year they were passed, were obtained from a variety of sources, including state legislative databases (see note for each state) and a map of student nondiscrimination laws produced by the Human Rights Campaign (Human Rights Campaign 2010b).

101. Macgillivray 2004; "High Plains School District," "High Plains," and various names for individuals and groups mentioned in the following discussion are pseudonyms assigned by Ian Macgillivray to protect privacy.

102. National Center for Lesbian Rights and Gay, Lesbian, and Straight Education Network, n.d.a.; *Ray v. Antioch,* 107 F. Supp.2d 1165 (N.D. Cal. 2000).

103. American Civil Liberties Union Foundation, n.d.

104. *Ariz. Rev. Stat.* § 15-716 (2003).

105. *Cal. Educ. Code* § 51550 (West 2003).

106. *Nev. Rev. Stat.* 389.065 (2003).

107. *Utah Code Ann.* § 53A-13-101 (2003).
108. Alan Guttmacher Institute 2003.
109. *Mass. Gen. Laws,* ch. 71, § 32A (2003).
110. An Act Relative to Parental Notification and Consent, H. 1445 (proposed 2003).
111. *S.C. Code Ann.* § 59-32-30(A)(5) (Law, Co-op 2003).
112. *Ariz. Rev. Stat.* § 15-716(C) (2003).
113. *Ala. Code* § 16-40A-2(c)(8) (2003).
114. *Tex. Health and Safety Code Ann.* § 163.002(8) (Vernon 2003).
115. *Utah Admin. Code* R277-474-3(A)(2) (2003); *Utah Code Ann.* § 53A-13-101 (2003).
116. *Lawrence v. Texas,* 123 S. Ct. 2472 (2003).
117. Human Rights Watch 2002.
118. Ibid.
119. Ibid.
120. Winerip 2003a.
121. Pharr 1997.
122. Bonauto 2002.
123. California Safe Schools Coalition, n.d.b.
124. Gay, Lesbian, and Straight Education Network 2004a.
125. Ibid.
126. 365gay.com 2005.
127. American Civil Liberties Union of Arkansas 2005.

CHAPTER 4

1. Price and Telljohan 1991.
2. Telljohann and Price 1993.
3. Harris 1997.
4. Ibid.
5. Griffin 1992.
6. Sheldon 2001.
7. Holmes and Slap 1998.
8. Stevenson 2000.
9. Groth and Birnbaum 1978; Jenny and Roesler 1994.
10. Finkelhor 1994; Stevenson 2000.
11. Finkelhor 1994.
12. Stevenson 2000.
13. Ibid.
14. Jenny and Roesler 1994.
15. Groth and Birnbaum 1978.
16. Pharr 1997.
17. Telljohan and Price 1993; Walling 1993.
18. Nesmith, Burton, and Cosgrove 1999.
19. Diaz and Ayala 2001.
20. Munoz-Plaza, Quinn, and Rounds 2002.
21. Ibid.

22. Fontaine 1998; Ginsberg 1999.
23. Bochenek and Brown 2001.
24. Kosciw, Diaz, and Greytak 2008.
25. Lipkin 1999.
26. Russell 2001.
27. Russell, Seif, and Truong 2001.
28. Diaz and Ayala 2001.
29. Woog 1995.
30. Rofes 2000.
31. Blumenfeld 1994. When he made the decision to come out in 1993, Peter Atlas was a math teacher at Concord Carlisle Regional High School in Massachusetts.
32. Ibid.
33. Pettett 2005.
34. Blumenfeld 1994; D'Augelli 1996; Walling 1993.
35. Lipkin 1994.
36. Fontaine 1998.
37. Bochenek and Brown 2001.
38. California Safe Schools Coalition and Tides Center 2005.
39. Gay, Lesbian, and Straight Education Network and Harris Interactive 2008.
40. Szalacha 2001a; Perrotti and Westheimer 2001.
41. American Civil Liberties Union 2002; Goldstein 2001.
42. Goldstein 2001.
43. Bochenek and Brown 2001.
44. Ibid.
45. American Civil Liberties Union 2002.
46. Ibid.
47. New York City Department of Education 2009.
48. Ibid.
49. Greytak and Kosciw 2010.
50. Ibid.
51. Ibid.
52. Ginsberg 1999.
53. For more information on these other organizations that participated in the LGBT civil rights movement prior to the Stonewall Riots of 1969, see, in this book's list for further reading, Marcus 1992 and D'Emilio 1983.
54. Proctor and Groze 1994; Rubin 1995.
55. National Education Association 2002.
56. Russel, Kostroski, et al. 2006.
57. Macgillivray and Jennings 2008.
58. Cited in ibid.
59. Ibid.
60. Kosciw, Diaz, and Greytak 2008.
61. Ibid.
62. Ibid.
63. Lipkin 1994.
64. 603 *Mass. Regs. Code* § 26.00 (2003) (Access to Equal Educational Opportunity).

65. Perrotti and Westheimer 2001.
66. Ibid.
67. GSA Network, n.d.
68. Kosciw, Diaz, and Greytak 2008.
69. Uribe and Harbeck 1992.
70. New York City Department of Education 2009.
71. Ibid.
72. Ibid.
73. Greytak and Kosciw 2010.
74. New York City Department of Education 2009.
75. New York City Department of Education 2010.
76. Ibid.
77. Blumenfeld 1994.
78. Gay, Lesbian, and Straight Education Network, n.d.a.
79. Griffin and Ouellett 2002.
80. Gay, Lesbian, and Straight Education Network, n.d.b.
81. More information about the GSA Network, including access to its California state directory of GSAs and an interactive map of state networks across the country, is available at http://gsanetwork.org/.
82. Kosciw, Diaz, and Greytak 2008.
83. Ginsberg 1999.
84. Radkowsky and Siegel 1997.
85. Griffin and Ouellett 2002.
86. Bulion 2000.
87. Szalacha 2001b.
88. MacGillivray 2007.
89. Lee 2002.
90. Griffin et al. 2003.
91. Gay, Lesbian, and Straight Education Network 2007.
92. Walls, Stacey, and Wisneski 2008.
93. Shahum 1996.
94. Human Rights Resource Center 2000.
95. Shahum 1996.
96. Bennett-Haigney 1996.
97. The suit was filed by the American Civil Liberties Union (North Carolina and Utah chapters), Lambda Legal Defense and Education Fund, and the National Center for Lesbian Rights. The law firm of Heller Ehrman White & McAuliffe was also involved.
98. *E. High Gay/Straight Alliance v. Bd. of Educ.*, No. CIV. 2:98-CV-193J, 1999 WL 1390255 (D. Utah 1999).
99. Shahum 1996.
100. Hetrick-Martin Institute, n.d.b.
101. Hetrick-Martin Institute, n.d.a.
102. Ibid.
103. Winerip 2003b.
104. Hetrick-Martin Institute, n.d.b.
105. Ibid.
106. Hetrick-Martin Institute, n.d.c.

107. Information included in this profile is from a personal interview conducted with Luis A. in August 2010.

108. *New York Times* 2003.

109. *Wall Street Journal* 2003.

110. *Daily News* 2003.

111. Osborne 2003.

112. Bronski 2003.

113. 365gay.com 2003.

CHAPTER 5

1. White House 2002.

2. *No Child Left Behind Act of 2001, U.S. Code* 115 (2002), § 1425.

3. U.S. Department of Education 2002c.

4. White House 2002.

5. Ibid.

6. U.S. Department of Education 2002.

7. Ibid.

8. ABCNews.com 2002.

9. *Everson v. Bd. of Educ. of Ewing,* 330 U.S. 1 (1947).

10. *Zelman v. Simmons-Harris,* 234 F.3d 945 (6th Cir. 2000), *rev'd,* 536 U.S. 639 (2002).

11. Gay, Lesbian, and Straight Education Network 2001b.

12. *Zelman v. Simmons-Harris.*

13. US Charter Schools 2010.

14. Ibid.

15. Nathan 1999.

16. Finn, Manno, and Vanourek 2000.

17. This profile was originally published by the National Gay and Lesbian Task Force in Cianciotto and Cahill 2003 (see this book's list for further reading).

18. National Education Association, n.d.

19. American Federation of Teachers, n.d.

20. Casey 2000.

21. Ibid.

22. Gay, Lesbian, and Straight Education Network 2001b.

23. Simpson 2002.

24. American Association of University Women 2003; *United States v. Virginia,* 518 U.S. 515 (1996).

25. American Association of University Women 2003.

26. Gandy 2002.

27. Teicher 2003.

28. Ibid.

29. American Association of University Women Educational Foundation, n.d.

30. American Association of University Women 2003.

31. Ibid.

32. Bailey 1996.

33. Datnow, Hubbard, and Woody 2001.

34. White House 2002.

35. U.S. Department of Education 2002a.

36. Fleming 2000; U.S. Congress 1987.

37. National Association for Multicultural Education 2003.

38. Bohn and Sleeter 2002.

39. Ibid., quoting Rich 1986 (see this book's list for further reading).

40. Bohn and Sleeter 2002.

41. Taylor 1990.

42. Garofalo et al. 1998; Russell, Seif, and Truong 2001.

43. For a biography of Walt Whitman, see, in this book's list for further reading, Schmidgall 1997.

44. For a biography of Gertrude Stein, see, in this book's list for further reading, Souhami 2000 or Hobhouse 1975.

45. In this book's list for further reading, see De Veaux 2004 for a biography of Audre Lorde, Lorde 1982 for her autobiography.

46. For biographical information on Emma Goldman, see the Emma Goldman Papers, available at http://sunsite.berkeley.edu/Goldman.

47. For a biography of Magnus Hirschfeld, see, in this book's list for further reading, Wolff 1987.

48. For a biography of Bayard Rustin, see, in this book's list for further reading, D'Emilio 2003.

49. *No Child Left Behind Act of 2001,* § 1425.

50. Heins, Cho, and Feldman 2006.

51. Johnson 2000.

52. Silver, n.d.

53. Johnson 2000.

54. Ibid.

55. *Reno v. Am. Civil Liberties Union,* 521 U.S. 844 (1997).

56. American Civil Liberties Union 1997.

57. Beeson 2001.

58. Ibid.

59. For a list of Beacon Press's publications, see http://www.beacon.org.

60. For a list of the Sexual Health Network's publications, see http://www.sexualhealth.com.

61. Thornburgh and Lin 2002.

62. Electronic Frontier Foundation and Online Policy Group 2003.

63. *United States v. Am. Library Assoc.,* 537 U.S. 1170 (2003).

64. Miner 1998.

65. Ibid.

66. Spear 1999.

67. Ibid.

68. N2H2, n.d.

69. Gay, Lesbian, and Straight Education Network 2001a.

70. *Consumer Reports* 2001.

71. Electronic Frontier Foundation and Online Policy Group 2003.

72. Ibid.

73. Ibid.

74. ConsumerReports.org 2005.

75. Gay, Lesbian, and Straight Education Network 2001a.

76. U.S. Department of Education 2002b.

77. *No Child Left Behind Act of 2001*, § 1425.

78. *Hate Crimes Statistics Act of 1990*, *U.S. Code* 28 (2003), § 534 (passed 1990); *No Child Left Behind Act of 2001*, § 1425.

79. *Romer v. Evans*, 517 U.S. 620 (1996).

80. National Center for Lesbian Rights and Gay, Lesbian, and Straight Education Network, n.d.b.

81. *No Child Left Behind Act of 2001*, § 1425.

82. *U.S. Code* 20 (2003), § 1232h(b).

83. *No Child Left Behind Act of 2001*, § 1425.

84. *Alaska Stat.* § 14.03.110 (Michie 2002); *N.J. Stat. Ann.* § 18A: 36-34 (West 2001); *Utah Code Ann.* § 53A-13-302 (1999).

85. State of Alaska Department of Health and Social Services 2010.

86. *No Child Left Behind Act of 2001*, § 1425.

87. Ibid.

88. Ibid.

89. Ibid.

90. *Boy Scouts of Am. v. Dale*, 530 U.S. 640 (2000); May 2001.

91. *No Child Left Behind Act of 2001*, § 9525 (equal access to public school facilities).

92. *U.S. Code* 36 (2003), § 10101.

93. *No Child Left Behind Act of 2001*, HR 1, 107th Cong., 1st sess., *Congressional Record* 147, no. 7, daily ed. (May 23, 2001): H 2618.

94. Ibid.

95. Ibid.

96. Ibid.

97. Murphy and Anders 2001.

98. Jones 2002.

99. Frank 2010.

100. *No Child Left Behind Act of 2001*, HR 1, 107th Cong., 1st sess., *Congressional Record* 147, no. 7, daily ed. (May 22, 2001): H 2535.

101. Gailey 2002.

102. *No Child Left Behind Act of 2001*, HR 1, 107th Cong., 1st sess., *Congressional Record* 147, no. 7, daily ed. (May 22, 2001): H 2535.

CHAPTER 6

1. January 2010 letter from the Sexuality Information and Education Council of the United States and other groups to President Obama and congressional leaders.

2. Brückner and Bearman 2005.

3. Sexuality Information and Education Council of the United States 2008a.

4. Ibid.

5. Sexuality Information and Education Council of the United States 2010.

6. Sexuality Information and Education Council of the United States 2008a.
7. Sexuality Information and Education Council of the United States 2008b.
8. Sexuality Information and Education Council of the United States 2008d.
9. Sexuality Information and Education Council of the United States 2007b.
10. Stein 2008.
11. Mathematica Policy Research 2007; Kirby 2001; Hauser 2004.
12. Mathematica Policy Research 2007.
13. Sexuality Information and Education Council of the United States 2007b.
14. Bearman and Brückner 2001.
15. Centers for Disease Control and Prevention 2010.
16. The examples in the text are taken from Kempner 2001a and Kempner 2001b.
17. Meenan 2003a.
18. Ibid.
19. Strunsky 2003.
20. Fouratt 2003.
21. Strunsky 2003.
22. Meenan 2003a.
23. Strunsky 2003.
24. Cogswell and Simo 2003.
25. Meenan 2003b.
26. Boykin 2003.
27. Ibid.
28. Jenny and Roesler 1994; Holmes and Slap 1998. See also "Social Science Research Finds No Link between Sexual Orientation and Child Sexual Abuse" in chapter 3.
29. Sexuality Information and Education Council of the United States 2007a.
30. Sexuality Information and Education Council of the United States 2008c.
31. Planned Parenthood 2009.
32. Centers for Disease Control and Prevention 2008a.
33. New York City Department of Health and Mental Hygiene 2009.
34. Centers for Disease Control and Prevention 2010.
35. Weinstock, Berman, and Cates 2004.
36. Guttmacher Institute 2010.
37. Kosciw, Diaz, and Greytak 2008.
38. Goodenow 2007.
39. Ryan et al. 2009.
40. Ibid.

CHAPTER 7

1. Lesbian, Gay, and Bisexual (LGB) Youth Sexual Orientation Measurement Work Group 2003.
2. This research meeting was hosted by the National Gay and Lesbian Task Force while coauthor Sean Cahill served as director of the organization's Policy Institute.
3. Kaiser 2003.

4. Fram 2003.

5. Ibid.

6. *Departments of Labor, Health and Human Services, and Education, and Related Agencies Appropriations Act of 2004,* HR 2660, 108th Cong., 1st sess., *Congressional Record* 149, no. 13, daily ed. (July 10, 2003): H 6574.

7. Setoodeh 2008.

8. Remafedi et al. 1992; Rowell 1996.

9. Barney 2004.

10. *Departments of Labor, Health and Human Services, and Education, and Related Agencies Appropriations Act of 2004,* HR 2660, 108th Cong., 1st sess., *Congressional Record* 149, no. 13, daily ed. (July 10, 2003): H 6575.

11. Krieger 2000.

12. Sell and Becker 2001.

13. Ibid.

14. Russell, Seif, and Truong 2001.

15. Reis and Saewyc 1999.

16. Sell and Becker 2001.

17. Sell 1997.

18. Friedman et al. 2004.

19. Ryan 2002.

20. Ibid.

21. Diaz 1998. Diaz's research provides an important framework for conceptualizing and conducting in-depth qualitative research.

22. Ryan 2002.

23. Babbie 2002.

24. Deshler and Ewert 1995.

25. Babbie 2002.

26. Russell, Seif, and Truong 2001.

27. Kosciw, Diaz, and Greytak 2008.

28. See, in this book's list for further reading, Putnam, Liss, and Landsverk 1996, cited in Elze 2003.

29. Fisher 1993, cited in Elze 2003.

30. Elze 2003.

31. Martin and Meezan 2003.

CHAPTER 8

1. Ryan 2000.

2. Ryan 2002.

3. Ibid.

4. See Diaz 1998; Diaz and Ayala 2001.

5. Ryan 2002.

6. Kosciw, Diaz, and Greytak 2008.

7. Russell, Seif, and Truong 2001.

8. Reis and Saewyc 1999.

9. Massachusetts Department of Education 2002.

10. Vermont Department of Health Office of Alcohol and Drug Abuse Programs 2002.

11. Noel and Sable 2009.

12. Cianciotto 2006; Dang and Frazer 2004.

13. Kosciw, Diaz, and Greytak 2008.

14. Pohan and Bailey 1997.

15. Ibid.

16. Zubowski 2009.

17. Wright 2009.

18. Zubowski 2009.

19. Rofes 1999.

20. Ibid.

21. Diaz and Ayala 2001.

22. Rofes 1999.

23. Kosciw, Diaz, and Greytak 2008.

24. Diaz and Ayala 2001.

25. Email correspondence with Connie Cordovilla, American Federation of Teachers, October 2003.

26. Griffin and Ouellett 2002.

27. Szalacha 2001b.

28. U.S. Equal Employment Opportunity Commission 2003.

29. National Center for Lesbian Rights and Gay, Lesbian, and Straight Education Network 2003.

30. Hunter 1999.

31. Russell 2005.

32. Resnick 2000; Lesbian, Gay, and Bisexual (LGB) Youth Sexual Orientation Measurement Work Group 2003.

33. Resnick et al. 1997.

34. Diaz and Ayala 2001.

35. Borowsky, Ireland, and Resnick 2001.

36. Lesbian, Gay, and Bisexual (LGB) Youth Sexual Orientation Measurement Work Group 2003.

37. ABC News.com 2000.

38. Lum, n.d.

39. Ibid.

40. Cassels 2000.

41. Lum, n.d.

42. Fuller 2002.

43. *Journal of Gay and Lesbian Issues in Education,* n.d. (see this book's list of further reading).

44. Ibid.

45. Ibid.

46. Russell 2005.

47. Ibid.

48. Ibid.

49. Lesbian, Gay, and Bisexual (LGB) Youth Sexual Orientation Measurement Work Group 2003.

CHAPTER 9

1. White House 2010.
2. Hensel 2010.
3. McKinley 2010; Burford 2010.
4. itgetsbetterproject.org, n.d.
5. Obama 2010. The video of President Obama's It Gets Better message and videos created by Vice President Biden and other members of the Obama administration are available at http://www.whitehouse.gov/issues/civil-rights/it-gets-better.
6. Schindler 2010.
7. Grossman and D'Augelli 2006.
8. Gay Men's Health Crisis 2010.

Bibliography

ABCNews.com. 2000. A profile of courage: High school athlete reveals homosexuality; Community rallies behind him. June 22. Retrieved September 29, 2003, from http://abcnews.go.com/onair/2020/2020_000622_coreyjohnson_feature.html.

ABCNews.com. 2002. Supreme Court OKs vouchers that send kids to religious schools. June 28. Retrieved August 20, 2003, from http://abcnews.go.com/sections/us/DailyNews/scotus_vouchers020627.html.

Alan Guttmacher Institute. 2003. *State policies in brief.* August 1. Retrieved August 11, 2003, from http://www.guttmacher.org/pubs/spib_SE.pdf.

American Association of University Women. 2003. Single-sex education. January. Retrieved August 8, 2003, from http://www.aauw.org/takeaction/policyissues/pdfs/SingleSexEducation.pdf.

American Association of University Women Educational Foundation. 1993. *Hostile hallways: The AAUW survey on sexual harassment in America's schools.* Washington, DC: Harris/Scholastic Research.

American Association of University Women Educational Foundation. n.d. Report finds separating by sex not the solution to gender inequality in school. Retrieved October 19, 2003, from http://www.aauw.org/about/newsroom/press_releases/sspr.cfm.

American Civil Liberties Union. 1997. Supreme Court rules: Cyberspace will be free! ACLU hails victory in Internet censorship challenge. June 26. Retrieved August 22, 2003, from http://archive.aclu.org/news/n062697a.html.

American Civil Liberties Union. 2002. *Making schools safe.* New York: American Civil Liberties Union. Electronic version.

American Civil Liberties Union. 2003a. ACLU secures sweeping changes in Arkansas school district. July 17. Retrieved July 29, 2003, from http://aclu.org/news/NewsPrint.cfm?ID=13163&c=106.

American Civil Liberties Union. 2003b. ACLU sues Arkansas school district to guarantee gay student's rights to be "out" at school. April 8. Retrieved October 7, 2003, from http://www.aclu.org/LesbianGayRights/LesbianGayRights.cfm?ID=12298&c=106.

American Civil Liberties Union. 2010. Senate introduces bill to protect LGBT students against discrimination. May 20. Retrieved September 25, 2010, from http://www.commondreams.org/newswire/2010/05/20-9.

American Civil Liberties Union Foundation. n.d. *The cost of harassment: A fact sheet for lesbian, gay, bisexual, and transgender high school students.* Retrieved

October 10, 2010, from http://www.aclu.org/files/pdfs/lgbt/schoolsyouth/costofharassment.pdf.

American Civil Liberties Union of Arkansas. 2005. 2005 legislative session. Retrieved December 6, 2006, from http://www.acluarkansas.org/Legislation/Legislation.htm.

American Civil Liberties Union of Northern California. 2003. Federal appeals court says schools must protect gay students from harassment. April 8. Retrieved October 21, 2003, from http://www.aclunc.org/pressrel/030409-flores.html.

American Federation of Teachers. n.d. Charter schools. Retrieved October 19, 2003, from http://www.aft.org/issues/charterschools.html.

American Psychiatric Association. 1997. *The diagnostic and statistical manual of the American Psychiatric Association.* 4th ed. Washington, DC: American Psychiatric Association.

Babbie, E. 2002. *The basics of social research.* Belmont, CA: Wadsworth.

Bailey, S. M. 1996. Shortchanging girls and boys. *Educational Leadership* 53 (8): 76.

Barney, D. D. 2004. Health risk-factors for gay American Indian and Alaska Native adolescent males. *Journal of Homosexuality* 46 (1/2): 137–57.

Battle, J., Cohen, C. J., Warren, D., Fergerson, G., and Audam, S. 2001. *Say it loud, I'm black and I'm proud: Black Pride Survey 2000.* New York: National Gay and Lesbian Task Force Policy Institute.

Bauermeister, J. A., Johns, M. M., Sandfort, G. M. T., Eisenberg, A., Grossman, A. H., and D'Augelli, A. R. 2010. Relationship trajectories and psychological well-being among sexual minority youth. *Journal of Youth and Adolescence* 39 (10): 1148–63.

Bearman, P., and Brückner, H. 2001. Promising the future: Virginity pledges and the transition to first intercourse. *American Journal of Sociology* 106 (4): 859–912.

Bedell, J. I. 2003. Personal liability of school officials under § 1983 who ignore peer harassment of gay students. *University of Illinois Law Review* 3:829–62.

Beeson, A. 2001. Round two: Cyber-censorship returns to Supreme Court. Retrieved August 25, 2003, from http://archive.aclu.org/court/beeson_01.html.

Bennett, L. 1997. Break the silence. *Teaching Tolerance Magazine* 12. Retrieved August 18, 2006, from http://www.tolerance.org/magazine/number-12-fall-1997/break_silence.

Bennett-Haigney, L. 1996. Young activists fight intolerance in Utah. *National NOW Times,* May. Retrieved September 30, 2003, from http://www.now.org/nnt/05-96/kelliut.html.

Biblarz, T. J., and Stacey, J. 2010. How does the gender of parents matter? *Journal of Marriage and Family* 72 (1): 3–22.

Blackless, M., Charuvastra, A., Derryck, A., Fausto-Sterling, A., Lauzanne, K., and Lee, E. 2000. How sexually dimorphic are we? *American Journal of Human Biology* 12:151–66.

Blumenfeld, W. J. 1994. "Gay/straight" alliances: Transforming pain to pride. *High School Journal* 77 (1/2): 113–21.

Bochenek, M., and Brown, A. W. 2001. *Hatred in the hallways: Violence and dis-*

crimination against lesbian, gay, bisexual, and transgender students in U.S. schools. New York: Human Rights Watch. Retrieved August 18, 2006, from http://www.hrw.org/reports/2001/uslgbt/toc.htm.

Bohn, A., and Sleeter, C. 2002. Standards and multiculturalism. *Rethinking Schools Online* 16 (3). Retrieved August 25, 2003, from http://www.rethinkingschools .org/archive/16_03/Mult163.shtml.

Bonauto, M. 2002. Background information on "no promo homo" policies. September 16. Retrieved September 25, 2010, from http://www.glsen.org/cgi-bin/iowa/all/news/record/30.html.

Bontempo, D. E., and D'Augelli, A. R. 2002. Effects of at-school victimization and sexual orientation on lesbian, gay, or bisexual youths' health risk behavior. *Journal of Adolescent Health* 30 (5): 364–74.

Borowsky, I. W., Ireland, M., and Resnick, M. D. 2001. Adolescent suicide attempts: Risks and protectors. *Pediatrics* 107 (3): 485–93.

Bos, H. M. W., van Balen, F., Gartrell, N. K., and Peyser, H. 2008. Children in planned lesbian families: A cross-cultural comparison between the United States and Netherlands. *American Journal of Orthopsychiatry* 78 (2): 211–19.

Boss, R. W. n.d. Meeting CIPA requirements with technology. Public Library Association. Retrieved September 3, 2010, from http://www.ala.org/ala/mgrps/ divs/pla/plapublications/platechnotes/internetfiltering.cfm.

Boykin, K. 2003. She didn't have to die. May 13. Retrieved October 8, 2003, from http://www.keithboykin.com/arch/000737.html.

Bronski, M. 2003. Rethinking the Harvey Milk School: Not-so-fast times at Queermont High. *Boston Phoenix*, August 8–14. Retrieved August 19, 2006, from http://www.bostonphoenix.com/boston/news_features/other_stories/ documents/03073221.asp.

Brückner, H., and Bearman, P. 2005. After the promise: The STD consequences of adolescent virginity pledges. *Journal of Adolescent Health* 36:271–78.

Bulion, L. 2000. Gay-straight alliances: Ground zero for school tolerance. December 19. Retrieved July 15, 2003, from http://www.education-world.com/a_ issues/issues149.shtml.

Burford, M. 2010. The surge in gay teen suicide. AOLHealth.com, October 12. Retrieved October 13, 2010, from http://www.aolhealth.com/2010/10/12/gay-teen-suicide-surge.

California Safe Schools Coalition. n.d.a. Legal protections for transgender and other gender non-conforming youth (Excerpted from *Beyond the binary, a tool-kit for gender identity activism in schools*). Retrieved September 21, 2010, from http://www.casafeschools.org/resourceguide/LegalProtections.html.

California Safe Schools Coalition. n.d.b. *School safety and violence prevention for lesbian, gay, bisexual, and transgender students: A question and answer guide for California school officials and administrators.* San Francisco: California Safe School Coalition. Retrieved October 9, 2010, from http://casafeschools .org/LegalQA.pdf.

California Safe Schools Coalition and Tides Center. 2005. *District policies and trainings.* California Safe Schools Research Brief No. 1. San Francisco: California Safe Schools Coalition and Tides Center. Retrieved October 10, 2010, from http://www.casafeschools.org/DistPolFACTSHEET_rev1a.pdf.

Callahan, C. J. 2001. Protecting and counseling gay and lesbian students. *Journal of Humanistic Counseling, Education, and Development* 40 (1): 5–10.

Casey, L. 2000. The charter conundrum. *Rethinking Schools Online* 14 (3). Retrieved August 29, 2003, from http://www.rethinkingschools.org/archive/14_03/char143.shtml.

Casper, V., and Schultz, S. B. 1999. *Gay parents/straight schools: Building communication and trust.* New York: Teachers College Press.

Cassels, P. 2000. A brave athlete, supportive school. *Bay Windows,* March 20.

Centers for Disease Control and Prevention. 2008. *HIV incidence.* Retrieved February 14, 2010, from http://www.cdc.gov/hiv/topics/surveillance/ incidence .htm.

Centers for Disease Control and Prevention. 2010. *2009 National Youth Risk Behavior Survey overview.* Retrieved December 8, 2010, from http://www.cdc .gov/HealthyYouth/yrbs/pdf/us_overview_yrbs.pdf.

Cianciotto, J. 2006. Hispanic and Latino same-sex couple households in the United States: A report from the 2000 census. In M. Dupuis and W. A. Thompson, eds., *Defending Same-Sex Marriage,* vol. 3, *The Freedom-to-Marry Movement: Education, Advocacy, Culture, and the Media.* Westport, CT: Praeger.

Clair, R. n.d. Making school safe for queer kids. *Curve.* Retrieved October 16, 2003, from http://www.curvemag.com/Detailed/7.html.

Clatts, M. C., Goldsamt, L., Yi, H., and Gwadz, M. V. 2005. Homelessness and drug abuse among young men who have sex with men in New York City: A preliminary epidemiological trajectory. *Journal of Adolescence* 28 (2): 201–14.

Cloud, J. 1998. Trans across America: Watch out, Pat Buchanan; Ridiculed for years, "transgenders" are emerging as the newest group to demand equality. *Time,* July 20.

Cochran, B. N., Stewart, A. J., Ginzler, J. A., and Cauce, A. M. 2002. Challenges faced by homeless sexual minorities: Comparison of gay, lesbian, bisexual, and transgender homeless adolescents with their heterosexual counterparts. *American Journal of Public Health* 92 (5): 773–76.

Cogswell, K., and Simo, A. 2003. Erasing Sakia: Who's to blame? *Gully,* June 6. Retrieved October 14, 2003, from http://www.thegully.com/essays/gay mundo/030606_sakia_gunn_murder.html.

Consumer Reports. 2001. Digital chaperones for kids: Which Internet filters protect the best? Which get in the way? March. Retrieved October 19, 2003, from http://www.consumerreports.org/main/content/display_report.jsp?FOLDER percent3C percent3Efolder_id=348251&bmUID=1066584995177.

ConsumerReports.org. 2005. Filtering software: Better, but still fallible. June. Retrieved September 3, 2010, from http://hs.yarmouth.k12.me.us/Pages/ YSD_YHSTechnology/presources/ConsumerReports.FilteringSo.pdf.

Corliss, H. L., Rosario, M., Wypij, D., Fisher, L. B., and Austin, S. B. 2008. Sexual orientation disparities in longitudinal alcohol use patterns among adolescents: Findings from the growing up today study. *Archives of Pediatric and Adolescent Medicine* 162 (11): 1071–78.

Currah, P., and Minter, S. 2001. *Transgender equality: A handbook for activists and policymakers.* New York: National Gay and Lesbian Task Force and National Center for Lesbian Rights.

Daily News. 2003. School's gay, that's okay. Editorial. August 7, 26.

Dang, A., and Frazer, S. 2004. *Black same-sex households in the United States: A report from the 2000 census.* New York: National Gay and Lesbian Task Force Policy Institute and the National Black Justice Coalition.

Datnow, A., Hubbard, L., and Woody, E. 2001. Is single gender schooling viable in the public sector? Unpublished report, University of Illinois, Champaign-Urbana.

D'Augelli, A. R. 1996. Enhancing the development of lesbian, gay, and bisexual youths. In E. Rothblum and L. Bonds, eds., *Prevention of heterosexism and homophobia.* Newbury Park, CA: Sage.

D'Augelli, A. R. 1998. Developmental implications of victimization of lesbian, gay, and bisexual youths. In G. M. Herek, ed., *Stigma and Sexual Orientation.* Newbury Park, CA: Sage.

D'Augelli, A. R., Grossman, A. H., Salter, N. P., Vasey, J. J., Starks, M. T., and Sinclair, K. O. 2005. Predicting suicide attempts of lesbian, gay, and bisexual youth. *Suicide and Life-Threatening Behavior* 35 (6): 646–61.

D'Augelli, A. R., Grossman, A. H., and Starks, M. T. 2006. Childhood gender atypicality, victimization, and PTSD among lesbian, gay, and bisexual youth. *Journal of Interpersonal Violence* 21 (11): 1462–82.

D'Augelli, A. R., Hershberger, S. L., and Pilkington, N. W. 1998. Lesbian, gay, and bisexual youth and their families: Disclosure of sexual orientation and its consequences. *American Journal of Orthopsychiatry* 68 (3): 361–71.

D'Augelli, A. R., and Patterson, C. J., eds. 2001. *Lesbian, gay, and bisexual identities and youth: Psychological perspectives.* New York: Oxford University Press.

D'Augelli, A. R., Pilkington, N. W., and Hershberger, S. L. 2002. Incidence and mental health impact of sexual orientation victimization of lesbian, gay, and bisexual youths in high school. *School Psychology Quarterly* 17 (2): 148–67.

Deshler, D., and Ewert, M. 1995. Participatory action research: Traditions and major assumptions. Retrieved September 15, 2011, from http://www.Actmad.net/Madness_library/POV/DESHLER.PAR.

Diaz, E. M., and Kosciw, J. G. 2009. *Shared differences: The experiences of lesbian, gay, bisexual, and transgender students of color in our nation's schools.* New York: Gay, Lesbian, and Straight Education Network.

Diaz, R. 1998. *Latino gay men and HIV: Culture, sexuality, and risk behavior.* New York: Routledge.

Diaz, R., and Ayala, G. 2001. *Social discrimination and health: The case of Latino gay men and HIV risk.* New York: National Gay and Lesbian Task Force Policy Institute.

Di Ceglie, D., Freedman, D., McPherson, S., and Richardson, P. 2002. Children and adolescents referred to a specialist gender identity development service: Clinical features and demographic characteristics. *International Journal of Transgenderism* 6 (1): 14–20. Retrieved July 30, 2003, from http://www.symposion.com/ijt/ijtvo06no01_01.htm.

Dube, E. M., and Savin-Williams, R. C. 1999. Sexual identity development among ethnic sexual-minority male youths. *Developmental Psychology* 35 (6): 1389–98.

DuRant, R. H., Krowchuk, D. P., and Sinal, S. H. 1998. Victimization, use of violence, and drug use at school among male adolescents who engage in same-sex sexual behavior. *Journal of Pediatrics* 133 (1): 113–18.

Edwards, W. 1996. A sociological analysis of an invisible minority group: Male adolescent homosexuals. *Youth and Society* 27 (3): 229–51.

Electronic Frontier Foundation and Online Policy Group. 2003. *Internet blocking in public schools: A study of Internet access in educational institutions*. San Francisco, CA: Electronic Frontier Foundation and Online Policy Group. Retrieved August 25, 2003, from http://www.eff.org/Censorship/Censorware/net _block_report/net_block_report.pdf.

Elze, D. E. 2003. 8,000 miles and still counting . . . : Reaching gay, lesbian, and bisexual adolescents for research. In W. Meezan and J. I. Martin, eds., *Research methods with gay, lesbian, bisexual, and transgender populations*. Binghamton, NY: Haworth.

Family Research Council. 2003. Prevention of harassment and intimidation in public schools (HB 345): Hearings before the Ways and Means Committee of the Maryland House of Delegates (testimony of Peter Sprigg). Retrieved October 17, 2003, from http://www.frc.org/get.cfm?i=TS03C1.

Faulkner, A. H., and Cranston, K. 1998. Correlates of same-sex behavior in a random sample of Massachusetts high school students. *American Journal of Public Health* 88 (2): 262–66.

Feinstein, R., Greenblatt, A., Hass, L., Kohn, S., and Rana, J. 2001. *Justice for all: A report on lesbian, gay, bisexual, and transgendered youth in the New York juvenile justice system*. New York: Urban Justice Center.

Ferrero, E., Freker, J., and Foster, T. 2002. *Too high a price: The case against restricting gay parenting*. New York: ACLU Lesbian and Gay Rights Project.

Finerman, S. 2001. Sexual minority students and peer sexual harassment in high school. *Journal of School Social Work* 11 (2): 50–69.

Finerman, S. 2002. Sexual harassment between same-sex peers: Intersection of mental health, homophobia, and sexual violence in schools. *Social Work* 47 (1): 65–74.

Finerman, S., and Bennett, L. 1998. Implications of peer sexual harassment between same-sex teens. Paper presented at the International Social Work Research Conference, Miami, FL.

Finkelhor, D. 1994. The future of children: Sexual abuse of children. *Journal of Psychology and Human Sexuality* 4 (2): 46–47.

Finn, C. E., Manno, B. V., and Vanourek, G. 2000. *Charter schools in action: Renewing public education*. Princeton, NJ: Princeton University Press.

Fisher, C. B. 1993. Integrating science and ethics in research with high-risk children and youth. *Social Policy Report* (Society for Research in Child Development) 7 (4): 1–27.

Fleming, J. 2000. Affirmative action and standardized test scores. *Journal of Negro Education* 69 (1–2): 27–37.

Fontaine, J. 1998. Evidencing a need: School counselors' experiences with gay and lesbian students. *Professional School Counseling* 1 (3): 8–14.

Fouratt, J. 2003. Thousands mourn Sakia. *Gay City News*, May 23–29.

Fram, A. 2003. House rejects conservative bid to block four federal grants for sex research. Associated Press, July 10.

Frank, N. 2010. *Don't ask, don't tell: Detailing the damage.* Santa Barbara, CA: Palm Center, University of California–Santa Barbara. Retrieved September 8, 2010, from http://www.palmcenter.org/files/DetailingCostofDADT.pdf.

Friedman, M. 2010. N.J. Assembly, Senate pass "Anti-Bullying Bill of Rights" in wake of Tyler Clementi's death. nj.com, November 22. Retrieved December 8, 2010, from http://www.nj.com/news/index.ssf/2010/11/nj_assembly_passes_anti-bullyi.html.

Friedman, M. S., Silvestre, A. J., Gold, M. A., Markovic, N., Savin-Williams, R. C., Huggins, J., and Sell, R. L. 2004. Adolescents define sexual orientation and suggest ways to measure it. *Journal of Adolescence* 27 (3): 303–17.

Fuller, D. 2002. A new dimension in snapshot of gay teenagers. *New York Times,* December 24, 7.

Gailey, P. 2002. Schools shouldn't be wary of military recruiters. *St. Petersburg (FL) Times,* December 1, 3D.

Gandy, K. 2002. Segregation won't help. *USA Today,* May 10. Available at http://www.now.org/press/inTheNews/20020510.html.

Gardner, R. 2002. Destination graduation: Dropout prevention New York State style. Paper presented at the annual conference of the Centers for Disease Control and Prevention, Division of Adolescent and School Health, Washington, DC.

Garner, A. 2002. Don't "protect" me; give me your respect. *Newsweek,* February 11.

Garofalo, R., Wolf, R. C., Kessel, S., Palfrey, J., and DuRand, R. H. 1998. The association between health risk behaviors and sexual orientation among a school-based sample of adolescents. *Pediatrics* 101 (5): 895–902.

Garofalo, R., Wolf, R. C., Wissow, L. S., Woods, E. R., and Goodman, E. 1999. Sexual orientation and risk of suicide attempts among a representative sample of youth. *Archives of Pediatrics and Adolescent Medicine* 153 (15): 487–501.

Gartrell, N., and Bos, H. 2010. US national longitudinal lesbian family study: Psychological adjustment of 17-year-old adolescents. *Pediatrics* 126 (1): 28–36.

Gartrell, N., Rodas, C., Deck, A., Peyser, H., and Banks, A. 2005. The national lesbian family study: 4. Interviews with the 10-year-old children. *American Journal of Orthopsychiatry* 75 (4): 518–24.

Gates, G. J. 2010. *Sexual minorities in the 2008 General Social Survey: Coming out and demographic characteristics.* Los Angeles: Williams Institute. Retrieved January 23, 2010, from http://www2.law.ucla.edu/williamsinstitute/pdf/Sexual-Minorities-2008-GSS.pdf.

Gay, Lesbian, and Straight Education Network. 2001a. *Internet filtering software.* Retrieved September 3, 2010, from http://www.glsen.org/binary-data/GLSEN_ATTACHMENTS/file/282-1.PDF.

Gay, Lesbian, and Straight Education Network. 2001b. Parental "choice," school "choice," and school vouchers. Retrieved August 20, 2006, from http://www.glsen.org/cgi-bin/iowa/all/library/record/513.html.

Gay, Lesbian, and Straight Education Network. 2004a. GLSEN decries Alabama lawmaker's homophobic bill to ban and destroy books. December 2. Retrieved January 24, 2005, from http://www.glsen.org/cgi-bin/iowa/all.library/record/1755.html.

Gay, Lesbian, and Straight Education Network. 2004b. *State of the states, 2004: A policy analysis of lesbian, gay, bisexual, and transgender (LGBT) safer schools issues.* New York: Gay, Lesbian, and Straight Education Network. Retrieved September 23, 2010, from http://www.glsen.org/binary-data/GLSEN_ATTACH MENTS/file/338-3.PDF.

Gay, Lesbian, and Straight Education Network. 2007. *Gay-straight alliances: Creating safer schools for LGBT students and their allies.* GLSEN Research Brief. New York: Gay, Lesbian, and Straight Education network. Retrieved October 11, 2010, from http://www.glsen.org/binary-data/GLSEN_ATTACHMENTS/ file/000/000/930-1.pdf.

Gay, Lesbian, and Straight Education Network. 2009a. *The experiences of lesbian, gay, bisexual and transgender middle school students.* GLSEN Research Brief. New York: Gay, Lesbian, and Straight Education Network. Retrieved September 1, 2010, from http://www.glsen.org/binary-data/GLSEN_ATTACH MENTS/file/000/001/1475-1.pdf.

Gay, Lesbian, and Straight Education Network. 2009b. Sirdeaner Walker testimony at strengthening school safety through prevention of bullying hearing. July 8. Retrieved September 25, 2010, from http://www.glsen.org/cgi- bin/iowa/all/news/record/2450.html.

Gay, Lesbian, and Straight Education Network. n.d.a. About gay-straight alliances (GSAs). Retrieved August 20, 2003, from http://GLSEN.org/templates/stu dent/record.html?section=48&record=145.

Gay, Lesbian, and Straight Education Network. n.d.b. Background and information about gay-straight alliances. Retrieved January 13, 2010, from http:// www.glsen.org/cgi-bin/iowa/all/library/record/2336.html.

Gay, Lesbian, and Straight Education Network and Harris Interactive. 2008. *The principal's perspective: School safety, bullying, and harassment: A survey of public school principals.* New York: Gay, Lesbian, and Straight Education Network and Harris Interactive.

Gay Men's Health Crisis. 2010. *New York City policy agenda 2010–2011.* Retrieved September 14, 2011, from http://www.gmhc.org/files/editor/file/a_pa_city agenda2010(1).pdf.

Gender PAC. 2002. Time for schools to stand up to gender stereotyping in the classroom. July 15. Retrieved August 2, 2002, from http://www.gpac.org/ archive/news/index.html?cmd=view&archive=news&msgnum=0411.

Georgia Department of Education. 2010. *Policy for prohibiting bullying, harassment and intimidation.* Retrieved September 20, 2011, from http://public .doe.k12.ga.us/.

Gibson, P. 1989. Gay male and lesbian youth suicide. In *Report of the Secretary's Task Force on Youth Suicide* (DHHS Publication No. ADM 89-1623), vol. 3, pp. 3-110–3-142. Washington, DC: Department of Health and Human Services.

Gilliam, J. 2002. Respecting the rights of LGBTQ youth, a responsibility of youth- serving professionals. *Transitions: A Newsletter of Advocates for Youth* 14 (4): 1–2.

Ginsberg, R. 1999. In the triangle/out of the circle: Gay and lesbian students facing the heterosexual paradigm. *Educational Forum* 64:46–56.

Goldstein, N. 2001. *Zero indifference: A how-to guide for ending name-calling in schools.* New York: Gay, Lesbian, and Straight Education Network. Retrieved August 19, 2006, from http://www.glsen.org/cgi-bin/iowa/all/library/record/850.html.

Goodenow, C. 2007. Protective and risk factors for HIV-related behavior among adolescent MSM. Paper presented at the National HIV Prevention Conference, Atlanta, GA.

Green, R. 1998. Transsexuals' children. *International Journal of Transgenderism* 2 (3). Retrieved August 30, 2011, from http://www.iiav.nl/ezines/web/IJT/97-03/numbers/symposium/ijtc0601.htm.

Greene, B. 1997. Ethnic minority lesbians and gay men. In B. Greene, ed., *Ethnic and cultural diversity among lesbians and gay men.* Thousand Oaks, CA: Sage.

Greytak, E. A., and Kosciw, J. G. 2010. *Year one evaluation of the New York City Department of Education Respect for All training program.* New York: Gay, Lesbian, and Straight Education Network. Retrieved October 10, 2010, from http://www.glsen.org/binary-data/GLSEN_ATTACHMENTS/file/000/001/1633-2.PDF.

Greytak, E. A., Kosciw, J. G., and Diaz, E. M. 2009. *Harsh realities: The experiences of transgender youth in our nation's schools.* New York: Gay, Lesbian, and Straight Education Network. Retrieved September 23, 2010, from http://www.glsen.org/binary-data/GLSEN_ATTACHMENTS/file/000/001/1375-1.pdf.

Griffin, P. 1992. From hiding out to coming out: Empowering lesbian and gay educators. In K. Harbeck, ed., *Coming out of the classroom closet.* New York: Haworth.

Griffin, P., Lee, C., Waugh, J., and Beyer, C. 2003. Describing roles that gay-straight alliances play in schools: From individual support to school change. *Journal of Gay and Lesbian Issues in Education* 1 (3): 7–22.

Griffin, P., and Ouellett, M. L. 2002. Going beyond gay-straight alliances to make schools safe for lesbian, gay, bisexual, and transgender students. *Angles* 6 (1): 1–8.

Grossman, A. H., and D'Augelli, A. R. 2006. Transgender youth: Invisible and vulnerable. *Journal of Homosexuality* 51 (1): 111–28.

Grossman, A. H., and D'Augelli, A. R. 2007. Transgender youth and life-threatening behaviors. *Suicide and Life-Threatening Behavior* 37 (5): 527–37.

Groth, A. N., and Birnbaum, H. J. 1978. Adult sexual orientation and attraction to underage persons. *Archives of Sexual Behavior* 7 (3): 175–81.

Grov, C., Bimbi, D. S., Nain, J. E., and Parsons, J. T. 2006. Race, ethnicity, gender, and generational factors associated with the coming-out process among gay, lesbian, and bisexual individuals. *Journal of Sex Research* 43 (2): 115–21.

GSA Network. n.d. GSA directory. Retrieved September 25, 2010, from http://gsanetwork.org/civicrm/profile?q=civicrm/profile&force=1&gid=5&crmRowCount=10000.

Guttmacher Institute. 2010. *State policies in brief: Sex and STI/HIV education.* January 1. Retrieved February 14, 2010, from http://www.guttmacher.org/statecenter/spibs/spib_SE.pdf.

Harris, M. B. 1997. *School experiences of gay and lesbian youth: The invisible minority.* New York: Harrington Park.

Hauser, D. 2004. *Five years of abstinence-only-until-marriage education: Assessing the impact.* Washington, DC: Advocates for Youth. Retrieved December 8, 2010, from http://www.advocatesforyouth.org/index.php?option=com_content&task=view&id=623&Itemid=177.

Heins, M., Cho, C., and Feldman, A. 2006. *Internet filters: A public policy report.* 2nd ed. New York: Brennan Center for Justice at NYU School of Law. Retrieved October 10, 2010, from http://www.fepproject.org/policyreports/filters2.pdf.

Hensel, K. 2010. Teen suicide victim hangs himself from barn rafters. WISHTV.com, September 16. Retrieved December 8, 2010, from http://www.wishtv.com/dpp/news/local/east_central/teen-suicide-victim-hangs-himself-from-barn-rafters.

Herdt, G., and Boxer, A. 1996. *Children of horizons.* 2nd ed. Boston: Beacon.

Hetrick-Martin Institute. n.d.a. About HMI and HMS. Retrieved August 22, 2003, from http://www.hmi.org/GeneralInfoAndDonations/AboutHMIAndHMS/default.aspx.

Hetrick-Martin Institute. n.d.b. The Harvey Milk High School. Retrieved September 25, 2010, from http://www.hmi.org/Page.aspx?pid=230.

Hetrick-Martin Institute. n.d.c. LGBTQ youth statistics. Retrieved August 22, 2003, from http://www.hmi.org/Community/LGBTQYouthStatistics/default.aspx.

Holmes, W. C., and Slap, G. B. 1998. Sexual abuse of boys: Definitions, prevalence, correlates, sequelae, and management. *Journal of the American Medical Association* 280 (21): 1855–62.

Human Rights Campaign. 2010a. Safe schools improvement act. June 28. Retrieved September 25, 2010, from http://www.hrc.org/laws_and_elections/12142.htm.

Human Rights Campaign. 2010b. Statewide school laws and policies. June 24. Map. Retrieved September 25, 2010, from http://www.hrc.org/documents/school_laws.pdf.

Human Rights Campaign. 2010c. Student non-discrimination act. June 28. Retrieved September 25, 2010, from http://www.hrc.org/laws_and_elections/14126.htm.

Human Rights Resource Center. 2000. *Lesbian, gay, bisexual, and transgender rights: A human rights perspective, activity 3.* Retrieved October 21, 2003, from http://www1.umn.edu/humanrts/edumat/hreduseries/TB3/act3/act3f.htm.

Human Rights Watch. 2002. *Ignorance Only: HIV/AIDS, Human Rights, and Federally Funded Abstinence-Only Programs in the United States; Texas: A Case Study.* Reports: United States, vol. 14, no. 5(G). Retrieved August 19, 2006, from http://hrw.org/reports/2002/usa0902/.

Hunter, J. 1999. Beyond risk: Refocus research on coping. *Journal of the Gay and Lesbian Medical Association* 3 (3): 75–76.

Hunter, J., and Mallon, G. P. 2000. Lesbian, gay, and bisexual adolescent development: Dancing with your feet tied together. In B. Greene and G. L. Croom, eds., *Education research and practice in lesbian, gay, bisexual, and transgendered psychology.* Thousand Oaks, CA: Sage.

Hunter, J., and Schaecher, R. 1987. Stressors on lesbian and gay adolescents in schools. *Social Work in Education* 9 (3): 180–90.

Intersex Society of North America. 2003. Frequency: How common are intersex conditions? Retrieved August 4, 2003, from http://www.isna.org/faq/frequency.html.

Intersex Society of North America. n.d. What is an intersex condition? What do these diagnoses mean? Retrieved October 18, 2003, from http://www.isna.org/faq/faq-medical.html#what.

Irvine, J. M. 2001. Educational reform and sexual identity. In A. R. D'Augelli and C. J. Patterson, eds., *Lesbian, gay, and bisexual identities and youth.* New York: Oxford University Press.

itgetsbetterproject.org. n.d. What is the It Gets Better Project? Retrieved December 8, 2010, from http://www.itgetsbetter.org/pages/about-it-gets-better-project/.

James, S. D. 2009. When words can kill: "That's so gay." ABCNews.com, April 14. Retrieved February 14, 2010, from http://abcnews.go.com/Health/Mind MoodNews/story?id=7328091&page=1.

Jenny, C., and Roesler, T. A. 1994. Are children at risk for sexual abuse by homosexuals? *Pediatrics* 94 (1): 44.

Johnson, M. J. 2000. Letter to the House and Senate on Internet blocking/filtering requirements. July 25. Retrieved August 20, 2003, from http://www.aclu.org/news/NewsPrint.cfm?ID=8968&c=252.

Johnson, S. M., and O'Conner, E. 2002. *The gay baby boom.* New York: New York University Press.

Jones, C. T. 2002. [Dear colleague letter]. March 25. Retrieved August 11, 2003, from http://www.ed.gov/offices/OCR/boyscouts_letter.html.

Jordan, K. M. 2000. Substance abuse among gay, lesbian, bisexual, transgender, and questioning adolescents. *School Psychology Review* 29 (2): 201–6.

Journal of Gay and Lesbian Issues in Education. n.d. Beyond risk: Resilience in the lives of sexual minority youth. Call for papers and forthcoming thematic special feature. Retrieved August 20, 2006, from http://www.jtsears.com/JGLI Ethemes4.htm.

Joyner, C. 2010. Miss. school district settles lesbian prom-date case. *USA Today,* July 20. Retrieved September 25, 2010, from http://www.usatoday.com/news/nation/2010-07-20-lesbian-prom-lawsuit_N.htm.

Kaiser, J. 2003. Politics and biomedicine: Studies of gay men, prostitutes come under scrutiny. *Science* 300:403.

Keaton, P. 2010. *Numbers and types of public elementary and secondary education agencies from the Common Core of Data: School year 2008–09* (NCES 2010-346). Table 2. Number of operating public elementary and secondary local education agencies and number of students in membership, by agency type and state or jurisdiction: School year 2008–09. National Center of Education Statistics, Institute of Education Sciences, U.S. Department of Education. Washington, DC. Retrieved September 15, 2011, from http://nces.ed.gov/pubs2010/2010346.pdf.

Kempner, M. 2001a. Controversy over CDC's Research to Classroom Project. *SIECUS Report* 29 (6): 9–11.

Kempner, M. 2001b. State-level debates over abstinence-only-until-marriage. *SIECUS Report* 29 (6): 7.

Kirby, D. 2001. *Emerging answers: Research findings on programs to reduce teen pregnancy.* Washington, DC: National Campaign to Prevent Teen Pregnancy. Retrieved December 8, 2010, from http://www.thenationalcampaign.org/EA2007/EA2007_full.pdf.

Kissen, R. 1999. Children of the future age: Lesbians and gay parents talk about school. In W. J. Letts and J. T. Sears, eds., *Queering elementary education: Advancing the dialogue about sexualities and schooling.* New York: Rowman and Littlefield.

Kitts, R. L. 2005. Gay adolescents and suicide: Understanding the association. *Adolescence* 40 (159): 621–29.

Kosciw, J. G., and Diaz, E. M. 2008. *Involved, invisible, ignored: The experiences of lesbian, gay, bisexual, and transgender parents and their children in our nation's K–12 schools.* New York: Gay, Lesbian, and Straight Education Network. Retrieved September 25, 2010, from http://www.glsen.org/binary-data/GLSEN_ATTACHMENTS/file/000/001/1104-1.pdf.

Kosciw, J. G., Diaz, E. M., and Greytak, E. A. 2008. *2007 National School Climate Survey: The experiences of lesbian, gay, bisexual and transgender youth in our nation's schools.* New York: Gay, Lesbian, and Straight Education Network. Retrieved July 23, 2010, from http://www.glsen.org/binary-data/GLSEN_AT TACHMENTS/file/000/001/1290-1.pdf.

Krieger, N. 2000. Counting accountability: Implications of the new approaches to classifying race/ethnicity in the 2000 census. *American Journal of Public Health* 90 (11):1687–89.

Lambda Legal Defense and Education Fund. 1996a. *Nabozny v. Podlesny.* Retrieved July 28, 2003, from http://www.lambdalegal.org/cgi-bin/iowa/cases/record?record=54.

Lambda Legal Defense and Education Fund. 1996b. *Romer v. Evans.* Retrieved October 9, 2010, from http://www.lambdalegal.org/in-court/cases/romer-v-evans.html.

Lambda Legal Defense and Education Fund. 2001. *Youth in the margins.* New York: Lambda Legal Defense and Education Fund.

Lambda Legal Defense and Education Fund and Gay, Lesbian, and Straight Education Network. 2001. *A guide to effective statewide laws/policies: Preventing discrimination against LGBT students in K–12 schools.* New York: Lambda Legal Defense and Education Fund and Gay, Lesbian, and Straight Education Network. Retrieved August 18, 2006, from http://www.lambdalegal.org/binary-data/LAMBDA_PDF/pdf/61.pdf.

Leach, C. 2002. Transgender youth and the role of service providers. *Transitions: A Newsletter of Advocates for Youth* 14 (4): 12–13.

Leck, G. M. 2000. Heterosexual or homosexual? Reconsidering binary narratives on sexual identities in urban schools. *Education and Urban Society* 32 (3): 324–48.

Lee, C. 2002. The impact of belonging to a high school gay/straight alliance. *High School Journal* 85 (3): 13–26.

Lemp, G. F., Hirozawa, A. M., Givertz, D., Nieri, G. N., Anderson, L., Lindegren, M. L.,

Janssen, R. S., and Katz, M. 1994. Seroprevalence of HIV and risk behaviors among young homosexual and bisexual men: The San Francisco/Berkeley Young Men's Survey. *Journal of the American Medical Association* 272 (6): 449–54.

Lesbian, Gay, and Bisexual (LGB) Youth Sexual Orientation Measurement Work Group. 2003. *Measuring sexual orientation of young people in health research.* San Francisco: Gay and Lesbian Medical Association. Retrieved September 16, 2003, from http://www.stophiv.com/lgbtc/measure_young2003.pdf.

Letts, W. J., and Sears, J. T. 1999. *Queering elementary education: Advancing the dialogue about sexualities and schooling.* New York: Rowman and Littlefield.

Lewin, T. 2003. Arkansas school is accused of harassing a gay student. *New York Times,* March 25. Retrieved October 7, 2003, from http://www.nytimes.com/2003/03/25/education/25GAY.html.

Lipkin, A. 1994. The case for a gay and lesbian curriculum. *High School Journal* 77 (1/2): 95–107.

Lipkin, A. 1999. Know sexual identity, homosexual adjustment issues before counseling LGBT youth. *Brown University Child and Adolescent Behavior Letter* 15 (12): 1.

Lum, M. n.d. Corey Johnson: Confident, courageous, and coming to Texas. Retrieved September 29, 2003, from http://www.txtriangle.com/archive/921/coverstory.htm.

Macgillivray, I. K. 2004. *Sexual orientation and school policy: A practical guide for teachers, administrators, and community activists.* New York: Rowman and Littlefield.

MacGillivray, I. K. 2007. *Gay-straight alliances: A handbook for students, educators, and parents.* New York: Harrington Park.

Macgillivray, I. K., and Jennings, T. 2008. A content analysis exploring lesbian, gay, bisexual, and transgender topics in foundations of education textbooks. *Journal of Teacher Education* 59 (2): 170–89.

Mallon, G. P. 1998. *We don't exactly get the welcome wagon: The experiences of gay and lesbian adolescents in child welfare systems.* New York: Columbia University Press.

Mallon, G. P. 1999. *Social services with transgendered youth.* Binghamton, NY: Harrington Park.

Martin, J. I., and Meezan, W. 2003. Applying ethical standards to research and evaluations involving lesbian, gay, bisexual, and transgender populations. In W. Meezan and J. I. Martin, eds., *Research methods with gay, lesbian, bisexual, and transgender populations.* Binghamton, NY: Haworth.

Massachusetts Department of Education. 1999. *Massachusetts high school students and sexual orientation results of the 1999 Youth Risk Behavior Survey.* Boston: Massachusetts Department of Education. Electronic version.

Massachusetts Department of Education. 2000. *1999 Massachusetts Youth Risk Behavior Study.* Boston: Massachusetts Department of Education. Electronic version.

Massachusetts Department of Education. 2002. *2001 Massachusetts Youth Risk Behavior Survey results.* Malden, MA: Massachusetts Department of Education. Retrieved August 18, 2006, from http://www.doe.mass.edu/cnp/hprograms/yrbs/.

Mathematica Policy Research. 2007. *Impacts of four Title V, Section 510 abstinence education programs.* Princeton, NJ: Mathematica Policy Research. Retrieved February 14, 2010, from http://www.mathematica-mpr.com/publications/pdfs/impactabstinence.pdf.

May, M. 2001. Conservative caveats threaten schools: They lose millions if scouts are banned from using space. *San Francisco Chronicle,* December 23, A3.

Mays, V. M., Chatters, L. M., Cochran, S. D., and Mackness, J. 1998. African American families in diversity: Gay men and lesbians as participants in family networks. *Journal of Comparative Family Studies* 29 (1): 73–87.

McCready, L. 2001. When fitting in isn't an option, or Why black queer males at a California high school stay away from Project 10. In K. K. Kumashiro, ed., *Troubling intersections of race and sexuality: Queer students of color and anti-oppressive education.* New York: Rowman and Littlefield.

McGuire, J. K., Dixon, A., and Russell, S. T. 2009. *School safety for middle school students.* California Safe Schools Coalition Research Brief No. 11. San Francisco: California Safe Schools Coalition. Retrieved September 25, 2010, from http://casafeschools.org/CSSC_Research_Brief_11.pdf.

McKinley, J. 2010. Suicides put light on pressures of gay teenagers. *New York Times,* October 3. Retrieved October 13, 2010, from http://www.nytimes.com/2010/10/04/us/04suicide.html?_r=1&scp=1&sq=gay%20suicide&st=cse.

Meek, J. 2000. Brockton students protect transgendered classmate. *Brockton (MA) Enterprise,* November 17.

Meenan, M. 2003a. Lesbian teen dies in hate stabbing. *Gay City News,* May 16–23.

Meenan, M. 2003b. Tears and then, perhaps, respect. *Gay City News,* May 23–29.

Meyer, E. J. 2010. *Gender and sexual diversity in schools.* Explorations of Educational Purpose, vol. 10. New York: Springer.

Miner, B. 1998. Internet filtering: Beware the cyber censors. *Rethinking Schools Online* 12 (4). Available at http://www.rethinkingschools.org/restrict.asp?path=archive/12_04/net.shtml.

Moon, M. W., McFarland, W., Kellogg, T., Baxter, M., Katz, M. H., MacKellar, D., and Valleroy, L. A. 2000. HIV risk behavior of runaway youth in San Francisco: Age of onset and relation to sexual orientation. *Youth and Society* 32 (2): 184–212.

Mosher, W., Chandra, A., and Jones, J. 2005. *Sexual Behavior and Selected Health Measures: Men and Women 15–44 Years of Age, United States, 2002.* Advance Data from Vital and Health Statistics No. 362. Hyattsville, MD: U.S. Department of Health and Human Services, Centers for Disease Control and Prevention.

Mottet, L. 2004. The education and policy needs of transgender individuals. *SIECUS Report* 32 (4): 35–38.

Munoz-Plaza, C., Quinn, S., and Rounds, K. 2002. Lesbian, gay, bisexual, and transgender students: Perceived social support in the high school environment. *High School Journal* 85 (4): 52–63.

Murphy, L., and Anders, C. 2001. Letter to the Senate on First Amendment issues in Sen. Helms' "Boy Scouts of America Equal Access Act" amendment to ESEA. May 21. Retrieved July 29, 2003, from http://www.aclu.org/news/NewsPrint.cfm?ID=284&c=106.

Nathan, J. 1999. *Charter schools: Creating hope and opportunity for American education.* San Francisco: Jossey-Bass.

National Association for Multicultural Education. 2003. Resolutions and position papers. February 1. Retrieved July 15, 2003, from http://www.nameorg.org/resolutions/definition.html.

National Center for Lesbian Rights. 2002. *Harassment and discrimination: A legal overview.* Retrieved October 16, 2003, from http://www.nclrights.org/publications/pubs/harass-overview0902.pdf.

National Center for Lesbian Rights and Gay, Lesbian, and Straight Education Network. n.d.a. *Fifteen expensive reasons why safe schools legislation is in your state's best interest.* Retrieved September 25, 2010, from http://www.nclrights.org/site/DocServer/15reasons.pdf?docID=1621.

National Center for Lesbian Rights and Gay, Lesbian, and Straight Education Network. n.d.b. *Inclusion of enumerated categories in safe school legislation/policies.* Retrieved September 2, 2003, from http://www.nclrights.org/publications/pubs/inclusion.pdf.

National Education Association. 2002. *Report of the NEA task force on sexual orientation.* Retrieved August 21, 2003, from http://www.nea.org/nr/02taskforce.html.

National Education Association. n.d. Charter schools. Retrieved October 19, 2003, from http://www.nea.org/charter/.

National Safe Schools Partnership. 2007. *Bridging the gap in federal law: Promoting safe schools and improved student achievement by preventing bullying and harassment in our schools.* Retrieved September 25, 2010, from http://www.glsen.org/binary-data/GLSEN_ATTACHMENTS/file/000/000/912-1.pdf.

Nesmith, A., Burton, D. L., and Cosgrove, T. J. 1999. Gay, lesbian, and bisexual youth and young adults: Social support in their own words. *Journal of Homosexuality* 37:95–108.

Newman, B. S., and Muzzonigro, P. G. 1993. The effects of traditional family values on the coming out process of gay male adolescents. *Adolescence* 23 (109): 213–27.

New York City Department of Education. 2009. Mayor, chancellor, and city council speaker announce expansion of anti-harassment initiative in city schools: Second phase of "Respect for All" initiative expands trainings for school staff, creates new accountability standards. October 2. Retrieved October 11, 2010, from http://schools.nyc.gov/Offices/mediarelations/NewsandSpeeches/2009-2010/Anti-Harassment_initiative_expansion.htm.

New York City Department of Education. 2010. Department of Education launches first annual "Respect For All Week": Respect for All Week will kick off on March 8 and run through March 12, 2010. March 8. Retrieved October 10, 2010, from http://schools.nyc.gov/Offices/mediarelations/NewsandSpeeches/2009-2010/rfaweek030810.htm.

New York City Department of Health and Mental Hygiene. 2009. *HIV epidemiology and field services semiannual report.* October. Retrieved February 14, 2010, from http://www.nyc.gov/html/doh/downloads/pdf/dires/dires-2009-report-semi2.pdf.

New York Times. 2003. The Harvey Milk High School. Editorial. August 3.

No Child Left Behind Act of 2001. 115 *U.S.C.* (2002).

Noel, A. M., and Sable, J. 2009. *Public elementary and secondary school student enrollment and staff counts from the Common Core of Data: School year 2007–08*. NCES 2010-309. Washington, DC: National Center for Education Statistics, Institute of Education Sciences, U.S. Department of Education. Retrieved January 12, 2010, from http://nces.ed.gov/pubsearch/pubsinfo.asp?pubid=2010309.

N2H2. n.d. Bess™ filtering for schools. Retrieved August 21, 2003, from http://www.n2h2.com/products/bess.php?device=school.

Obama, B. 2010. It Gets Better video transcript. October 21. Retrieved December 9, 2010, from http://www.whitehouse.gov/it-gets-better-transcript.

Online Safety and Technology Working Group. 2010. *Youth safety on a living Internet: Report of the Online Safety and Technology Working Group*. Retrieved December 9, 2010, from http://www.ntia.doc.gov/reports/2010/OSTWG_Final_Report_060410.pdf.

Osborne, D. 2003. Diaz bashes Milk school. *Gay City News*, August 15–21.

Patterson, C. J. 1995. *Lesbian and gay parenting: A resource for psychologists*. Washington, DC: American Psychological Association. Retrieved August 18, 2006, from http://www.apa.org/pi/parent.html.

Patterson, C. J. 2006. Children of lesbian and gay parents. *Current Directions in Psychological Science* 15 (5): 241–44.

Patterson, C. J. 2009. Children of lesbian and gay parents: Psychology, law, and policy. *American Psychologist* 64 (8): 725–36.

Perrin, E. C., and Committee on Psychosocial Aspects of Child and Family Health. 2002. Co-parent or second-parent adoption by same-sex parents. *Pediatrics* 109 (2): 341–44.

Perrotti, J., and Westheimer, K. 2001. *When the drama club is not enough: Lessons from the Safe Schools Program for Gay and Lesbian Students*. Boston: Beacon.

Pettett, C. 2005. Homophobia and harassment in school age populations. *American Sexuality Magazine* 1 (2).

Pharr, S. 1997. *Homophobia: A weapon of sexism*. Inverness, CA: Chardon.

Pilkington, N. W., and D'Augelli, A. R. 1995. Victimization of lesbian, gay, and bisexual youth in community settings. *Journal of Community Psychology* 23 (1): 34–56.

PlanetOut. 2000. Trans teen's school dress allowed. October 13. Retrieved October 1, 2003, from http://www.planetout.com/pno/news/article.html?date=2000/10/13/1.

Planned Parenthood. 2009. Planned parenthood statement on President Obama's 2010 budget. May 8. Retrieved May 8, 2009, from http://www.plannedparenthood.org/about-us/newsroom/press-releases/planned-parenthood-statement-president-obamas-2010-budget-26882.htm.

Pohan, C. A., and Bailey, N. J. 1997. Opening the closet: Multiculturalism that is fully inclusive. *Multicultural Education* 5 (1): 12–15.

Price, J. H., and Telljohan, S. K. 1991. School counselors' perceptions of adolescent homosexuals. *Journal of School Health* 61 (10): 433–8.

Proctor, C., and Groze, V. K. 1994. Risk factors for suicide among gay, lesbian, and bisexual youths. *Social Work* 39 (5): 504–13.

Radkowsky, M., and Siegel, L. J. 1997. The gay adolescent: Stressors, adaptations, and psychosocial interventions. *Clinical Psychology Review* 17 (2): 191–216.

Ray, N. 2007. *Lesbian, gay, bisexual, and transgender youth: An epidemic of homelessness.* New York: National Gay and Lesbian Task Force Policy Institute.

Reis, B., and Saewyc, E. 1999. *Eighty-three thousand youth: Selected findings of eight population-based studies as they pertain to antigay harassment and the safety and well-being of sexual minority students.* Seattle: Safe Schools Coalition of Washington.

Remafedi, G. 1987. Male homosexuality: The adolescent perspective. *Pediatrics* 79 (3): 326–30.

Remafedi, G. 1994. Predictors of unprotected intercourse among gay and bisexual youth: Knowledge, beliefs, and behavior. *Pediatrics* 94 (2/1): 163–68.

Remafedi, G., Resnick, M., Blum, R., and Harris, L. 1992. Demography of sexual orientation in adolescents. *Pediatrics* 89 (4): 714–21.

Resnick, M. D. 2000. Protective factors, resiliency, and healthy youth development. *Adolescent Medicine: State of the Art Reviews* 11 (1): 157–64.

Resnick, M. D., Bearman, P. S., Blum, R. W., Bauman, K. E., Harris, K. M., Jones, J., et al. 1997. Protection of adolescents from harm: Findings from the national longitudinal study on adolescent health. *Journal of the American Medical Association* 278 (10): 823–32.

Rideout, V., Foehr, U., and Roberts, D. 2010. *Generation M² media in the lives of 8- to 18-year-olds.* Menlo Park, CA: Henry J. Kaiser Family Foundation. Retrieved December 9, 2010, from http://www.kff.org/entmedia/upload/8010.pdf.

Rofes, E. 1999. What happens when kids grow up? The long-term impact of an openly gay teacher on eight students' lives. In W. J. Letts and J. T. Sears, eds., *Queering elementary education: Advancing the dialogue about sexualities and schooling.* Lanham, MD: Rowman and Littlefield.

Rofes, E. 2000. Young adult reflections on having an openly gay teacher during early adolescence. *Education and Urban Society* 32 (3): 399.

Rosario, M., Rotheram-Borus, M. J., and Reid, H. M. 1996. Gay-related stress and its correlates among gay and bisexual male adolescents of predominantly black and Hispanic background. *Journal of Community Psychology* 24 (2): 136–59.

Rosario, M., Schrimshaw, E. W., and Hunter, J. 2005. Psychological distress following suicidality among gay, lesbian, and bisexual youths: Role of social relationships. *Journal of Youth and Adolescence* 34 (2): 149–61.

Rowell, R. 1996. *HIV prevention for gay/bisexual/two-spirit Native American men.* Oakland, CA: National Native American AIDS Prevention Center.

Rubin, S. A. 1995. Children who grow up with gay or lesbian parents: How are today's schools meeting this "invisible" group's needs? Master's thesis, University of Wisconsin-Madison. ERIC Document Reproduction Service No. ED386290.

Russell, S. T. 2001. LGBTQ youth are at risk in U.S. school environment. *SIECUS Report* 29 (4): 19–22.

Russell, S. T. 2005. Beyond risk: Resilience in the lives of sexual minority youth. *Journal of Gay and Lesbian Issues in Education* 2 (3): 5–18.

Russell, S. T., Clarke, T. J., and Laub, C. 2009. *Understanding school safety and the intersections of race, ethnicity, and sexual orientation.* California Safe Schools Coalition Research Brief No. 10. San Francisco: California Safe Schools Coalition. Retrieved September 24, 2010, from http://www.casafeschools.org/CSSC_Research_Brief_10.pdf.

Russell, S. T., Franz, B. T., and Driscoll, A. K. 2001. Same-sex romantic attraction and experiences of violence in adolescence. *American Journal of Public Health* 91 (6): 903–6.

Russell, S. T. and Joyner, K. 2001. Adolescent sexual orientation and suicide risk: Evidence from a national study. *American Journal of Public Health* 91 (8): 1276–81.

Russel, S. T., Kostroski, O., McGuire, J. K., Laub, C., and Manke, E. 2006. *LGBT issues in the curriculum promotes school safety.* California Safe Schools Coalition Research Brief No. 4. San Francisco: California Safe Schools Coalition. Retrieved October 10, 2010, from http://www.casafeschools.org/FactSheet-curriculum.pdf.

Russell, S. T., McGuire, J. K., Larriva, J., Laub, C., Manke, E., and Rosen, A. 2009. *School safety for students with LGBT parents.* California Safe Schools Coalition Research Brief No. 6. San Francisco: California Safe Schools Coalition. Retrieved September 24, 2010, from http://www.casafeschools.org/FactSheet6_Pages.pdf.

Russell, S. T., McGuire, J. K., Laub, C., Manke, E., O'Shaughnessy, M., Heck, K., and Calhoun, C. 2006. *Harassment in schools based on actual or perceived sexual orientation: Prevalence and consequences.* California Safe Schools Coalition Research Brief No. 2. San Francisco: California Safe Schools Coalition. Retrieved September 25, 2010, from http://casafe schools.org/CSSC_Research_Brief_2.pdf.

Russell, S. T., McGuire, J. K., Toomey, R., and Anderson, C. R. 2010. *Gender nonconformity and school safety: Documenting the problem and steps schools can take.* California Safe Schools Coalition Research Brief No. 12. San Francisco: California Safe Schools Coalition. Retrieved September 24, 2010, from http://casafeschools.org/CSSC_Research_Brief_12.pdf.

Russell, S. T., Seif, H., and Truong, N. L. 2001. School outcomes of sexual minority youth in the United States: Evidence from a national study. *Journal of Adolescence* 24 (1): 111–27.

Russell, S. T., Talmage, C., Laub, C., and Manke, E. 2009. *The economic costs of bullying at school.* California Safe Schools Coalition Research Brief No. 5. San Francisco: California Safe Schools Coalition. Retrieved September 25, 2010, from http://casafeschools.org/FactSheet5rev2.pdf.

Russell, S. T, and Truong, N. L. 2001. Adolescent sexual orientation, race and ethnicity, and school environments: A national study of sexual minority youth of color. In K. K. Kumashiro, ed., *Troubling intersections of race and sexuality: Queer students of color and anti-oppressive education.* Lanham, MD: Rowman and Littlefield.

Russell, S. T., Truong, N. L., and Driscoll, A. K. 2002. Adolescent same-sex romantic attractions and relationships: Implications for substance use and abuse. *American Journal of Public Health* 92 (2): 198–202.

Ryan, C. 2000. Analysis of the content and gaps in the scientific and professional literature on the health and mental health concerns of lesbian, gay, and bisexual youth. Unpublished manuscript, American Psychological Association's Healthy Lesbian, Gay, and Bisexual Students Project.

Ryan, C. 2002. *A review of the professional literature and research needs of LGBT youth of color.* Washington, DC: National Youth Advocacy Coalition.

Ryan, C., and Futterman, D. 1998. *Lesbian and gay youth: Care and counseling.* New York: Columbia University Press.

Ryan, C., and Futterman, D. 2001. Social and developmental challenges for lesbian, gay, and bisexual youth. *SIECUS Report* 29 (4): 4–18.

Ryan, C., Huebner, D., Diaz, R. M., and Sanchez, J. 2009. Family rejection as a predictor of negative health outcomes in white and Latino lesbian, gay, and bisexual young adults. *Pediatrics* 123 (1): 346–52.

Ryan, D., and Martin, A. 2000. Lesbian, gay, bisexual, and transgender parents in the school system. *School Psychology Review* 29 (2): 207–16.

Sable, J., and Hill, J. 2006. *Overview of public elementary and secondary students, staff, schools, school districts, revenues, and expenditures: School year 2004–05 and fiscal year 2004* (NCES 2007-309). Table 1. Public school student membership in the United States and other jurisdictions, by grade and state or jurisdiction: School year 2004–05. U.S. Department of Education. Washington, DC: National Center for Education Statistics. Retrieved September 15, 2011, from http://nces.ed.gov/pubs2007/2007309.pdf.

Safe Schools Coalition of Washington State. 1999. *They don't even know me: Understanding antigay harassment and violence in schools.* Seattle: Safe Schools Coalition of Washington State. Retrieved August 18, 2006, from http://www.safeschoolscoalition.org/theydontevenknowme.pdf.

Safe Schools Improvement Act of 2007. H.R. 3132. 110th Cong., 1st sess.

Safe Schools Improvement Act of 2009. H.R. 2262, 111th Cong., 1st sess.

Safe Schools Improvement Act of 2010. S. 3739. 111th Cong., 2nd sess.

Savin-Williams, R. C. 1998. The disclosure to families of same-sex attractions by lesbian, gay, and bisexual youths. *Journal of Research on Adolescence* 8 (1): 49–68.

Savin-Williams, R. C. 2001a. A critique of research on sexual-minority youths. *Journal of Adolescence* 24 (1): 5–13.

Savin-Williams, R. C. 2001b. Suicide attempts among sexual minority youths: Population and measurement issues. *Journal of Consulting and Clinical Psychology* 69 (6): 983–91.

Savin-Williams, R. C. 2006. *The new gay teenager.* Cambridge, MA: Harvard University Press.

Savin-Williams, R. C., and Dube, D. M. 1998. Parental Reactions to their child's disclosure of a gay/lesbian identity. *Family Relations* 47 (1): 7–13.

Savin-Williams, R. C., and Lenhart, R. E. 1990. AIDS prevention among lesbian and gay youth: Psychosocial stress and health care intervention guidelines. In D. G. Ostrow, ed., *Behavioral aspects of AIDS.* New York: Plenum.

Scanlan-Stefanakos, V. 2001. Youth trans-action. *Advocate,* April 10.

Schindler, P. 2010. Paterson signs anti-bullying law; Enactment of Dignity for All Students Act caps decade-long struggle. *Gay City News,* September 8. Retrieved September 17, 2010, from http://gaycitynews.com/articles/2010/09/ 08/gay_city_news/news/doc4c8806211b448873523799.txt.

Schneider, M. E., and Owens, R. E. 2000. Concern for lesbian, gay, and bisexual kids: The benefits for all children. *Education and Urban Society* 32 (3): 349–68.

Sears, J. T. 1994. Challenges for educators: Lesbian, gay, and bisexual families. *High School Journal* 77 (1/2): 138–54.

Sell, R. L. 1997. The Sell Assessment of Sexual Orientation: Background and scoring. *Archives of Sexual Behavior* 26 (6): 643–58.

Sell, R. L., and Becker, J. B. 2001. [Data on sexual orientation for inclusion in Department of Health and Human Services databases]. Unpublished.

Setoodeh, R. 2008. Young, gay, murdered. *Newsweek,* July 19. Retrieved February 14, 2010, from http://www.newsweek.com/id/147790.

Sexuality Information and Education Council of the United States. 2006. *It gets worse: A revamped federal abstinence-only program goes extreme.* Retrieved August 5, 2009, from http://www.siecus.org/_data/global/images/Revamped _Abstinence_Only_Goes_Extreme.pdf.

Sexuality Information and Education Council of the United States. 2007b. *SIECUS Public Policy Office fact sheet.* Retrieved February 14, 2010, from http://www.siecus.org/_data/global/images/research_says.pdf.

Sexuality Information and Education Council of the United States. 2008a. A brief history: Abstinence-only-until-marriage funding. Retrieved February 14, 2010, from http://www.nomoremoney.org/index.cfm?pageid=947.

Sexuality Information and Education Council of the United States. 2008b. State of sex ed in Illinois supports needed end to abstinence-only funding. Retrieved February 14, 2010, from http://www.siecus.org/index.cfm?fuseaction=Fea ture.showFeature&featureid=1743&pageid=525&parentid=523.

Sexuality Information and Education Council of the United States. 2008c. *We're outta here: 25 states withdraw from crumbling Title V abstinence-only-until-marriage program.* Retrieved January 23, 2009, from http://siecus.org/_data/ global/images/25%20States%20Out%2010%208.pdf.

Sexuality Information and Education Council of the United States. 2008d. Sexuality education and abstinence-only-until-marriage programs in the states: An overview: Fiscal year 2008 edition. Retrieved September 20, 2011, from http://siecus.org/index.cfm?fuseaction=Page.viewPage&PageID=1164.

Sexuality Information and Education Council of the United States. 2010. SIECUS fact sheet: State by state decisions: The Personal Responsibility Education Program and Title V Abstinence-Only Program. Retrieved September 20, 2011, from http://siecus.org/index.cfm?fuseaction=Page.viewPage&PageID=1272.

Shahum, L. 1996. MoJo's July Hellraiser. *Mother Jones,* July/August. Retrieved September 29, 2003, from http://www.motherjones.com/mother_jones/JA96/ shahum.html.

Sheldon, L. P. 2001. Homosexuals recruit public school children. *Traditional Values Coalition Special Report* 18 (11).

Silenzio, V. M. B., et al. 2007. Sexual orientation and risk factors for suicidal ideation and suicide attempts among adolescents and young adults. *American Journal of Public Health* 97 (11): 2017–19.

Silver, J. n.d. Movie day at the Supreme Court, or "I know it when I see it": A history of the definition of obscenity. Retrieved August 21, 2003, from http://li brary.lp.findlaw.com/articles/file/00982/008860/title/subject/topic/constitu tionalpercent20law_first percent20amendment percent20-percent20freedom percent20of percent20speech/filename/constitutionallaw_1_86#edn1.

Simmons, T., and O'Connell, M. 2003. *Married-couple and unmarried-partner households: 2000.* Washington, DC: United States Census Bureau. Retrieved September 18, 2003, from http://www.census.gov/prod/2003pubs/censr- 5.pdf.

Simpson, M. D. 2002. Review of selected provisions of the Elementary and Secondary Act (ESEA). National Education Association. Paper presented at the annual meeting of the National Organization of Lawyers for Educational Associations, Anchorage, AK.

Smith, P., Mahdavi, J., Carvalho, M., Fisher, S., Russell, S., and Tippett, N. 2007. Cyberbullying: Its nature and impact in secondary school pupils. *Journal of Child Psychology and Psychiatry* 49 (4): 376–85.

SpeakTruth.com. n.d. Alana Flores. Retrieved October 16, 2003, from http:// www.speak-truth.com/bio/flores_alana.html.

Spear, J. 1999. How filtering software impacts our schools. In Gay and Lesbian Alliance Against Defamation, *Access denied, version 2.0: The continuing threat against Internet access and privacy and its impact on the lesbian, gay, bisexual, and transgender community.* Los Angeles: Gay and Lesbian Alliance Against Defamation.

Stacey, J., and Biblarz, T. 2001. (How) does the sexual orientation of the parent matter? *American Sociological Review* 66 (2): 159–83.

Stader, D. L., and Graca, T. J. 2007. Student-on-student sexual orientation harassment: Legal protections for sexual minority youth. *Clearing House* 80 (3): 117–22.

State of Alaska Department of Health and Social Services. 2010. *Fact sheet: 2009 Alaska youth risk behavior surveys.* Retrieved September 13, 2011, from http://www.hss.state.ak.us/press/2010/YRBSfact%20sheet_010710.pdf.

Stein, N. 1999. *Classrooms and courtrooms: Facing sexual harassment in K–12 schools.* New York: Teachers College Press.

Stein, R. 2008. Premarital abstinence pledges ineffective, study finds. *Washington Post,* December 29. Retrieved January 29, 2009, from http://www.washington post.com/wp-dyn/content/article/2008/12/28/AR2008122801588.html.

Stevenson, M. R. 2000. Public policy, homosexuality, and the sexual coercion of children. *Journal of Psychology and Human Sexuality* 12 (4): 8.

Strunsky, S. 2003. A young lesbian's stabbing death is far from resolved. Associated Press, August 9. Retrieved August 21, 2006, from the *Bucks County (PA) Courier Times* website, http://www.phillyburbs.com/pb-dyn/news/104-0809 2003-139007.html.

Student Nondiscrimination Act of 2010. H.R. 4530, 111th Cong., 2nd sess.

Student Nondiscrimination Act of 2010. S. 3390, 111th Cong., 2nd sess.

Szalacha, L. 2001a. Safe Schools Program for Gay and Lesbian Students. *Girls Coalition of Greater Boston Newsletter,* Fall. Electronic version.

Szalacha, L. 2001b. The sexual diversity climate of Massachusetts' secondary schools and the success of the Safe Schools Program for Gay and Lesbian Students. PhD diss., Harvard University.

Tasker, F. 2010. Same-sex parenting and child development: Reviewing the contribution of parental gender. *Journal of Marriage and Family* 72 (1): 35–40.

Taylor, O. L. 1990. *Cross-cultural communication: An essential dimension of effective education.* Rev. ed. Washington, DC: Mid-Atlantic Equity Center. Retrieved August 20, 2006, from http://www.maec.org/cross/.

Teicher, S. A. 2003. The case for single-sex schools. *Christian Science Monitor,* July 1.

Telingator, C. J., and Patterson, C. 2008. Children and adolescents of lesbian and gay parents. *Journal of the American Academy of Child and Adolescent Psychiatry* 47 (12): 1364–68.

Telljohann, S. K., and Price, J. H. 1993. A qualitative examination of adolescent homosexuals' life experiences: Ramifications for secondary school personnel. *Journal of Homosexuality* 26 (1): 41–56.

Thornburgh, D., and Lin, H. S., eds. 2002. *Youth, pornography, and the Internet.* Washington, DC: National Academic Press.

365gay.com. 2003. School for gay students to close. August 7. Retrieved December 8, 2010, from http://www.gaypasg.org/gaypasg/PressClippings/2003/August%202003/School%20For%20Gay%20Students%20To %20Close.htm.

365gay.com. 2005. Antigay textbook bill sparks fiery debate. January 25. Retrieved January 28, 2005, from http://www.365gay.com/newscon05/01/012505books .htm.

Thurlow, C. 2001. Naming the "outsider within": Homophobic pejoratives and the verbal abuse of lesbian, gay, and bisexual high school pupils. *Journal of Adolescence* 24 (1): 25–38.

Troiden, R. R. 1989. The formation of homosexual identities. *Journal of Homosexuality* 17 (1/2): 43–74.

Uribe, V. 1994. Project 10: A school-based outreach to gay and lesbian youth. *High School Journal* 77 (1/2): 108–12.

Uribe, V., and Harbeck, K. 1992. Addressing the needs of lesbian, gay, and bisexual youth: The origins of Project 10 and school-based intervention. In K. Harbeck, ed., *Coming out of the classroom closet.* New York: Haworth.

US Charter Schools. 2010. Answers to frequently asked questions. Retrieved January 15, 2010, from http://www.uscharterschools.org/pub/uscs_docs/o/faq.html#8.

U.S. Congress. 1987. House of Representatives. *Sex and race differences on standardized tests: Oversight hearings before the Subcommittee on Civil and Constitutional Rights of the Committee on the Judiciary.* 100th Cong., 1st sess. ERIC Document Reproduction Service No. ED312276.

U.S. Department of Education. 2001. Office of Civil Rights. *Revised sexual harassment guidance: Harassment of students by school employees, other students, or third parties.* Washington, DC: U.S. Department of Education, Office of Civil Rights. Retrieved August 19, 2006, from http://www.ed.gov/offices/OCR/archives/pdf/shguide.pdf.

U.S. Department of Education. 2002a. *Fact sheet: No Child Left Behind Act.* Retrieved July 11, 2003, from http://www.ed.gov/offices/OESE/esea/factsheet .html.

U.S. Department of Education. 2002b. *No Child Left Behind: A desktop reference*

(Section IV-A: Safe and Drug-Free Schools and Communities). Retrieved September 2, 2003, from http://www.ed.gov/offices/OESE/reference/4a.html.

U.S. Department of Education. 2002c. *The No Child Left Behind Act of 2001.* Retrieved July 16, 2003, from http://www.ed.gov/offices/OESE/esea/NCLBexec summ.pdf.

U.S. Department of Education, National Center for Education Statistics. 2003. *Digest of education statistics, 2002.* Table 38. Enrollment in public elementary and secondary schools, by grade and state: Fall 2000. Retrieved September 15, 2011, from http://nces.ed.gov/pubs2003/2003060b.pdf.

U.S. Equal Employment Opportunity Commission. 2003. EEOC settles color harassment lawsuit with Applebee's Neighborhood Bar and Grill. August 7. Retrieved October 23, 2003, from http://www.eeoc.gov/press/8-07-03.html.

Varney, J. A. 2001. Undressing the normal: Community efforts for queer Asian and Asian American youth. In K. K. Kumashiro, ed., *Troubling intersections of race and sexuality: Queer students of color and anti-oppressive education.* New York: Rowman and Littlefield.

Vermont Department of Health. 2002. Office of Alcohol and Drug Abuse Programs. *2001 Vermont Youth Risk Behavior Survey.* Burlington, VT: Vermont Department of Health, Office of Alcohol and Drug Abuse Programs. Retrieved August 18, 2006, from http://healthvermont.gov/pubs/ Publications .aspx.

Villarroel, M. A., Turner, C. F., Eggleston, E., Al-Tayyib, A., Rogers, S. M., Roman, A. M., Cooley, P. C., and Gordek, H. 2006. Same-gender sex in the United States: Impact of T-ACASI on prevalence estimates. *Public Opinion Quarterly* 70 (2): 166–96.

Wainright, J. L., and Patterson, C. J. 2006. Delinquency, victimization, and substance use among adolescents with female same-sex parents. *Journal of Family Psychology* 20 (3): 526–30.

Wainright, J. L., and Patterson, C. J. 2008. Peer relations among adolescents with female same-sex parents. *Developmental Psychology* 44 (1): 117–26.

Walling, D. R. 1993. *Gay teens at risk.* Bloomington, IN: Phi Delta Kappa Educational Foundation.

Walls, N. E., Stacey, F., and Wisneski, H. 2008. Suicidal ideation and attempts among sexual minority youths receiving social services. *Social Work* 53 (1): 21–29.

Wall Street Journal. 2003. Choice, if you're gay. Editorial. August 21.

Walsh, J. 1996. Profiles in Courage: Jamie Nabozny, 20, of Minneapolis, Minnesota. *Oasis,* February. Retrieved October 6, 2003, from http://www.youth .org/loco/PERSONProject/Alerts/States/Minnesota/jamie.html.

Walsh, M. 1994. Harassment suit rejected. *Education Week,* October 19, 10.

Weinstock, H., Berman, S. and Cates, W. 2004. Sexually transmitted diseases among American youth: Incidence and prevalence estimates, 2000. *Perspectives on Sexual and Reproductive Health,* 36 (1): 6–10.

White House. 2002. President signs landmark No Child Left Behind education bill. January 8. Retrieved October 18, 2003, from http://www.whitehouse.gov/ news/releases/2002/01/20020108-1.html.

White House. 2010. Office of the Press Secretary. Remarks of President Barack

Obama—as prepared for delivery—back to school speech. September 14. Retrieved December 8, 2010, from http://www.whitehouse.gov/the-press-office/2010/09/13/remarks-president-barack-obama-prepared-delivery-back-school-speech.

Wilson, W. L. 2009. A parent's worst nightmare: The real story behind Carl Walker-Hoover's suicide. Essence.com, April 16. Retrieved February 14, 2010, from http://www1.essence.com/news_entertainment/news/articles/carl_walker_hoover_suicide.

Winerip, M. 2003a. Promoting tolerance, not paying heed. *New York Times,* February 5, B9.

Winerip, M. 2003b. A safe haven finds itself under siege. *New York Times,* August 27, B1.

Woog, D. 1995. *School's out: The impact of gay and lesbian issues on America's schools.* Boston: Alyson.

Wright, J. 2009. Bus driver fired for doing nothing to prevent Jayron Martin's attack. DallasVoice.com, December 4. Retrieved February 14, 2010, from http://www.dallasvoice.com/instant-tea/_/jayron-martin/.

Zubowski, C. 2009. Student attacked with metal pipe said school administrators did nothing to help. KHOU.com, November 18. Retrieved February 14, 2010, from http://www.khou.com/home/Student-allegedly-chased-beat-with-metal-pipe-says-school-administrators-did-nothing-to-help-70430507.html.

Further Reading

The following citations were referenced in this book as sources for additional reading and information.

Bradford, J., Barrett, K., and Honnold, J. A. 2002. *The 2000 Census and Same-Sex Households: A User's Guide.* New York: National Gay and Lesbian Task Force Policy Institute, Survey and Evaluation Research Laboratory, and Fenway Institute.

Carter, K. 1997. Gay slurs abound. *Des Moines Register,* March 7, B1.

Cianciotto, J., and Cahill, S. *Education policy: Issues affecting lesbian, gay, bisexual, and transgender youth.* New York: National Gay and Lesbian Task Force Policy Institute, 2003. Available at http://www.thetaskforce.org/downloads/reports/reports/EducationPolicy.pdf.

D'Emilio, J. 1983. *Sexual politics, sexual communities: The making of a homosexual minority in the United States, 1940–1970.* Chicago: University of Chicago Press.

D'Emilio, J. 2003. *Lost prophet: The life and times of Bayard Rustin.* New York: Free Press.

De Veaux, A. 2004. *Warrior poet: A biography of Audre Lorde.* New York: W. W. Norton.

Dylan, Nicole. 2004. City enters partnership to assist lesbian and gay homeless youth. *Nation's Cities Weekly* 27:8.

Emma Goldman Papers. Available at http://sunsite.berkeley.edu/Goldman.

Hoagwood, K., Jensen, P. S., and Fisher, C. B., eds. *Ethical issues in mental health research with children and adolescents.* Mahwah, NJ: Lawrence Erlbaum Associates.

Hobhouse, J. 1975. *Everybody who was anybody.* New York: Putnam.

Hutchins, L., and Kaahumanu, L. 1991. *Bi any other name: Bisexual people speak out.* Los Angeles: Alyson.

Lorde, A. 1982. *Zami: A new spelling of my name.* Trumansburg, NY: Crossing.

Marcus, E. 1992. *Making history: The struggle for gay and lesbian equal rights, 1945–1990.* New York: HarperCollins.

Miller, M., André, A., Ebin, J., and Bessonova, L. 2007. *Bisexual health: An introduction and model practices for HIV/STI prevention programming.* New York: National Gay and Lesbian Task Force Policy Institute, Fenway Institute at Fenway Community Health, and BiNet USA.

Patterson, C. J. (2000). Family relationships of lesbian and gay men. *Journal of Marriage & Family,* 62(4), 1052–70.

Putnam, F. W., Liss, M. B., and Landsverk, J. 1996. Ethical issues in maltreatment research. In K. Hoagwood, P. S. Jensen, and C. B. Fisher, eds., *Ethical issues in mental health research with children and adolescents*. Mahwah, NJ: Lawrence Erlbaum Associates.

Rich, A. 1986. Invisible in academe. In *Blood, bread, and poetry: Selected prose, 1979–1985*. New York: W. W. Norton.

Schmidgall, G. 1997. *Walt Whitman: A gay life*. New York: Plume.

Souhami, D. 2000. *Gertrude and Alice*. London: Phoenix.

Wolff, C. 1987. *Magnus Hirschfeld: A portrait of a pioneer in sexology*. London: Quartet Books.

Case Law Citations

Boyd County High Sch. Gay Straight Alliance v. Bd. of Educ. of Boyd County, Ky., 258 F. Supp. 667 (E.D. Ky. 2003).

Boy Scouts of Am. v. Dale, 530 U.S. 640 (2000).

Colin v. Orange Unified Sch. Dist., 83 F. Supp. 2d 1135 (C.D. Calif. 2000).

Doe v. Brockton Sch. Comm., No. 2000-J-638, 2000 WL 33342399 (Mass. App. Ct. 2000).

Doe v. Yunits, No. 001060A, 2000 WL 33162199 (Mass. Super. Ct. 2000), *aff'd, Doe v. Brockton Sch. Comm.,* No. 2000-J-638, 2000 WL 33342399 (Mass. App. Ct. 2000).

E. High Gay/Straight Alliance v. Bd. of Educ., No. CIV. 2:98-CV-193J, 1999 WL 1390255 (D. Utah 1999).

Everson v. Bd. of Educ. of Ewing, 330 U.S. 1 (1947).

Flores v. Morgan Hill Unified Sch. Dist., 324 F.3d 1130 (9th Cir. 2003).

Lawrence v. Texas, 123 S. Ct. 2472 (2003).

Mclaughlin v. Bd. of Educ. of Pulaski County Special Sch. Dist., No. 4:03-CV-00244GTE, 2003 WL 21182283 (E.D. Ark. 2003).

Nabozny v. Podlesny, 92 F.3d 446 (7th Cir. 1996).

Ray v. Antioch, 107 F. Supp.2d 1165 (N.D. Cal. 2000).

Reno v. Am. Civil Liberties Union, 521 U.S. 844 (1997).

Romer v. Evans, 517 U.S. 620 (1996).

Seamons v. Snow, 864 F. Supp. 1111 (D. Utah 1994).

United States v. Am. Library Assoc., 537 U.S. 1170 (2003).

United States v. Virginia, 518 U.S. 515 (1996).

Zelman v. Simmons-Harris, 234 F.3d 945 (6th Cir. 2000), *rev'd,* 536 U.S. 639 (2002).

Index